LOCAL CITIZENSHIP IN A GLOBAL AGE

Although it is usually assumed that only the federal government can confer citizenship, localities often give residents who are noncitizens at the federal level the benefits of local citizenship: access to medical care, education, housing, security, labor and consumer markets, and even voting rights. In this work, Kenneth Stahl demonstrates that while the existence of these "noncitizen citizens" has helped to reconcile competing commitments within liberal democracy to equality and community, the advance of globalization and the rise of nationalist political leaders like Donald Trump has caused local and federal citizenship to clash. For nationalists, localities' flexible approach to citizenship is a Trojan horse undermining state sovereignty from within, while liberals see local citizenship as the antidote to a reactionary ethnic nationalism. This book should be read by anyone who wants to understand why citizenship has become one of the most important issues in national politics today.

KENNETH A. STAHL is a Professor of Law and Director of the Environmental, Land Use, and Real Estate Law certificate program at Chapman University Dale E. Fowler School of Law. His research combines doctrinal analysis with insights from disciplines including urban sociology, geography, economics, and the humanities. Professor Stahl's work has been widely published in many law reviews.

Local Citizenship in a Global Age

KENNETH A. STAHL

Chapman University Dale E. Fowler School of Law

CAMBRIDGE
UNIVERSITY PRESS

University Printing House, Cambridge CB2 8BS, United Kingdom

One Liberty Plaza, 20th Floor, New York, NY 10006, USA

477 Williamstown Road, Port Melbourne, VIC 3207, Australia

314–321, 3rd Floor, Plot 3, Splendor Forum, Jasola District Centre, New Delhi – 110025, India

79 Anson Road, #06–04/06, Singapore 079906

Cambridge University Press is part of the University of Cambridge.

It furthers the University's mission by disseminating knowledge in the pursuit of education, learning, and research at the highest international levels of excellence.

www.cambridge.org
Information on this title: www.cambridge.org/9781107156463
DOI: 10.1017/9781316661352

© Kenneth A. Stahl 2020

First published 2020

A catalogue record for this publication is available from the British Library.

Library of Congress Cataloging-in-Publication Data
NAMES: Stahl, Kenneth A., 1974– author.
TITLE: Local citizenship in a global age / Kenneth A. Stahl, Chapman University Dale E. Fowler School of Law.
DESCRIPTION: 1. | New York : Cambridge University Press, 2020. | Includes bibliographical references and index.
IDENTIFIERS: LCCN 2019044104 (print) | LCCN 2019044105 (ebook) | ISBN 9781107156463 (hardback) | ISBN 9781316609927 (paperback) | ISBN 9781316661352 (epub)
SUBJECTS: LCSH: Citizenship–United States. | Aliens–Civil rights–United States. | Aliens–Political activity–United States. | Local government–Law and legislation–United States. | Federal government–United States.
CLASSIFICATION: LCC KF4700 .S73 2020 (print) | LCC KF4700 (ebook) | DDC 342.7308/3–dc23
LC record available at https://lccn.loc.gov/2019044104
LC ebook record available at https://lccn.loc.gov/2019044105

ISBN 978-1-107-15646-3 Hardback
ISBN 978-1-316-60992-7 Paperback

For My Family

Contents

Figures and Tables

Figures

Tables

Acknowledgments

I am extremely grateful for all the comments, questions, and encouragement I received while writing this book from colleagues and friends, including but surely not limited to, Andy Ayers, Deepa Badrinarayana, Vicki Been, Richard Briffault, Sara Bronin, Janet Calvo, Nestor Davidson, Chris Elmendorf, Priya Gupta, Ernesto Hernandez-Lopez, Antonia Layard, John Travis Marshall, Sara Mayeux, Timothy Meyer, Robert Mikos, Ashira Ostrow, Marc Poirier, J. B. Ruhl, Rich Schragger, Dan Sharfstein, Anika Singh Lemar, Susanna Kim Ripken, Sarah Schindler, Chris Serkin, Christopher Slobogin, Kevin Stack, Rick Su, Zephyr Teachout, Ingrid Wuerth, and Kellen Zale.

Dan Sharfstein graciously invited me to present a very early draft at Vanderbilt University Law School's George Barrett Social Justice Program, where I received excellent comments from many colleagues. Nestor Davidson also graciously invited me to present an early draft at the inaugural Fordham Urban Law Center Author Workshop Series, where I also received outstanding feedback. Robin Malloy and the editors of SYRACUSE LAW REVIEW were kind enough to invite me to speak at their lecture series and with colleagues about the book at a very early stage. I am also grateful to the UNIVERSITY OF DETROIT MERCY LAW REVIEW for inviting me to speak about the book at its symposium on sanctuary cities. I had the pleasure of presenting drafts of various parts of the book at the 5th and 7th Annual State and Local Government Law Works in Progress Conference, the Law and Society Association annual meeting, the Association of Law, Culture and the Humanities annual meeting, and Georgia State University's Comparative Urbanism: Global Perspectives conference.

This project was generously supported by the law school administration at Chapman University Dale E. Fowler School of Law, for which I thank Deans Matt Parlow and Tom Campbell, and associate Deans Donald Kochan, Marisa Cianciarulo, and Danny Bogart. The staff of the Hugh and Hazel

Darling Library, especially Sherry Leysen, provided outstanding research assistance. Emilie Garber provided very thoughtful proofreading and comments. I would also like to thank Matt Gallaway and the entire team at Cambridge University Press for a delightful editorial experience. My greatest debt is to my family, thanks to whom all good things are possible.

Introduction

In November 2016, at the same moment Donald Trump was elected President of the United States on a virulently anti-immigrant platform, the city of San Francisco adopted a ballot measure granting all residents with children attending local public schools the right to vote in school board elections, regardless of their immigration status.[1] The ballot measure got little media attention and will probably have little effect on school board elections in San Francisco. Nevertheless, it helps clarify why local policies regarding the status of immigrants, exemplified above all by the decision of many cities (including San Francisco) to declare themselves "sanctuary cities" and limit law enforcement cooperation with federal immigration authorities, have become perhaps the most contentious set of issues on the national political stage. In short, these policies raise the fraught question of who is a citizen.

As the immigrant population in the United States has grown in the last several decades, the line between citizens and noncitizens has blurred, with noncitizens increasingly being granted access to opportunities often associated with citizenship. Many local governments have been at the forefront of this trend, issuing municipal identification cards to immigrants, providing immigrant children with English-language education, translating official documents and materials into foreign languages, enforcing mandates against discrimination based on immigration status, providing emergency health care treatment to immigrants, and barring law enforcement from inquiring about individuals' immigration status.[2] These benefits are among the core

---

[1] *See* Madison Park, *Noncitizens in San Francisco Can Register to Vote, but Only for School Board Elections*, CNN.COM (July 20, 2018, 12:00 AM), https://www.cnn.com/2018/07/20/us/noncitizens-vote-san-francisco/index.html.

[2] *See, e.g.*, ABIGAIL FISHER WILLIAMSON, WELCOMING NEW AMERICANS? LOCAL GOVERNMENTS AND IMMIGRANT INCORPORATION (2018). Local governments are *required* to provide some of the listed benefits, such as emergency medical care and education to noncitizens. Others, like

1

components of what T. H. Marshall famously called the "social rights" of citizenship, rights that have become ever more salient as the state has taken increasing responsibility for the welfare of its members.[3]

With the extension of social rights to noncitizens, participation in the political process has taken on special significance as the mark of what distinguishes citizens from noncitizens. Though noncitizens had the right to vote in many states prior to the twentieth century, no state today permits noncitizens to vote in state elections, and noncitizens have been prohibited from voting in federal elections since the 1990s.[4] The Supreme Court has upheld the exclusion of noncitizens from political participation (broadly understood not just as voting, but also holding public positions like police officers and public school teachers), writing that "[t]he exclusion of aliens from basic governmental processes is not a deficiency in the democratic system but a necessary consequence of the community's process of political self-determination."[5] Yet, San Francisco is one of several American cities to grant noncitizens the right to vote in certain local elections, and it may soon become a trend. Since San Francisco's move in 2016, at least five other municipalities have also extended the franchise to noncitizens, and many cities have considered doing the same in just the last few years.[6] In essence, these cities are conferring a form of *local*

---

issuing municipal identification cards and requiring law enforcement to refrain from cooperating with immigration authorities, have usually been voluntarily adopted by cities. On the importance of this distinction, see Rose Cuison Villazor, *What Is a "Sanctuary"?* 61 SMU L. Rev. 133, 153 (2008). I address this distinction further later and argue that there is less to the distinction than may initially appear.

[3] *See* T. H. Marshall, *Citizenship and Social Class, in* Class, Citizenship, and Social Development 65 (1964).

[4] 18 U.S.C. § 611.

[5] Cabell v. Chavez-Salido, 454 U.S. 432, 439 (1982) (excluding aliens from serving as probation officers); Foley v. Connelie, 435 U.S. 291 (1978) (police officers); Ambach v. Norwick, 441 U.S. 68 (1979) (schoolteachers).

[6] New York allowed noncitizens to vote in school board elections before it abolished its elected school board for unrelated reasons. *See* Joshua A. Douglas, *The Right to Vote under Local Law*, 85 Geo. Wash. L. Rev. 1039, 1063–64 (2017). While Chicago Board of Education members are appointed, noncitizen parent and community representatives may participate in the election of the same to certain Local School Councils. *Id.* at 1063–64; *see also* Chi. Pub. Schs., Office of Local Sch. Council Relations, 2018 Local School Council Election Guide 16–18 (2018) [https://perma.cc/LM62-SV2S].

The city of Detroit and ten Maryland municipalities, in addition to San Francisco, currently allow noncitizens to vote in certain elections. Detroit, Mich., Code § 14-6-10 (2017) (district council elections); Barnesville, Md., Charter, § 74-3 (1991) [https://perma.cc/5NRN-ZJZL] (election of commissioners); Garrett Park, Md., Charter, art. III, § 78-20 (2018) [https://perma.cc/A7DU-SDDC] (town elections); Glen Echo, Md., Charter, art. V, § 501(2) (1997) [https://perma.cc/GQ4W-HWQR] (town elections); Hyattsville, Md., Charter Amendment Res. 2016-02 (Dec. 5, 2016) [https://perma.cc/4K3X-2LV3] (city elections);

citizenship on people who are not citizens, and in some cases are barred from ever becoming citizens, at the national level.

Among the Americans who elected Donald Trump President, there is a seething anxiety over the perception that the meaning of citizenship is being diluted by the expansion of the benefits of citizenship to noncitizens. This anxiety often manifests in the form of falsified stories about noncitizens illegally voting in federal elections, draining welfare coffers without paying

MARTIN'S ADDITIONS, MD., CHARTER, art. III, § 301 (2018) [https://perma.cc/5DSU-C8N5] (council elections); MOUNT RAINIER, MD., CHARTER AMEND. RES. 1-2016 (Jan. 3, 2017) [https://perma.cc/Q5SB-UBY3] (city elections); RIVERDALE PARK, MD., CHARTER, art. V, § 501 (2018) [https://perma.cc/RJ47-LBQL] (town elections); SOMERSET, MD., CHARTER, art. V, § 83-21 (2017) [https://perma.cc/8JAA-ZJ8W] (town elections); TAKOMA PARK, MUNI. CHARTER, art. VI, § 601(a), 603(b) (2019) (city elections); TOWN OF CHEVY CHASE, CHARTER, art. IV, § 401 (2019) (town elections); S.F., CAL., MUN. ELECS. CODE art. X, §§ 1001–1005 (2019) (school board elections).

Of the ten Maryland municipalities, five of them have voted to grant suffrage rights to noncitizens since November 2016. *See* GARRETT PARK, MD. (adopting a Resolution Amending Section 78-20 of Article III of the Garrett Park Charter: Qualifications of Voters on July 10, 2017) [https://perma.cc/3P55-T6BB]; HYATTSVILLE, MD. (adopting Charter Amendment Resolution 2016-02 on Dec. 5, 2016) [https://perma.cc/4K3X-2LV3]; MOUNT RAINIER, MD. (adopting Charter Amendment Resolution 1-2016 on Jan. 3, 2017) [https://perma.cc/Q5SB-UBY3]; RIVERDALE PARK, MD. (adopting Charter Amendment Resolution 2018-CR-01 on May 7, 2018) [https://perma.cc/5DNQ-UYFB]; CHEVY CHASE TOWN, MD. (adopting a Resolution to Amend Section 401 of the Charter of the Town of Chevy Chase on Dec. 10, 2018) [https://perma.cc/MSD9-FE85].

Montpelier, Vermont, also voted in 2018 to amend its city charter and allow noncitizens to vote, though that charter change requires state approval. MONTPELIER, VT., Art. III Ballot Measure (Nov. 6, 2018) [https://perma.cc/7MJH-U729] (asking whether to amend Charter sections 5-1501 through 5-1504); *see also* H. 207, Gen. Assemb., 2019–2020 Sess. (Vt. 2019) [https://perma.cc/GN58-9UMF].

Other cities, including Portland, Maine; College Park, Maryland; and Winooski, Vermont, have debated enfranchising noncitizens since 2016. *See* PORTLAND, ME., CITY COUNCIL, Agenda Order 29-18/19 (discussing an "Order Placing Charter Amendment on November 6, 2018, Municipal Ballot re: Immigrant Voting") (Aug. 13, 2018) [https://perma.cc/G887-FZD6]; COLLEGE PARK, MD., CITY COUNCIL, Item No. 17-CR-02 (Sept. 12, 2017) (minutes) [https://perma.cc/F9Q2-GE99]; WINOOSKI, VT., CITY COUNCIL, Agenda Item No. IX.c. (discussing a "Charter Change to Allow for All Resident (Non-Citizen) Voting") (Sept. 17, 2018) (minutes) [https://perma.cc/N37G-HFTX].

In Massachusetts, where cities must request permission from the state to make changes to their election rules, two cities (Amherst and Wayland) have sent petitions to the state legislature requesting permission to extend the franchise to noncitizens since 2016, and two others (Boston and Somerville) have debated doing the same. *See* AMHERST, MASS., SELECT BD. MINUTES, ANNUAL TOWN MEETING – REQUEST FOR SPECIAL ACT 3 (June 5, 2017) [https://perma.cc/7TJY-5QKQ]; WAYLAND, MASS., ANN. TOWN MEETING Agenda Art. 10 (Apr. 2, 2017) [https://perma.cc/LZC6-KDH7]; BOS., MASS., CITY COUNCIL, Agenda Item No. 0240 (July 10, 2018) [https://perma.cc/R9C7–44MZ]; SOMERVILLE, MASS. BD. OF ALDERMEN, MAYOR'S REQUEST Agenda Item 206804 (Apr. 11, 2019) [https://perma.cc/A5MK-FTXF]; *see also* H. 3745, 190th Gen. Ct. (Mass. 2017-18); H. 659, 191st Gen. Ct. (Mass. 2019).

taxes, taking jobs from American citizens, and committing crimes. For that
reason, at the very same time that many cities are blurring the line between
citizens and noncitizens, the Trump administration is seeking to draw that
line more sharply. Trump has called for the restriction of legal immigration to
the lowest levels since the xenophobic immigration laws of the 1920s. His
provocation of a government shutdown over a southern border wall, the
abhorrent Muslim ban, the separation of families at the border, and the
relentless demonizing of "illegal" immigrants are all intended to relieve
nativist anxiety by creating an unambiguous, often racially defined, distinction
between citizens and noncitizens. Relatedly, Trump has relentlessly attacked
"sanctuary cities" for resisting that distinction, frequently attempting to tie
urban gun violence with liberal immigration policies.[7]

This synopsis of our current political environment illustrates the two central
arguments of this book. First, although it is commonly believed that nations
alone can confer citizenship, citizenship is actually distributed at multiple
scales simultaneously, and often on divergent grounds. In essence, we practice
"citizenship federalism." Second, local and federal governments tend to
distribute citizenship in ways that are not only divergent but actually in direct
contradiction, which means that political conflict is prone to erupt between
these two scales over their different understandings of citizenship. Although,
in the United States, state governments are the building blocks of federalism
and historically an important repository of citizenship as well, in practice today
citizenship is largely being defined at the local and federal levels, with states
playing a more passive role.

That the modern debate over citizenship largely takes the form of a conflict
between federal and local governments reflects the historical fact that cities
and nation-states have long had distinctive "spheres of citizenship," in Yishai
Blank's phrase.[8] For centuries, cities have been dependent on foreign trade to
survive and could never rely on borders to buffer themselves against global
forces; as a result, they have generally made membership in the urban political
community widely available to all those who choose to reside or do business in
the city. The modern nation-state, on the other hand, is entirely a creature of

---

[7] For some overviews of immigration policy under Trump, see SARAH PIERCE & ANDREW
    SELEE, MIGRATION POLICY INSTITUTE, IMMIGRATION UNDER TRUMP: A REVIEW OF POLICY
    SHIFTS IN THE YEAR SINCE THE ELECTION (December 2017), https://www.migrationpolicy.org/
    research/immigration-under-trump-review-policy-shifts. For a sampling of some of Trump's
    tweets about one of his favorite targets, the city of Chicago, see Kori Rumore, *When Trump
    Talks about Chicago, We Track It*, CHI. TRIBUNE (Mar. 28, 2019, 8:10 AM), https://www
    .chicagotribune.com/news/local/breaking/ct-trump-tweets-quotes-chicago-htmlstory.html.
[8] *See* Yishai Blank, *Spheres of Citizenship*, 8 THEORETICAL INQUIRIES L. 411 (2007).

its borders, predicated on the idea that the state's sovereign authority and the nation's territorial reach extend the full length of, and are bounded by, the lines dividing them from adjacent nation-states. Thus, it has been considered essential to the very idea of the nation-state that the government must be able to differentiate members from nonmembers on the basis of specific national traits that demonstrate a deep connection to the territory.[9]

The conceptual divide between cities and nation-states over the meaning of citizenship remains evident today. In the United States and many other places, for example, federal governments have the plenary authority to limit mobility of noncitizens across their borders, and citizenship is granted based on ascriptive criteria such as birth, lineage, or an extensive process of naturalization designed to demonstrate fealty to the civic ideals of the state. Subnational governments such as states and local governments, however, generally have no authority to limit mobility into or out of their territory and must extend the status and benefits of state and local citizenship to all national citizens who are resident within the jurisdiction's territory (and often to noncitizen residents as well).[10] In short, while national citizenship is ascriptive and "closed" based on shared identity and an organic sense of belonging, local citizenship is consensual and "open" based on residence and mobility.

Until recently, there was no conflict between the two modes of citizenship because they were perceived as complementary. Closure at the federal level facilitated openness at the local level. According to Michael Walzer's famous formulation,

> Neighborhoods can be open only if countries are at least potentially closed. Only if the state makes a selection among would-be members and guarantees the loyalty, security and welfare of the individuals it selects, can local communities take shape as "indifferent" associations, determined solely by personal preference and market capacity.[11]

Although this formulation is deficient and perhaps "chimerical," as Linda Bosniak argues[12] (see Chapter 2), it worked well enough for a long time to contain some of the inherent contradictions of citizenship. Today, however, the local and national modes of citizenship are being drawn into direct conflict by the effects of "globalization," that is, our era of relatively free

---

[9] *See id.*; Saskia Sassen, Territory, Authority, Rights 6, 36, 40–54, 64–67 (updated ed. 2008).

[10] See the discussion in Chapter 2.

[11] Michael Walzer, Spheres of Justice 38–39 (1983).

[12] *See* Linda Bosniak, *Being Here: Ethical Territoriality and the Rights of Immigrants, in* Citizenship between Past and Future 123, 128 (Engin Isin et al. eds. 2008).

trade, free immigration, capital mobility, and global cultural and technological integration. As borders have opened and economies have been largely restructured into knowledge- and service-based systems, cities have enjoyed almost all of the economic growth, benefitting from the entrepreneurship and innovation fostered by mobility and the close proximity of strangers in urban quarters, "the strength of weak ties" in the memorable phrase of sociologist Mark Granovetter.[13] Due to a steady stream of immigrants and professionals in the finance, service, and technology industries, these cities have become younger, more ethnically diverse, and more open to new ideas. Cities that have thrived in recent years as a result of their openness have sought, for both instrumental and ideological reasons, to expand the boundaries of citizenship, as phenomena like the rise of sanctuary cities and San Francisco's recent ballot measure attest.[14]

For many other places, especially rural communities and smaller metropolitan areas, globalization has been perceived as a curse rather than a blessing. As the global knowledge-based economy favors places where large numbers of people cluster, it disfavors places where they are more thinly populated. A recent report demonstrates that half of the job growth in the United States since 2010 has been concentrated in seventy-three counties comprising just a third of the nation's population, all of which are among the country's densest urban areas.[15] As labor and capital have concentrated in larger metropolitan areas, they have emptied out these smaller places. Between 2010 and 2014, rural areas lost an average of 33,000 people per year, a period during which cities gained as many as 2.3 million people per year.[16] Persistent population loss has caused these places to become whiter, older,

---

[13] Mark S. Granovetter, *The Strength of Weak Ties*, 78 Am. J. Soc. 1360 (1973).

[14] *See* Kenneth Stahl, *Preemption, Federalism and Local Democracy*, 44 Fordham Urb. L.J. 133, 150–51 (2017); Richard Florida, Who's Your City (2008); Cristina M. Rodriguez, *The Significance of the Local in Immigration Regulation*, 106 Mich. L. Rev. 567, 577 (2008) (describing the appeal of sanctuary and other immigrant-friendly policies for "global cities").

[15] *See* Richard Florida, *Geographic Inequality Is Swallowing the Recovery*, CityLab (May 23, 2016), http://www.citylab.com/politics/2016/05/there-are-more-losers-than-winners-in-americas-economic-recovery-due-to-geographic-inequality/483989/ [https://perma.cc/56XL-WZFU]. Florida also notes increasing inequality in job growth between the twenty largest counties nationwide and the rest of the country. *Id.*

[16] *See* Alana Semuels, *The Graying of Rural America*, CityLab (Jun. 2, 2016), http://www.citylab.com/housing/2016/06/the-graying-of-rural-america/485288/ [https://perma.cc/9MAQ-TFN8] (on rural population loss); Emily Badger, *Metropolitan Areas Are Now Fueling Virtually All of America's Population Growth*, Wash. Post (Mar. 27, 2014), https://www.washingtonpost.com/news/wonk/wp/2014/03/27/metropolitan-areas-are-now-fueling-virtually-all-of-americas-population-growth/ [https://perma.cc/9ENF-LHDJ] (on urban population growth).

less educated, and more insulated from cultural change. Along with "brain drain" and economic depression, residents of these places sense that they are losing social status and their traditional moral values to a vacuous urban culture obsessed with transitory prosperity.[17] In an effort to slow the pace of demographic and economic change, places like Hazleton, Pennsylvania, and Farmers Branch, Texas, attempted to enact their own immigration policies but were stymied by the courts because, as noted before, local borders are required to be formally open.[18]

Feeling themselves to be the collateral damage of globalization's winner-take-all culture, many people in these smaller metropolitan areas have turned a resentful eye toward cities and their vaunted openness. They blame cities' expansive approach to citizenship and, relatedly, cities' increasing ethnic and racial diversity, for the economic and moral decline of their communities.[19] Donald Trump was elected President of the United States, largely thanks to people from those smaller metropolitan areas hit hard by globalization, on the strength of promises to revitalize these forgotten places, turn back the tide of demographic change, and punish cities.[20] One way Trump has done this, in addition to blowing up trade deals, tightening immigration laws, and attacking sanctuary cities, has been to assert or otherwise imply that minorities and urban dwellers can never be "real" citizens. He has denounced immigrants in racial or religious terms, calling Mexicans "rapists," deriding protections for immigrants from "shithole" countries, and falsely claiming that Muslim prayer

---

[17] *See* Stahl, *supra* note 14, at 152–56.

[18] For context on the Hazleton and Farmers Branch cases, see Stella Burch Elias, *The New Immigration Federalism*, 74 OHIO ST. L.J. 703 (2013).

[19] *See generally* Ashley Jardina, WHITE IDENTITY POLITICS 207–11 (2019) (observing that globalization enhanced the sense among Trump's white supporters that the white race was losing status); KATHERINE J. CRAMER, THE POLITICS OF RESENTMENT (2016) (describing "rural consciousness" in Wisconsin that drives political participation, characterized by resentment of perceived urban values, antipathy toward government, and racist attitudes).

[20] *See* James Surowiecki, *Losers!*, NEW YORKER (June 6 & 13, 2016), http://www.newyorker.com/magazine/2016/06/06/losers-for-trump [https://perma.cc/VS6F-4QMR] (noting that Trump's campaign was driven by a sense of loss among his supporters); David Dudley, *The GOP Is Afraid of My City*, CITYLAB (July 22, 2016), http://www.citylab.com/crime/2016/07/the-gop-is-afraid-of-baltimore-chicago-detroit-st-louis/492671 [https://perma.cc/PWG3-QDUQ] (arguing that Trump's anti-urban platform was aimed at scaring rural voters who are terrified of cities); Vann R. Newkirk II, *Mayors vs. Trump*, CITYLAB (July 27, 2016), http://www.citylab.com/politics/2016/07/cities-mayors-trump/493211 [https://perma.cc/DQ9F-43V6] (observing that Trump's campaign message on crime, immigration, and other issues was essentially anti-urban); Josh Stephens, *Trump to Cities: You're Dead to Me*, PLANETIZEN (July 26, 2016, 8:00 AM), http://www.planetizen.com/node/87620/trump-cities-you're-dead-me [https://perma.cc/ANF8-NR57] (comparing Trump's "law and order" message to its Nixonian forerunner in the 1970s and noting the anti-urban roots of the message).

rugs were found at the southern border. The clear implication is that Mexican-Americans, Muslims, and refugees from places like Haiti are unworthy of being true citizens. Likewise, he has persistently attacked prominent black Americans for being violent, unpatriotic, or dumb. And he has smeared cities like San Francisco and Chicago as "disgusting," "a disaster," and "worse than Afghanistan."[21]

The urban expansion of citizenship thus leads to its opposite, a retrenchment of a backward-looking, place-bound, and racialized conception of citizenship. Securing national borders and instilling a shared sense of national identity rooted in seemingly primordial characteristics provides a form of solace as well as a bulwark against these unwanted cultural and economic changes. The city, with its open borders, cosmopolitan values, and flexible approach toward citizenship, appears to be the embodiment of all the evils of globalization. In a vicious circle, cities redouble their commitment to openness, inviting still more recriminations. Local and national citizenship have thus become irreconcilable.

I.1 THE DIFFERENCE BETWEEN LOCAL CITIZENSHIP AND URBAN CITIZENSHIP

My contention that our current political crisis is partially a conflict over the meaning of citizenship is a departure from the existing literature dealing with the subject of local citizenship.[22] Within this body of literature, much of which builds on the French theorist Henri LeFebvre's idea of "the right to the city," local citizenship is exemplified by the ancient Greek city-states, where residents met in public to deliberate on the political issues of the day. According to the literature, this active, participatory form of local citizenship was destroyed by capitalism and the modern state, which obliterated the public spaces in which people could gather and replaced them with enlarged private spaces for isolated consumption. Citizenship was transformed from the

---

[21] *See* Rumore, *supra* note 7.

[22] For characteristic examples of the literature described in this section, see Remaking Urban Citizenship: Organizations, Institutions and the Right to the City (Michael Peter Smith & Michael McQuarrie eds. 2012); Don Mitchell, The Right to the City: Social Justice and the Fight for Public Space 140 (2003); Democracy, Citizenship and the Global City (Engin Isin ed., 2000); Cities and Citizenship (James Holston ed. 1999); Richard T. Ford, *City-states and Citizenship*, in Citizenship Today: Global Perspectives and Practices 209, 210 (T. Alexander Aleinikoff & Douglas Klusmeyer eds., 2001); Mark Purcell, *Citizenship and the Right to the Global City*, 27.3 Int'l. J. Urb. & Regional Research 564 (2003).

collective, public-minded civic activity that characterized the city-states into a thinner conception based on individual rights and market freedom. As part of that transformation, citizenship was removed from the local level, the scale at which people could experience civic empowerment through face-to-face engagement with their peers, and located exclusively at the level of the nation-state, a scale at which relations are abstract and impersonal. When urban dwellers wrest the city's places away from capital and appropriate it for their own use, they are exercising their "right to the city," pushing back against the enervated modern conception of nation-state citizenship in an attempt to revive the older idea of local citizenship, a citizenship that is active, participatory, oppositional, and rooted in the city's public places. For this reason, most of the literature views local citizenship as something inherently "urban," arising out of the spontaneous interactions and mobilizations that characterize cities, and these writers tend to use the term "urban citizenship" rather than, as here, the broader term "local citizenship." Like myself, these writers tend to see federal citizenship in crisis as a result of globalization and population mobility, and they assert that urban citizenship could re-emerge out of the ashes of nation-state citizenship.[23]

In my view, this idea of "urban citizenship" misses a great deal about local citizenship and the relationship between local and federal citizenship. The nation-state has not destroyed or displaced local citizenship. What it has done is change the nature of local citizenship from the "republican" idea of active, participatory self-government to a more "liberal" idea of local citizenship based on residence, mobility, and market choice, as a complement to the identity and closure of federal citizenship. It is this liberal idea of local citizenship we now see cities embracing as they reap the benefits of globalization. However, liberal local citizenship is not specifically "urban." In fact,

---

[23] One recent work on urban citizenship that does not appear to have been influenced by LeFebvre is URBAN CITIZENSHIP AND AMERICAN DEMOCRACY (Amy Bridges & Michael Javen Fortner eds. 2016). However, this book also focuses on "urban" rather than "local" citizenship and, much like the work in the "right to the city" tradition, generally treats citizenship as synonymous with participation, consistent with the ancient republican tradition of citizenship. *See* Michael Javen Fortner, *Urban Autonomy and Effective Citizenship, in* URBAN CITIZENSHIP AND AMERICAN DEMOCRACY, *supra* note 23, at 23, 24 ("*effective citizenship* emphasizes individual engagement with city politics and the *capacity* of residents to determine the fate of their communities . . . ").

A few important works on local citizenship that appear to have avoided the trap of equating local citizenship with the citizenship of the ancient Greek city-state and understood that it can take a variety of forms include Blank, *supra* note 8; Monica W. Varsanyi, *Interrogating 'Urban Citizenship' vis-à-vis Undocumented Migration*, 10 Cit. Stud. 229 (2006); Rainer Baubock, *Reinventing Urban Citizenship*, 7 CIT. STUD. 139, 148, 151 (2003). Even in many of these pieces "urban citizenship" remains the predominant framing, as their titles illustrate.

although cities have been on the front lines of much of the current conflict over citizenship, local citizenship today may be embodied above all by the sprawling, auto-centered suburbs, which rarely offer genuine places of civic engagement but which, within our political and legal tradition, are seen as models of mobility and consumer choice.[24] Furthermore, as I have already indicated, cities in smaller metropolitan areas like Hazleton and Farmers Branch are also illustrative of liberal local citizenship insofar as they are legally constructed as "open" and mobile, and therefore barred from enacting their own immigration rules. While cities like San Francisco celebrate the open-ness of their citizenship policies, places like Hazleton and Farmers Branch may resent it, and that very resentment is part of what causes them to embrace the promise of a more ascriptive, closed citizenship offered by demagogues like Donald Trump.

Undoubtedly, scholars and advocates of urban citizenship would consider this new "local citizenship" unworthy of the name "citizenship." A citizenship chained to markets and consumption is a thin gruel compared to the "real" public-minded citizenship of the Greek city-state, a mockery of cities' proud tradition of civic activity and engagement. Whatever we think of it, however, the local citizenship I describe here *is* a form of citizenship. Descriptively, liberalism is as much a part of the tradition of citizenship and local life as republicanism. The idea that local citizenship is somehow antithetical to a modern preoccupation with markets and consumption belies the fact that cities have always been centers of market activity as much as political activity, and the public spaces where the Greeks practiced politics were the same places where they engaged in trade. Normatively, it is not clear that liberal local citizenship is inferior to republican "urban citizenship." Local govern-ments' embeddedness in global markets has induced a cosmopolitan view of citizenship that has inoculated them from the reactionary ethnic nationalism now gripping our federal government. Cities have maintained a positive attitude toward foreigners and an openness to diversity at least partly because of their dependence on trade. The many economic benefits that cities receive today from liberal trade and immigration policies have likewise induced a more open attitude toward citizenship. This is true not only of big "global cities" like New York and San Francisco but, as Abigail Fisher Williamson observes in a recent book, it is also true of smaller cities and towns, which have largely responded to immigrants by welcoming them (albeit often after an

---

[24] On the many contradictions of suburbia, see, for example, THE NEW SUBURBAN HISTORY (Kevin M. Kruse & Thomas J. Sugrue eds., 2006); ROBERT FISHMAN, BOURGEOIS UTOPIAS: THE RISE AND FALL OF SUBURBIA (1987).

initial period of hostility).[25] For that reason, many observers today see our local citizenship, the citizenship produced by trade and consumption and embeddedness in markets, as the last hope to save the future from the destructive path of ethnic nationalism.[26] By contrast, the idea of "urban citizenship," based as it is on an organic relationship between people and territory, risks sliding into an ascriptive form of nationalism. Nation-states around the world, not least among them the United States, are retreating into just such a primordial idea of citizenship rooted in place.

Nevertheless, the "urban citizenship" literature is a valuable critique of the excesses of liberal local citizenship and a reminder of local citizenship's potential. While municipalities' embeddedness in markets has perhaps immunized them against the perils of nationalism, it has also subjected them to a different danger, the danger of allowing the market to become the measure of all things. Something is clearly amiss when billionaires and soda companies devote millions to funding public schools, and Domino's Pizza sends out trucks to fix potholes on city streets.[27] The provision of basic city services has become far too dependent on the largesse of corporations and the wealthy. At the same time, cities like San Francisco piously call themselves "sanctuary cities" open to all comers while blocking the production of most new housing, making the city inaccessible to all but the very affluent. The clear message is that San Francisco will extend citizenship to all who can pay

---

[25] *See* Williamson, *supra* note 2, at 3, 134–35, 162–64, 176–77.

[26] *See* Benjamin R. Barber, If Mayors Ruled the World: Dysfunctional Nations, Rising Cities 116 (2013); Nilanjana Roy, *Cities Offer Sanctuary against the Insularity of Nationalism*, Fin. Times (Apr. 4, 2017), https://www.ft.com/content/b54093f0-191f-11e7-9c35-0dd2cb31823a; Robert Muggah & Misha Glenny, *Populism Is Poison. Plural Cities Are the Antidote*, World Econ. Forum (Jan. 4, 2017), https://www.weforum.org/agenda/2017/01/populism-is-poison-plural-cities-are-the-antidote/; Benjamin Barber, *In the Age of Donald Trump, the Resistance Will Be Localized*, The Nation (Jan. 18, 2017), https://www.thenation.com/article/in-the-age-of-donald-trump-the-resistance-will-be-localized/.

[27] In 2010, billionaire Mark Zuckerberg donated $100 million to create a foundation to improve public schools in the city of Newark, New Jersey, a move that is now widely considered to have been a failure. *See* Leanna Garfield, *Mark Zuckerberg Once Made a $100 Million Investment in a Major U.S. City to Help Fix Its Schools – Now the Mayor Says the Effort 'Parachuted' in and Failed*, Bus. Insider (May 12, 2018, 11:00 AM), https://www.businessinsider.com/mark-zuckerberg-schools-education-newark-mayor-ras-baraka-cory-booker-2018-5. More recently, basketball star LeBron James's foundation helped create the "I Promise" public school in Akron, Ohio, with encouraging results so far. *See* Erica L. Green, *Lebron James Opened a School that Was Considered an Experiment. It's Showing Promise*, N.Y. Times (Apr. 12, 2019), https://www.nytimes.com/2019/04/12/education/lebron-james-school-ohio.html. On Domino's crusade to fix potholes, see Andrew Zaleski, *Why Domino's Pizza Is Fixing Potholes Now*, CityLab.com (Jun. 14, 2018), https://www.citylab.com/transportation/2018/06/dominos-pizza-is-fixing-potholes-now-and-thats-fine/562829/.

to live there. This backsliding into market subservience is exactly what the urban citizenship literature protests against. The question that hangs over this book, then, is whether we can formulate a model of local citizenship that avoids the perils of both reactionary ethnic nationalism and market liberalism.

I.2 METHODOLOGICAL NOTE

My methodology differs somewhat from the urban citizenship literature. Where that literature largely emphasizes how citizenship arises from people's everyday practices and uses of public space, I focus primarily on the way that citizenship is inscribed in law, meaning case law as well as statutory and regulatory law. Citizenship is here a construct, a way of thinking that has been promulgated and popularized by state decision makers for reasons that suit the state's ideological needs. It is "top-down" rather than "bottom-up." Frances Olsen has referred to this type of construct as a "structure of consciousness," which she defines as "a shared vision of the social universe that underlies a society's culture and also shapes the society's view of what social relationships are 'natural' and, therefore, what social reforms are possible."[28] Though a product of elite ideology, a structure of consciousness takes root in the popular imagination, shaping the way people think and act. In the context of citizenship, once courts and decision makers constructed local citizenship as "liberal," rooted in mobility and interest, people adapted their understandings of local citizenship to fit the construct. For example, as Williamson reports, many municipalities have been induced to adopt a friendly attitude toward immigrants precisely because courts have barred them from erecting barriers to immigration. Therefore, understanding how local citizenship has been legally constructed is critically important to understanding how local citizenship is practiced. That is my task in Parts I and II of this book.

On the other hand, because citizenship is a structure of consciousness produced by elite ideology, it does not necessarily reflect empirical reality or the lived experience of people. According to Olsen, a structure of consciousness causes what Marx called "self-alienation," which "prevents us from realizing the range of choices available to us."[29] We have "impoverished notions of community and freedom."[30] For that reason, municipalities have

---

[28] Frances E. Olsen, *The Family and the Market: A Study of Ideology and Legal Reform*, 96 HARV. L. REV. 1497, 1498 (1983).

[29] *Id.* at 1563–64.

[30] *Id.* at 1566.

not always quiescently accepted their subjection to an elite construct of citizenship, but have frequently sought (usually unsuccessfully) to dismantle that construct and recover more robust notions of community and freedom. Therefore, after Parts I and II elaborate the ways that local citizenship has been legally constructed by elites in a top-down manner, Part III describes, in the tradition of the urban citizenship literature, how local governments and their residents have attempted to recover alternative modes of citizenship rooted in local knowledge, local practice, and local places.

I.3 PLAN OF THE BOOK

As described, this book is divided into three parts. Part I examines how the American legal and political tradition has attempted to mediate an internal contradiction in the meaning of citizenship by dividing the competing aspects of citizenship between the federal and local scales. That effort worked well enough for a time, but globalization has caused local and federal citizenship to clash and exposed the self-contradictory nature of modern citizenship. Chapter 1 explains how the modern state simultaneously maintains commitments to three different conceptions of citizenship that are all in some tension with each other: the republican, liberal, and ethno-nationalist models of citizenship. Liberalism stresses individual market freedom and natural rights; republicanism emphasizes collective civic activity; ethno-nationalism is based on solidarity and identity. We have managed to mitigate the inherent conflicts among these conceptions through the distinction, long central to the idea of citizenship, between the "public" and "private" spheres. Citizens live primarily private lives, where they are ruled by the marketplace and individual desires, but occasionally enter the public sphere to engage in politics, where they become part of an organic polity unified by a common sense of purpose and shared civic identity.

Chapter 2 then details how this distinction has been operationalized through jurisdictional scale, or federalism. Through a mosaic of laws regarding suffrage, immigration, education and public benefits, zoning, civil rights, and others, our system has designated federal citizenship as the public sphere of identity and civic activity, and local citizenship as the private sphere of the market and the family. The potential for conflict among the various conceptions of citizenship is muted because their contradictory components are divided into separate spheres and each is then confined to its designated sphere. This chapter also describes, however, how globalization has caused the public/private distinction to break down, and with it, the line between local and federal citizenship to become blurred. As that has happened, the contradictions among the three conceptions of citizenship have become more pronounced, resulting in a crisis in the meaning of citizenship and increasing hostility between cities and the state.

Chapter 3 presents a brief history of local citizenship that describes the process by which our ideas about citizenship came to be divided between federal and local scales. Our bifurcated conception of citizenship was a highly contingent product of the nation-state's long evolution from the ancient city-state. There was never a conscious decision to divide citizenship the way we did.

Part II illustrates the trajectory of local and federal citizenship with three case studies of classes of people who at some time or another enjoyed suffrage or other benefits of citizenship at the municipal level without enjoying them at the national level: women, noncitizens, and landowners. In each case, the reason for the divergent treatment of the class at issue has been the desire to steer among the various conceptions of citizenship by maintaining a firm distinction between the private sphere of local citizenship and the public sphere of federal citizenship. These three case studies also demonstrate the ways in which the public/private distinction has begun collapsing under the weight of globalization, destabilizing our understanding of citizenship.

Chapter 4 presents the historical case of woman suffrage. Though prior to the Nineteenth Amendment women were deemed unsuited for citizenship at the federal level because their designated place was exclusively within the private sphere of the home rather than the public sphere of politics, they nevertheless attained the right to vote in local elections in many places because the municipality was itself perceived as a private, home-like sphere dedicated to quotidian functions like the care of children that fell squarely within women's sphere. Granting women the right to vote in local elections was thus consistent with the idea that local citizenship was qualitatively distinct from federal citizenship.

A similar pattern is evident today in the case of noncitizen residents, as Chapter 5 illustrates. By the late nineteenth century the prevailing ethno-nationalist ethos of the day established that noncitizens, much like women, were incapable of federal citizenship because of both racial distinctions and questions about the loyalty of noncitizens. At the same time, however, local citizenship was coming to be understood as something entirely different, determined by mobility and choice rather than loyalty and identity. Some cities have accordingly granted the right of suffrage to noncitizen residents on the grounds that they share a common interest with other local residents in the provision of municipal services. Perhaps more importantly, cities are required to give noncitizens many "social rights" that have increasingly come to be synonymous with citizenship, like housing, education, and security. This chapter focuses on two of those rights, the right of education enshrined in the Supreme Court's decision in *Plyler v. Doe*,[31] and the right of security exemplified by the sanctuary city. In both cases, these rights have been conferred on noncitizens on the premise that social rights are incidents of residence rather than nationality. In order to make local citizenship a matter of private consumer choice, local services such as education and security are bundled together with residence so that local "consumer-voters" can more efficiently shop for municipalities in which to settle. Thus, noncitizen residents' enjoyment of local citizenship follows from local citizenship being perceived as private and liberal in nature.

Chapter 6 describes how some local governments have given rights of citizenship, including voting rights, to nonresident landowners. Indeed, some municipalities have actually *limited* the franchise exclusively to landowners. Once again, this is indicative of the distinctive nature of local citizenship. Property ownership ceased being a prerequisite for voting in state and federal elections by the 1850s, as citizenship was coming to be seen primarily in ethno-nationalist terms as a matter of shared identity. Local governments, reflecting their history as commercial entities, have been more open to tying the franchise to landownership, and as a de facto matter, many cities today use zoning regulations to ensure that anyone who cannot afford to purchase a home cannot acquire residence, and therefore the right to vote. This de facto property qualification for local citizenship illustrates that local citizenship is constructed as purely private and liberal, predicated upon consumer choice, mobility, and self-interest rather than identity.

Chapter 7 brings the three case studies of women, noncitizens, and landowners together to show how, as globalization has caused the public/private distinction to come apart, the distinctively local form of citizenship has seeped into the federal sphere and threatened the ethno-nationalist conception of citizenship. With increasing labor and capital mobility across national borders, nation-states confront the same pressures cities have long faced to confer citizenship on the basis of interest and choice rather than nationality, but there is fierce opposition to doing so on the grounds that it will undermine the basis of federal citizenship by fraying the ties of ethnicity, history, and territory that supposedly link the members of the state's "imagined community."[32] This opposition takes the form of growing animosity toward

---

[31] 457 U.S. 202 (1982).
[32] *See* BENEDICT ANDERSON, IMAGINED COMMUNITIES (1983).

free trade, immigration, and the cities that symbolize an open and flexible approach to citizenship.

While much of the frustration over the nature of citizenship today comes from the political right, it has long been echoed by observers on the political left who denounce the way cities have become trapped within a culture of "neoliberalism." In this view, a citizenship based on mobility and economic interest degrades both citizenship and the city by conceptualizing citizens as glorified consumers and the municipality as a passive and enervated receptacle for consumer demands. Furthermore, the liberal idea of local citizenship has effectively legitimized a widespread pattern of racial segregation by passing off racially identified spaces as the work of private consumer markets rather than government policy decisions. Liberalism is, it seems, as fraught with difficulties as ethnic nationalism. Accordingly, the advocates of "urban citizenship" described earlier have emphasized several alternative traditions of citizenship, rooted in local places, which may offer a pathway forward without the perils of either liberalism or nationalism.

Part III dives into some of these alternative traditions. As Chapter 8 explores, what unites them all is a rejection of the liberal idea of citizenship founded in consumption and markets as well as the ethno-nationalist idea of citizenship based on a "public" perceived as an organic unity. The public is apprehended instead as a place where strangers come together, and citizenship as an activity that occurs in those public places. In other words, the public is a *city*, and the citizen is a participant in a vibrant and diverse civic life rather than either a passive consumer or a nondescript entity subsumed within an organic polity. Unlike the liberal idea of local citizenship that privileges mobility solely for the white middle class, these alternative traditions seek to empower communities of color to chart their own destinies by asserting their rights to the city's places.

Chapter 9 revisits the republican conception of the citizen, a conception that has been largely muted in modern society in favor of the liberal and ethno-nationalist ideas. In recent years there has been an effort to "revive" republicanism as an alternative to both the consumerism and individualism of liberal citizenship and the unreflective jingoism of ethnic nationalism. Scholars like Michael Sandel have drawn on the republican tradition of city-state citizenship to call for a renewed commitment to a republican urban citizenship. In this vision, the city would have the means to protect itself against the forces of global capitalism and the disruptions of gentrification, and its public places – its parks, schools, and libraries – would be sites of civic activity where strangers could mingle without being judged either by their identity or their wallet. Unfortunately, however, the republican concern with protecting the city from the world leads it down the path to a quasi-nationalist xenophobia, in which outsiders are ostracized and scapegoated.

Chapter 10 introduces the "postmodern" conception of local citizenship. On this view, the city is a "fortuitous association" where people come together in all of their differences, and where members of marginalized groups exercise a form of citizenship by appearing in public and challenging their formal exclusion from political power. Unlike the republican idea, postmodern citizenship rejects walls and rejects the idea that the city should isolate itself from the world; it is open and borderless. Yet, for that very reason, postmodern citizenship is necessarily fragile and ephemeral. A borderless city risks diluting the normative subgroups that make it possible to tolerate the impersonality and anonymity of the city; if they lose their ability to withdraw into their subgroups, people may flee the city entirely for ethnically and racially homogenous suburbs.

Finally, Chapter 11 considers "differentiated" citizenship. This model would incorporate people into the political life of the city as members of their cultural subgroups rather than as individuals. Differentiated citizenship thus enables historically marginalized groups such as racial minorities to assert collective rights that have often been denied them under the individualistic liberal model. Among other rights, groups would have the ability to exercise control over places with which they share deep cultural, economic, and political ties. Differentiated citizenship thus attempts to steer between republican and postmodern citizenship. It calls for affirmative recognition of normative subgroups in society, but in such a manner that will incorporate those subgroups into political life, rather than enabling them to withdraw from political life. As such, differentiated citizenship rejects both the republican insistence on a homogenous political "community" that rigidly polices its borders as well as the postmodern refusal to draw any boundary lines at all. Ultimately, however, differentiated citizenship is problematic because it largely reinforces the marginalization of the groups it wishes to empower by legitimizing the status quo of racially identified places.

In a Conclusion, I argue that the reason these theories all fail is because attempting to excise liberalism from local citizenship is futile. Cities were built on commerce, and commerce is as much in the lifeblood of cities as politics is. But liberalism has never been *only* about commerce. It is also about equality. Because of its commitment to equality, liberalism has had a far better track record in advancing human freedom than any of its competitors. And as globalization has advanced, we may have gone too far down the path of liberalism to turn back. Embracing liberalism, while also committing to reforming it, will enable us to harness the best of local citizenship's historical legacy for a future in which the fate of citizenship and the nation-state are still uncertain.

PART I

Citizenship Federalism

Over the last decade, legal scholars have paid increasing attention to "immigration federalism," or the ways that immigration powers are divided among levels of government.[1] Little of this scholarship, however, has grappled with the question of "citizenship federalism," that is, how the division of powers over matters such as immigration reflects divergent ideas about citizenship.[2] Much like the sociologists in the "urban citizenship" tradition of LeFebvre, legal scholars have generally assumed that citizenship exists solely at the level of the nation-state.[3] For

[1] For representative examples, see Stella Burch Elias, *The New Immigration Federalism*, 74 Ohio St. L.J. 703 (2013); Rick Su, *Local Fragmentation as Immigration Regulation*, 47 Hous. L. Rev. 367 (2010); Clare Huntington, *The Constitutional Dimension of Immigration Federalism*, 61 Vand. L. Rev. 787, 812–23 (2008); Cristina M. Rodriguez, *The Significance of the Local in Immigration Regulation*, 106 Mich. L. Rev. 567 (2008); Juliet Stumpf, *States of Confusion: The Rise of State and Local Power Over Immigration*, 86 N.C. L. Rev. 1557 (2008).

[2] A few articles have addressed "citizenship federalism," but generally done so only briefly, or neglected the local context. See Vicki C. Jackson, *Citizenship and Federalism, in* CITIZENSHIP TODAY: GLOBAL PERSPECTIVES AND PRACTICES 127 (T. Alexander Aleinikoff & Douglas Klusmeyer eds., 2001) (discussing citizenship federalism primarily by contrasting *state* with federal citizenship, and concluding that federal citizenship is "primary"); see also Willem Maas, *Multilevel Citizenship, in* THE OXFORD HANDBOOK OF CITIZENSHIP 644 (Ayelet Shachar et al. eds. 2017); Monica W. Varsanyi, *Documenting Undocumented Migrants: The Matriculas Consulares as Neoliberal Local Membership*, 12 GEOPOLITICS 299 (2007); Yishai Blank, *Spheres of Citizenship*, 8 THEORETICAL INQUIRIES L. 411 (2007). Rainer Baubock, *Reinventing Urban Citizenship*, 7 CIT. STUD. 139, 148, 151 (2003). Two interesting law review symposium articles have very briefly discussed the possibility of "local citizenship." See Rose Cuizon Villazor, *"Sanctuary Cities" and Local Citizenship*, 37 FORDHAM URB. L.J. 573 (2010); Peter J. Spiro, *Formalizing Local Citizenship*, 37 FORDHAM URB. L.J. 559 (2010).

[3] A pair of recent articles addresses the question of state citizenship, but interestingly, they both see state citizenship as a dormant status that was once predominant and could potentially be revived in the future. See Maeve Glass, *Citizens of the State*, 85 U. Chi. L. Rev. 865 (2018); Peter L. Markowitz, *Undocumented No More: The Power of State Citizenship*, 67 Stan. L. Rev. 869 (2015); As I address at the end of Chapter 2, state citizenship is indeed dormant for a variety of reasons, but *local* citizenship remains an active status.

instance, in an essay entitled *City-States and Citizenship*, a rare example of legal scholarship that even addresses local citizenship, Richard T. Ford writes that "[a] characteristic of modernity is the close identification of citizenship with the nation-state," and that today, by contrast to ancient Athens, "only nations have citizens."[4] He further argues that as globalization destabilizes the nation-state, urban citizenship is likely to re-appear in something resembling its previous republican incarnation. In the future he imagines, "[u]rban citizenship would not replace citizenship, but rather supplement it. The city would become a place of stronger political affiliation and political power, reflecting the importance of the contemporary global village and the real virtues of decentralization of power."[5]

The goal of this Part is to demonstrate that local citizenship is neither an artifact of the republican past nor an aspiration for the global future, but a status that actually exists in the present. Matters such as immigration, the distribution of public benefits, land use, civil rights enforcement, security, education, the franchise, and others are divided between the federal government and local governments (as well as states, though these today play a more muted role), in a way that reflects divergent ideas about citizenship. As I discussed in the Introduction, the reason scholars like Ford may not have identified this division of power as "citizenship federalism" is because they see local citizenship as something quintessentially "urban" in nature. Local citizenship today, however, no longer conforms to the republican model of the ancient Greek city-state but is exemplified more by the suburb than the city.

Once I have established that local and federal citizenship actually coexist within our nation-state, we can then see how globalization is threatening that coexistence, causing the local and national ideas of citizenship to come directly into conflict and raising the question of what it means to be a citizen.

---

[4]   Richard T. Ford, *City-states and Citizenship*, in CITIZENSHIP TODAY: GLOBAL PERSPECTIVES
      AND PRACTICES 209, 210 (T. Alexander Aleinikoff & Douglas Klusmeyer eds., 2001).

[5]   *Ibid.* at 211; 224–25; 228.

1

Three Models of Citizenship

Citizenship is a protean concept. It has never had a fixed meaning. Nevertheless, students of citizenship have usefully identified several different models or ways of thinking about citizenship. In this chapter, I discuss three models that have been particularly important in the formation and maintenance of modern citizenship: the republican, liberal, and ethno-nationalist models. These three models conflict in various ways, but they have been reconciled in our political culture based on something they all share: Each model is the product of a distinction in western thought between the public and private spheres. The public/private distinction, accordingly, underpins the entire western idea of citizenship. As I shall elaborate in subsequent chapters, though, globalization is steadily undermining this distinction and, as it does so, the liberal, republican, and ethno-nationalist models have all begun to clash. The municipality, which is the fount of all our ideas about citizenship and has long straddled the public/private distinction, has become the key battleground in this conflict.

1.1 REPUBLICAN CITIZENSHIP

Drawing inspiration from the practice of direct democracy in the ancient Greek city-states, and embellished by luminaries of western philosophy like Machiavelli, Rousseau, and Hannah Arendt, the republican tradition holds that there is a public realm of civic participation and obligation that is sharply distinguishable from the private sphere of the family and economic life. In the public realm of the *polis*, man is a *citizen*, a wholehearted participant in the political life of the republic. In his capacity as a citizen, each man is expected to act selflessly and independently, to exercise his judgment as to the best interest of the *polis* without regard to his own personal financial or familial interest. Such personal matters are relegated to the private realm of the *oikos*, or home, where men are free to pursue their economic self-interest and enter relationships of dependence to advance that interest. The man only becomes a citizen when he leaves the dependent, self-seeking sphere of the *oikos* and enters the exalted sphere of the *polis*.[1]

The sharp distinction between *polis* and *oikos*, between public and private, led to a persistent preoccupation in republican thought with what became known as "corruption." The thin line between public and private was constantly threatened as private economic and familial concerns bled into the civic affairs of state, degrading and corrupting the purity of the public sphere. The concern with corruption became one of the hallmarks of republican ideology, echoing in the works of scholars over the centuries and powerfully influencing the framers of our Constitution. Zephyr Teachout argues convincingly that preventing corruption was one of the Framers' core concerns. As she argues, much of the Constitution's structure, from the separation of powers to the size of the houses of the legislature, from limitations on accepting foreign gifts to the frequency of elections, were designed to ensure that public officials served the public good and were not ensnared by the many temptations to serve their own self-interest. The framers also placed great reliance on the existence of a stable class of yeoman farmers who would maintain the independence and civic virtue of the republic. They worried that the rise of commerce and landless people would lead inexorably to a decline of civic virtue and an increase in corruption as people became obsessed with the pursuit of money.[2]

---

[1] The most significant contemporary analysis of the various models of citizenship is Linda Bosniak, *Citizenship Denationalized*, 7 IND. J. GLOBAL LEGAL STUD. 447 (2000). Bosniak largely eschews terminology like "liberal," "republican," and "ethno-nationalist," however, using more descriptive terms for these models like "citizenship as rights," "citizenship as political activity," and so on. Her discussion of the republican, or "citizenship as political activity," model is at pp. 470–79. Other important discussions of the republican tradition include Iseult Honohan, *Liberal and Republican Conceptions of Citizenship*, in THE OXFORD HANDBOOK OF CITIZENSHIP 83 (Shachar et al. eds. 2017); J. G. A. Pocock, *The Ideal of Citizenship Since Classical Times*, in THE CITIZENSHIP DEBATES 32 (Gershon Shafir ed., 1998); Adrien Oldfield, *Citizenship and Community*, in THE CITIZENSHIP DEBATES, *supra* at 79; DEREK HEATER, CITIZENSHIP (1990); HANNAH ARENDT, ON REVOLUTION (1963); HANNAH ARENDT, THE HUMAN CONDITION (1958); Rogers M. Smith, *"One United People:" Second-Class Female Citizenship and the American Quest for Community*, 1 YALE J. L. & HUM. 229, 236–39 (1989).

[2] *See* ZEPHYR TEACHOUT, CORRUPTION IN AMERICA: FROM BENJAMIN FRANKLIN'S SNUFF BOX TO CITIZENS UNITED (2014). *See also* LAURA S. UNDERKUFFLER, CAPTURED BY EVIL: THE IDEA OF CORRUPTION IN LAW (2013); GORDON S. WOOD, THE RADICALISM OF THE AMERICAN REVOLUTION (1991); J. G. A. POCOCK, THE MACHIAVELLIAN MOMENT: FLORENTINE POLITICAL THOUGHT AND THE ATLANTIC REPUBLICAN TRADITION (1975).

As the concern with landless people suggests, the corruption that republicans feared was not only the invasion of private concerns into the public sphere but the admission of impure classes of people into the exalted class of citizens. The independence from private concerns that was so vital to the *polis* was only possible because of the relations of strict dependence within the sphere of the *oikos* – the dominance of husband over wife, parent over child, master over slave, and so forth. Those deemed too bound up with the private sphere of the home and market to exercise true independence – most notably women, laborers, and non-citizens – were permanently excluded from the category of citizens. Indeed, the disfranchisement of these classes was a necessary precondition to the independence of the male citizen that ensured his civic-minded judgment. In early America, republican concerns about corruption led to the franchise being confined to property-owning or taxpaying males, and later the disfranchisement of paupers and immigrants. In short, the activity of citizenship that republicans sought to cultivate was only possible by making large numbers of people within the society ineligible for citizenship.[3]

1.2 LIBERAL CITIZENSHIP

The republican city-states of Ancient Greece were fairly short lived, but the republican tradition has lived on mostly as a critique and an aspirational counterpoint to the model of citizenship that displaced it, the "liberal" model. As the late Benjamin Barber observed, ancient Athenians were obsessed with independence because they had so little of it; already by the time of Pericles, Athens was being drawn into an empire that sapped the city-state's independence and gave rise to a new conception of citizenship that was based on one's status as a rights-bearing individual, rather than participation in civic affairs. In Roman times, when St. Paul protested an unjust arrest by calling himself a "citizen" of Rome, he meant not that he lived in the city or participated in its

---

[3] On the exclusion of women, slaves, workers, and others from republican citizenship *see* POCOCK, Note 2, at 34; ARLENE W. SAXONHOUSE, FEAR OF DIVERSITY: THE BIRTH OF POLITICAL SCIENCE IN ANCIENT GREEK THOUGHT (1992); HANNA FENICHEL PITKIN, FORTUNE IS A WOMAN: GENDER AND POLITICS IN THE THOUGHT OF NICCOLO MACHIAVELLI (1984); ARENDT, *supra* note 1, at 27. On the evolution of the property qualification for voting in America, see ALEXANDER KEYSSAR, THE RIGHT TO VOTE: THE CONTESTED HISTORY OF DEMOCRACY IN THE UNITED STATES (2000); Robert J. Steinfeld, *Property and Suffrage in the Early American Republic*, 41 STAN. L. REV. 335 (1989).

politics but that he was entitled to the rights and privileges the Roman Empire granted its members.[4]

This new liberal conception of citizenship was far better suited than the republican conception to a populous, diverse, and geographically dispersed polity, as well as a society engaged in commerce. Republican citizenship presupposed the small, relatively homogenous world of the ancient Greek city-state (Athens at its height is estimated to have had no more than 40,000 citizens) and was clearly unworkable in the modern world of large, diverse nation-states (a single Congressional district in California today has about 800,000 residents). But liberal citizenship could be extended far and wide, as in the case of St. Paul, without diluting what it meant to be a citizen. Furthermore, as a commercial economy replaced a primarily agrarian one, the ideal of a citizen who could devote countless leisure hours to public affairs as he passively earned income on his landed estate courtesy of the unpaid labor of slaves and women gave way to a new reality in which people were obsessed with profit – and in which many people did not own land. In the liberal theory made famous by John Locke, the role of government was to protect private property, not to be a forum for participation. Rather than a set of civic responsibilities, citizenship was the right of an individual to own private property and call upon the government to safeguard it. It was, in short, a status instead of an activity. This shift meant that unlike republicans, who saw the public sphere as the sphere of freedom and the private sphere as literally a de-privation, liberals viewed the private realm as the sphere of freedom and the public as a necessary evil that existed in order to enable that freedom.[5]

By the time of the American Revolution, it was already evident that society was moving towards what Gordon Wood calls "a consciously pluralistic, ethnic, interest-group politics." Self-interest in politics had become a fact of life. The Framers of our Constitution, while motivated by republican concerns about corruption, also recognized that they lived in a world of

---

[4]   *See* Benjamin R. Barber, Jihad v. McWorld 34 (1995); Pocock, *supra* note 2, at 37; On the liberal model of citizenship generally, see Rogers M. Smith, Civic Ideals: Conflicting Visions of Citizenship in U.S. History (1997); Bosniak, *supra* note 1, at 463–70; Honohan, *supra* note 1; Michael Walzer, *Citizenship*, in Political Innovation and Conceptual Change 211 (Terence Ball, et al. eds., 1989); Smith, *supra* note 1, at 233–36.

[5]   *See* Robert S. Dahl, Democracy and Its Critics (1989) (describing small size of Athenian Republic and unsuitability of republican government for large nation-states); Arendt, *supra* note 1 at 38 ("We no longer think primarily of deprivation when we use the word 'privacy,' and this is partly due to the enormous enrichment of the private sphere through modern individualism."); Sanford Levinson, *Suffrage and Community: Who Should Vote?*, 41 Fla. L. Rev. 545 (1989).

diversity and commercial acquisitiveness where civic virtue and direct public participation in political affairs were infeasible, and where politics was pervaded by interest. The classic expression of this ambiguity is James Madison's FEDERALIST 10, perhaps the most famous of the group of essays written to convince the voters of New York to approve the new Constitution. FEDERALIST 10 laments the rise of self-interested "factions" in politics but, rather than seeking to eradicate them, resigns itself to their inevitability.[6] Madison argues that a powerful federal government like the one created by the new Constitution would dilute the efficacy of factions by forcing them to compete for influence on a larger scale. The Constitution Madison and his compatriots were defending was, indeed, a thoroughly liberal document. It accepted and facilitated the rise of a commercial economy by giving the federal government a full complement of powers that promoted an integrated national economy and barred states from implementing protectionist measures that could disrupt that economy. Consistent with the liberal idea that citizenship is a status rather than an activity, the Constitution secured private property rights and a variety of personal rights against government intrusion while providing little in the way of opportunities for republican participation in the public sphere.[7]

The emergence of a market economy was linked as well with another liberal idea – equality. In a society where land was the primary source of wealth, it was also a source of social distinction – those who owned versus those who did not; those who worked the land versus those who profited from it. In a commercial economy, on the other hand, many people did not own land, and money became the great equalizer. As Gordon Wood writes, early Americans justified interest and moneymaking as "egalitarian and democratic." After all, "[w]hen people relate to each other only through interest, there is no obligation, no gratitude required; the relationship was to that extent equal."[8] The idea of market equality was consistent with the tradition of Lockean liberalism, which stressed that humans were naturally equal and only made unequal by political institutions. Natural equality was a point of emphasis during the Revolution, and afterwards, as the number of landless people proliferated, the argument for equality intensified. Property qualifications for voting, long justified on republican grounds that they were necessary to ensure an independent electorate, fell in the face of opposition from landless classes of people articulating claims about their natural rights.

---

[6] *See* THE FEDERALIST NO. 10, at 64 (James Madison) (Jacob E. Cooke ed., 1961).

[7] WOOD, *supra* note 2, at 243–70; SMITH, *supra* note 4, at 123–25.

[8] WOOD, *supra* note 2, at 337

By the end of the 1850s, nearly every state in the Union had abolished the property ownership and taxpaying requirement for voting.[9]

The intermingling of aspirations such as natural rights and equality with the grubby reality of market self-seeking caused liberalism to have some ambiguous implications. While some emphasize the immense "liberating potential" of liberalism's ideals, others, especially those who seek to revive the republican tradition, lament the loss of civic virtue and public participation, and the degraded nature of civic life in a society obsessed with earning and consuming. For the critics liberalism's promise of equality means only that each person "is weighed by his purse, not by his mind, and according to the preponderance of that, he rises or sinks in the scale of public opinion."[10]

1.3 ETHNO-NATIONALIST CITIZENSHIP

The republican and the liberal models of citizenship have existed alongside a third model, the ethno-nationalist model. Where republican theory envisions citizenship as an activity, and liberal theory views it as a status, the ethnonationalist conception considers citizenship a device for linking a group of people together under the banner of a shared culture or identity. By and large, this sense of shared identity is created by differentiating those who are included in the community from those who are excluded – that is, the citizen from the non-citizen. According to Liah Greenfeld, the term "nation" was initially used by the ancient Romans as a derogatory reference to *other* peoples; one defined one's own "nation" only in opposition to others.[11]

Like republican and liberal citizenship, ethno-nationalism has a deep foundation in the United States. Greenfeld traces the origins of nationalism to the time of the British King Henry VIII, when England broke away from the

---

[9] See KEYSSAR, *supra* note 3, at 3–42; Steinfeld, *supra* note 3, at 352–53. Keyssar notes that by the end of the 1850s, the only two property-owning requirements in the United States were restrictions on foreign-born voting in Rhode Island and a restriction on blacks voting in New York.

[10] See WOOD, *supra* note 2, at 243. Republicanism enjoyed a brief "revival" among legal academics during the 1980s, sparked by disillusionment with the Reagan administration. The revival and its flaws are helpfully described in LAURA KALMAN, THE STRANGE CAREER OF LEGAL LIBERALISM 132–63 (1996). The revival was criticized for, among other reasons, neglecting the "liberating potential" of liberalism. *See id.* at 177; *see also* Hendrik Hartog, *Imposing Constitutional Traditions*, 29 WM. & MARY L. REV. 78 (1987). I discuss the republican revival further in Chapter 9.

[11] See LIAH GREENFELD, NATIONALISM: FIVE ROADS TO MODERNITY 4 (1992). For general discussions of the ethno-nationalist model see Bosniak, *supra* note 1, at 479–88; SMITH, *supra* note 4, at 13–39; Smith, *supra* note 1, at 239–41.

Catholic Church and spread its own distinctive religious ideals. English nationalism accordingly involved a mix of chauvinism in which the English were the Bible's "chosen people" and an emerging liberal belief in rational individualism sparked by Protestantism's revolutionary claim that individuals could have an unmediated relationship with the divine.[12] The American colonists adopted this English version of nationalism, but the American commitment to individualism was so extreme that it threatened to undermine national cohesion. It was widely believed that independence from Britain would lead to the disintegration of America.[13] As Greenfeld notes, the common insistence in the years after independence that America was a *nation* contained "an element of wishful thinking" in a society that was extremely diverse and rife with religious conflict.[14] This wishful thinking became especially pronounced in the debates over the proposed US Constitution. In FEDERALIST 2, John Jay wrote that "Providence has been pleased to give this one connected country to one united people – a people descended from the same ancestors, speaking the same languages, professing the same religion, attached to the same principles of government, very similar in their manners and customs."[15] As Rogers Smith argues, FEDERALIST 2 was designed to rebut criticism from the anti-federalist camp that republican government could not succeed in a diverse civilization such as America.[16] Madison's FEDERALIST 10 was of course designed to do just the same, but the two essays attack the problem from opposite directions: Where FEDERALIST 10 accepts the diverse interests of the new republic and seeks to mute conflict among them through a strong federal government, FEDERALIST 2 confidently asserts that diversity itself is a non-issue because the population is mostly homogenous. In any event, Smith observes that, like liberal and republican citizenship, ethno-nationalism is also incorporated into our Constitution, for instance in the requirement that the President be a natural born citizen and that representatives in the House and Senate have seven years of citizenship in the United States.[17]

The ethno-nationalist conception of citizenship meshes with both the liberal and republican conceptions in interesting ways. On one hand, there is a relatively neat kinship between ethno-nationalist and republican

---

[12] *See* GREENFELD, *supra* note 11, at 50–87.

[13] *See id.* at 420–28.

[14] *Id.* at 424.

[15] THE FEDERALIST No. 2, at 9 (John Jay) (Jacob E. Cooke ed., 1961).

[16] Smith, *supra* note 1, at 239–40.

[17] SMITH, *supra* note 4, at 122–23, 128–34; Smith, *supra* note 1, at 239–41.

citizenship. The civic participation at the core of Republican citizenship presupposed, as ethno-nationalist citizenship does, a small and relatively homogenous citizenry. As we have seen, the classical republican tradition strictly excluded foreigners as well as others from admission to the sphere of citizenship. The republican insistence on separating the public from the private and its emphasis on the primacy of the public are also consistent with ethno-nationalism. Under the ethno-nationalist conception, the sphere of citizenship and politics must be strictly separated from the sphere of the market. Prominent theorists of nationalism such as Rousseau and Hegel posited that the "public" represents the organic unity of purpose that defines the nation as a nation. This unity is not simply a shared interest but a more transcendent affective bond that constitutes the people as a single organism. The particular economic concerns that individuals possess, even if widely shared, remain private and can never be the basis of citizenship. Hence, mere participation or influence in the marketplace has no effect on the nature of citizenship. Indeed, nationalism serves to protect its citizens against the impositions of the market.[18]

There is some daylight between the republican and ethno-nationalist conceptions of citizenship, however, insofar as the republican ideal presupposes relatively small, more immediate groupings of people such as the city-state in which citizens could actively participate, whereas nationalism, at least as Rousseau theorizes it, is based on an imagined relation between an abstract state and individuals who are relatively passive recipients of the state's largesse.[19] In that regard, nationalism is more akin to liberalism, which likewise sought to disempower intermediate organizations such as the city and create a direct relationship between individuals and the state.[20]

Liberalism and nationalism were, in fact, born together in England, and their relationship was solidified by the rise of capitalism. Capitalism exploded the hierarchical relationships of feudalism and displaced them with the individualized relationships of the marketplace. Meanwhile, the emergence of print media, what Benedict Anderson called "print-capitalism," knitted

---

[18] *See* Stanley I. Benn & Gerald F. Gaus, *The Liberal Conception of the Public and the Private, in* PUBLIC AND PRIVATE IN SOCIAL LIFE 31, 48–52 (S. I. Benn & G. F. Gaus eds., 1983).

[19] *See* GREENFELD, *supra* note 11, at 174 ("Rousseau advocates nothing less than a totalitarian state with no intermediate bodies between the central state and atomized individuals.")

[20] *See* Gerald E. Frug, *The City as a Legal Concept*, 93 HARV. L. REV. 1057, 1083–90 (1980) (asserting that liberal ideology used the public/private distinction to subordinate local governments and create an unmediated relationship between individuals and the state, because cities were seen as threatening to both state power and individual liberty).

diverse territories into a single economic and cultural unit, an "imagined community."[21] Nevertheless, there was always a latent tension between nationalism and liberalism. As reflected in the Lockean tradition, liberalism asserts that all human beings have natural rights and that the state exists in order to protect those pre-political rights. The state as such is a construct, a means of achieving individual freedom, rather than the embodiment of some primordial association.[22] Therefore, liberal citizenship should in principle be available to all regardless of nationality. Classical economists such as Adam Smith had great difficulty reconciling the liberal principles of free trade, which presupposed open borders and integrated markets, with a nationalist ideology predicated on protectionism and the idea of a "national economy." Yet, free trade and nationalism emerged at the same time. The nation-state was made consistent with liberal ideology on the uncomfortable principle that the nation-state was part of an evolutionary process from smaller to larger groupings that began with primitive village societies and would eventually end with world government.[23]

World government is hardly imminent today, however. As many observers have noted, most people do not conceive of themselves as citizens of the world, but as belonging to this or that place. Michael Walzer perceptively writes that if we are to think of our fellow citizens as our neighbors, we must first have an idea of what it means to be a neighbor.[24] Liberalism's vision of the state as simply a mechanism for private, individual aspirations risks suppressing the innate human desire for association and the need to belong to something greater than ourselves. As Rogers Smith argues, liberalism is rather unsatisfying for those seeking the succor of a community of shared values: "[L]iberalism's attractive insistence on at least a minimum of respect for all persons, inside and outside of one's political community, is in tension with a vivid belief in the importance of one's particular civic membership, one's citizenship."[25]

---

[21] *See* BENEDICT ANDERSON, IMAGINED COMMUNITIES (1983).

[22] *See* Smith, *supra* note 1, at 234 ("The thrust of classical liberalism's oppositional language of personal rights is to cast the claims of all types of associations, including political membership, as threats to personal liberty."); *see also* SMITH, *supra* note 4, at 77–82.

[23] *See* E. J. HOBSBAWM, NATIONS AND NATIONALISM SINCE 1780: PROGRAMME, MYTH, REALITY 25–28 (1990) (on liberal economists' struggles with nationalism); *ibid.* at 38–42 (on how liberalism was reconciled with nationalism); *see also* BARBER, *supra* note 4, at 158–68; YAEL TAMIR, LIBERAL NATIONALISM (1993).

[24] *See* Michael Walzer, *Spheres of Affection*, in FOR LOVE OF COUNTRY 125, 126 (Martha C. Nussbaum & Joshua Cohen eds. 2002).

[25] *See* Smith, *supra* note 1, at 230–31. *See also* Benjamin R. Barber, *Constitutional Faith*, in FOR LOVE OF COUNTRY, *supra* note 24, at 30, 34 ("Our attachments start locally and only then grow outward.")

As a result, people's attachments to their national cultures have generally increased as market liberalization has advanced.[26]

1.4 SYNTHESIZING THE CONCEPTIONS – THE PUBLIC/PRIVATE DISTINCTION

Comparing the three conceptions reveals several fault-lines in the idea of the nation-state and the meaning of modern citizenship. There is an enduring uncertainty about the boundary between the market and the state, the consumer and the citizen, the individual and the community. There is a tension between liberalism's emphasis on liberty and equality, nationalism's need to differentiate citizens from non-citizens, and republicanism's call for a vital sphere of public participation. Historically, these conflicts have been mediated in various ways. Perhaps the most significant mediating device has been the distinction long prevalent in western thought between the public and the private. As we have seen, the distinction the ancient Greeks drew between the public sphere of the *polis* and the private sphere of the *oikos* was essential to the republican idea of the citizen, and it has subsequently become inextricably bound up with the very concept of citizenship.

Before saying more, it's important to stress that the relationship between citizenship and the public/private distinction has two critical implications for the discussion of local citizenship that follows in the next several chapters. First, as we will see, within the American system of government citizenship is defined and distributed simultaneously at the federal and the local scales (and sometimes other scales as well). The bifurcation of citizenship between the federal and the local is predicated, in part, on the public/private distinction. Therefore, this bifurcated approach to citizenship has been the principal mechanism through which the public/private distinction mediates among the liberal, ethno-nationalist, and republican conceptions of citizenship. Under our federal system, the federal and the local occupy what Yishai Blank calls distinct "spheres of citizenship."[27] The federal is the public sphere of ethno-nationalist and republican citizenship; the local is the private sphere of liberal citizenship. Segregating the conceptions of citizenship between the spheres helps to mute the latent conflict among them. Second, during our age of globalization the public/private distinction is steadily eroding. As it does so, the distinction between local and national citizenship becomes blurred and

---

[26] *See, e.g.* MICHAEL IGNATIEFF, BLOOD AND BELONGING 152–55 (1993) (observing how Quebecois nationalist sentiment has intensified with increasing global economic integration).

[27] *See* Yishai Blank, *Spheres of Citizenship*, 8 THEORETICAL INQUIRIES L. 411 (2007).

the tensions among the various conceptions of citizenship become more pronounced. A crisis in what it means to be a citizen manifests as a crisis in the relationship between the nation-state and local governments.

A few caveats are in order. Initially, the fact that our system categorizes the national and the local spheres with different labels does not necessarily mean that municipalities or nation-states always conform to the labels they are assigned. To the contrary, municipalities in particular have frequently resisted being categorized in this way, as I explain in Part III. Though local citizenship is legally constructed as liberal in the ways I shall explain, local governments often act or attempt to act in ways that defy that label, such as adopting their own de facto immigration, trade, or foreign relations policies. Nevertheless, the immediate task in Parts I and II is to demonstrate that the separation of spheres is a "structure of consciousness" that shapes the way judges and policymakers approach citizenship and, often, the way the public thinks about citizenship as well.[28] Subsequently, Part III will demonstrate several ways in which municipalities have attempted to assault that structure of consciousness and implement alternative meanings of local citizenship. A second caveat has to do with the role of states. As the next chapter explains, state governments in the United States once played a dominant role in shaping citizenship, and may do so again. But in the present, they have been largely overshadowed by national and local definitions of citizenship.

To return to the matter at hand, the public/private distinction is a fundamental but notoriously ambiguous characteristic of the modern nation-state. The distinction is ambiguous because it is not a single binary but contains a multitude of overlapping distinctions. According to Jeff Weintraub, for example, the public/private distinction could refer to "[w]hat is hidden or withdrawn versus what is open, revealed, or accessible," or alternatively "[w]hat is individual, or pertains to an individual, versus what is collective, or what affects the interests of a collectivity of individuals."[29] As I explain later, it is within this second sense that the public/private distinction has operated to reconcile the liberal, republican, and ethno-nationalist conceptions of citizenship in the modern American nation-state. In general, this has meant that the public sphere is the sphere of government and politics, while the private sphere is the sphere of the marketplace and the family. Nevertheless, it is

---

[28] Frances E. Olsen's classic article *The Family and the Market: A Study of Ideology and Legal Reform*, 96 HARV. L. REV. 1497 (1983) argues that the conceptual separation of the family and the market functions as a structure of consciousness. I discuss this point further in Chapter 2.

[29] *See* Jeff Weintraub, *The Theory and Politics of the Public/Private Distinction, in* PUBLIC AND PRIVATE IN THOUGHT AND PRACTICE 1, 5 (Jeff Weintraub & Krishan Kumar eds., 1997).

useful to keep in mind the ambiguous nature of the public/private distinction because, as citizenship enters a period of crisis, it may be possible to reconceptualize citizenship by revisiting the public/private distinction. I will do just that in Part III. For now, though, the task is to see how the public/private distinction reconciles our different models of citizenship.

1.4.1 *The Liberal-Republican Synthesis*

The republican and liberal models of citizenship are often contrasted. Liberal citizenship emphasizes formal equality, where republican citizenship is based on the deep inequalities of the ancient household. Liberal citizenship emphasizes market striving, where republican citizenship emphasizes a citizenry that is liberated from the market to exercise civic virtue and pursue the public good. Nevertheless, it is far more accurate so see the liberal and republican conceptions of citizenship as complementary rather than contradictory. Both conceptions sharply distinguish the public sphere of the state from the private sphere of civil society. The difference is that the republican conception privileges the public realm, whereas the liberal conception privileges the private. In the republican tradition, humans achieve freedom through participation in the public realm, which must be kept free from corruption by the concerns of the private realm; in the liberal tradition, people achieve freedom in the private sphere of the market, and governmental power must be limited to prevent interference into that sphere. But the differing points of emphasis are less important than the shared faith that the distinction between public and private can preserve human freedom. In both conceptions, indeed, it is this distinction that creates the citizen. In the republican tradition, the citizen only exists in and because of the public realm; in the liberal tradition, the citizen is one who has rights *against* the public realm. In both traditions, what makes someone a citizen is the relation they have to a public sphere that is sharply distinguished from a private sphere.[30]

---

[30] Some useful discussions of the public/private distinction can be found in WEINTRAUB & KUMAR, *supra* note 29. The opening essay of the volume, Jeff Weintraub, *The Theory and Politics of the Public/Private Distinction, id.* at 1, is especially illuminating. *See also* MICHAEL WARNER, THE TROUBLE WITH NORMAL: SEX, POLITICS AND THE ETHICS OF QUEER LIFE 171–93 (1999); JEAN BETHKE ELSHTAIN, PUBLIC MAN, PRIVATE WOMAN: WOMEN IN SOCIAL AND POLITICAL THOUGHT (1993); Benn and Gaus, *supra* note 18. The classic treatment of the public/private distinction is Karl Marx, *On the Jewish Question, in* THE MARX-ENGELS READER 26 (Robert C. Tucker ed., 1978). For legal scholarship on the public/private distinction, *see* Kenneth A. Stahl, *Local Government, "One Person, One Vote," and the Jewish Question,* 49 HARV. C.R.-C.L. L. REV. 1 (2014); Joan Williams, *The Development of the Public/Private Distinction in American Law,* 64 TEX. L. REV. 225 (1985); Olsen, *supra* note 28; Frug, *supra* note 20.

The common thread running through the liberal and republican conceptions of citizenship makes it possible to fuse them into a single, liberal-republican idea of citizenship. As we have seen, the Framers of the US Constitution were thoroughgoing republicans who feared the "corruption" of the public sphere by the private and the decline of civic virtue in a commercial age. They were pragmatists, though, who were resigned to the belief that, for most people, civic virtue could not be resuscitated. They could not rely on the "independence" of citizens to assure public-mindedness. Rather than give up on their republican ideals, however, they sought to use the institutions of government to create structural barriers between the public and the private, so that the self-seeking of liberal society could be reconciled with the principles of republican government. Madison's FEDERALIST 10 embodies this liberal-republican compromise. Seen as "liberal" insofar as it recognizes the inevitability of private interest invading the public sphere and asserts the superiority of a large, diverse republic over a small, deliberative, and homogenous one, it is also republican in its faith that faction and interest can be mitigated and corruption of the public sphere avoided institutionally through the representative process. Madison expresses confidence that representation could ensure a virtuous civic realm because "representatives, whose enlightened views and virtuous sentiments render them superior to local prejudices" would counteract the self-interest of their constituents.[31] Ironically, of course, FEDERALIST 10 seeks to restore republican government by removing one of the essential components of republicanism – direct citizen participation in government.

As Zephyr Teachout writes, Madison and the other framers believed that incentive structures could profoundly affect how people behaved within the public sphere, and established the structure of government so that public and private interests would coincide.[32] As I have already noted, the Constitution is indeed structured in various ways to reduce temptations. Implicitly, it accepts that public officials will be tempted, that private concerns will always threaten to overwhelm public ones, and that we cannot expect any citizen's "independence" to guarantee civic virtue. Institutions must do the work that republican virtue no longer can. The Constitution's famed checks and balances – federalism, separation of powers, limited government, protection for private property – would protect the public good from the private self-interest of legislators.

---

[31] Madison, *supra* note 6, at 64.

[32] *See* TEACHOUT, *supra* note 2, at 46–47 ("Because men are not always virtuous, structures must be enacted in order to discourage self-serving behavior in public life.")

In our system, according to Michael Ignatieff, "virtuous institutions" redeem "unvirtuous men."[33]

In the years after the Constitution's ratification, the public/private distinction developed much further, cementing the rapprochement between liberal and republican conceptions of citizenship. The advance of liberal ideas made property appear to be less a guarantor of independence than just another private interest. As we have seen, most states abolished the property qualification for voting by the end of the 1850s, a major step towards separating the private sphere of property and commerce from the public sphere of government.[34] During the Jacksonian period, concerns that corporations were using the guise of the public interest to advance their own private ends led to a distinction between business corporations, which were designated private, and municipal corporations, which were labelled public.[35]

The public/private distinction reached its heyday during the Progressive era. The rise of the administrative state during an industrial age led simultaneously to liberal concerns about the state illegitimately redistributing private wealth and republican concerns that wealthy private interests and political machines were corrupting the public sphere. Observers lamented a loss of community resulting from rapid urbanization, leading to a new round of hand-wringing about the decline of civic virtue. Reflecting on widespread graft among public officials during the era of Tammany Hall and the political machine, reformers rejected Madison's conviction that legislators could be trusted to act in the public interest. These reformers sought a delegation of power to new institutions, administrative agencies staffed by public-minded experts. At the same time, courts introduced the public/private distinction into various areas of law in order to protect private markets from government interference and the public sphere from private interest.[36]

---

[33] *See* Michael Ignatieff, *The Myth of Citizenship, in* THEORIZING CITIZENSHIP 53, 63 (Ronald Beiner ed., 1995). *See also* WILL KYMLICKA, MULTICULTURAL CITIZENSHIP 175–76 (1995).

[34] The changing role of property in ideas about citizenship is discussed in more depth in Chapter 6.

[35] *See* Frug, *supra* note 20, at 1100–01; *see* also Herbert Hovenkamp, *The Classical Corporation in American Legal Thought*, 76 GEO. L.J. 1593, 1610–12 (1988) (discussing the backlash against corporate privilege and monopoly during the Jacksonian Era); HENDRIK HARTOG, PUBLIC PROPERTY AND PRIVATE POWER: THE CORPORATION OF THE CITY OF NEW YORK IN AMERICAN LAW 1730–1870, at 79–87 (1983).

[36] *See* MICHAEL SANDEL, DEMOCRACY'S DISCONTENT: AMERICA IN SEARCH OF A PUBLIC PHILOSOPHY 208–9 (1996) (observing that one response to social dislocation and loss of community in the late nineteenth and early twentieth century was to make government less dependent on virtue by vesting authority in experts); Morton J. Horwitz, *Republicanism and*

In modern times, the Supreme Court's celebrated line of cases requiring that state legislative bodies be apportioned according to the "one person, one vote" rule is another instance of the public/private distinction at work. In the face of objections that states should be able to allocate voting power to account for particular "interests," the Court held that legislatures must represent individuals rather than interests.[37] The one person/one vote rule thus conceptually segregates the private sphere of economic activity from the public sphere of political life.[38] The erection of a firm institutional barrier between public and private balances the republican and liberal conceptions of citizenship by allowing citizens to live primarily private lives, while occasionally calling on them to set aside their private interests and assume a separate identity as political actors. As Bruce Ackerman writes, the complex state of modern citizenship is captured in the evocative phrase "private citizen" – the individual is usually a "*private* citizen," but sometimes a "private *citizen*." In other words, under the public/private distinction the republican citizen and the liberal citizen are one.[39]

1.4.2 *The Nationalist-Republican Synthesis*

I mentioned earlier that the republican and ethno-nationalist conceptions of citizenship were relatively easy to synthesize because they both share an idea of the public as an organic whole, transcending the aggregated interests of individuals. Jean-Jacques Rousseau effectively fused the republican and nationalist conceptions of citizenship in his idea of the "general will." The nation "was conceptualized as an autonomous entity, existing above and independently of the wills of its individual members and dominating their wills."[40] The state is the vehicle through which this general will is enacted, and at the same time provides a boundary of the "people" that constitutes the nation. In contrast to the public sphere of the state is the private sphere of civil society, in which individuals pursue their own interests.[41]

Liberalism in American Constitutional Thought, 29 Wm. & Mary L. Rev. 57, 59–60 (1987); Morton J. Horwitz, *The History of the Public/Private Distinction*, 130 U. Pa. L. Rev. 1423, 1425–26 (1982) (public/private distinction grew out of a desire to curb the "dangerous and unstable redistributive tendencies of democratic politics").

[37] Reynolds v. Sims, 377 U.S. 533, 561 (1964) ("The rights allegedly impaired are individual and personal in nature.") I discuss the one person/one vote rule, and its application to local governments, more fully in Chapters 6 and 10.

[38] *See* Stahl, *supra* note 30, at 19–23; 44–48.

[39] *See* Bruce Ackerman, We the People: Foundations 295–314 (1991).

[40] *See* Greenfeld, *supra* note 11, at 175.

[41] *See* Benn & Gaus, *supra* note 18, at 51.

Like the liberal/republican synthesis, interestingly, the republican/ethno-nationalist synthesis has tended to subordinate republicanism. As Liah Greenfeld observes, the idea of the general will suppressed the traditional republican meaning of citizenship as "active participation in the formulation of the collective policy," in favor of servile obedience to the nation.[42] As we recall, the liberal-republican synthesis similarly displaced active participation with representative democracy and structural barriers to corruption. Republicanism's emphasis on direct citizen participation was ill-suited for a large and diverse nation-state, and its emphasis on civic virtue clashed with a capitalist society preoccupied with money and consumption. In modern times, liberal and ethno-nationalist ideas about citizenship have tended to predominate, and so that is the principal dynamic I address in the first two parts of this book. Part III will return to republican citizenship and evaluate whether it can perhaps be revived as an alternative to our fading liberal-nationalist model.

1.4.3 *The Liberal-Nationalist Synthesis*

Finally, the public/private distinction has also helped synthesize the liberal and ethno-nationalist conceptions of citizenship. While classical economists like Adam Smith puzzled over how liberalism could be reconciled with nationalism, others saw no contradiction, or at least elided it with less discomfort. The French revolutionaries, for example, believed nationalism to be the vehicle through which universal liberal ideals would be achieved – marrying the liberal goals of liberty and equality with the nationalist goal of fraternity. In their view, according to Benjamin Barber, the true cosmopolitan was someone "who thought *a la francaise*."[43] The paradox of liberal nationalism is probably best exemplified by the French Declaration of the Rights of Man, which asserted in grandiloquent terms the universal rights of men but then conferred such rights only on French citizens.[44]

---

[42] *Id.* at 175–76.

[43] BARBER, *supra* note 4, at 159.

[44] The contradiction inherent in the Declaration was insightfully explored in several works by Hannah Arendt, who assailed the Declaration on the grounds that it failed to provide protection for stateless persons. *See* HANNAH ARENDT, THE ORIGINS OF TOTALITARIANISM 290–302 (2nd ed. 1958); *id.* at 291 ("From the beginning the paradox involved in the declaration of inalienable human rights was that it reckoned with an 'abstract' human being who seemed to exist nowhere . . . ."); *id.* at 272 ("[T]he fact that the French Revolution had combined the rights of man with national sovereignty" indicated French belief that "true freedom true emancipation, and true popular sovereignty could be attained only with full national emancipation."); *id.* at 291 ("The whole question of human rights, therefore, was quickly and inextricably blended with the question of national emancipation; only the emancipated

This paradox has been muted by the public/private distinction. According to Linda Bosniak, our system attempts to balance nationalism with liberalism by conceptualizing citizenship as "hard on the outside but soft on the inside." That is to say, the state sets the terms of admission and naturalization on the "outside," but those on the "inside" are entitled to the state's protections to pursue their vision of the good life. The public sphere of immigration and naturalization is "hard," while the private sphere of market participation is "soft." Liberal nationalists see a single national identity and the protection offered by borders as a necessary context for the individual choice that liberalism promises. Will Kymlicka, who considers himself a liberal national-ist, frames the issue well:

> [W]e have a choice between, on the one hand, increased mobility and an expanded domain within which people are free and equal individuals, and, on the other hand, decreased mobility but a greater assurance that people can be free and equal members of their national culture. Most people in liberal democracies clearly favour the latter.[45]

Along similar lines, Yael Tamir writes that the liberal-nationalist conception of the citizen "portrays an autonomous person who can reflect on, evaluate, and choose his conception of the good, his ends, and his cultural and national affiliations, but is capable of such choices because he is situated in a particular social and cultural environment that offers him evaluative criteria."[46]

Probably the best known formulation of the "hard on the outside, soft on the inside" vision of citizenship comes from Michael Walzer, who conceptu-alizes the hard/soft dichotomy in terms of a vertical distinction between the nation and the locality:

> Neighborhoods can be open only if countries are at least potentially closed. Only if the state makes a selection among would-be members and guarantees the loyalty, security and welfare of the individuals it selects, can local communities take shape as 'indifferent' associations, determined solely by personal preference and market capacity.[47]

---

sovereignty of the people, of one's own people, seemed to be able to insure them."); HANNAH ARENDT, ON REVOLUTION 108 (1962); *id.* at 148–49 (discussing American Revolution's rejection of "rights of man" and preference for territorial sovereignty).

[45] WILL KYMLICKA, MULTICULTURAL CITIZENSHIP 93 (1995).

[46] TAMIR, *supra* note 23, at 33.

[47] MICHAEL WALZER, SPHERES OF JUSTICE 38–39 (1983) ; *see also* SASKIA SASSEN, TERRITORY, AUTHORITY, RIGHTS 6 (updated ed. 2008) (defining territorial sovereignty as referring to an entity that has "exclusive authority over a given territory and at the same time this territory is constructed as coterminous with that authority").

Though Walzer's framing is problematic for reasons I discuss later, it is also highly revealing. It suggests that citizenship, rather than existing solely at the scale of the nation, can exist at multiple scales simultaneously, creating what Yishai Blank calls "spheres of citizenship."[48] In Walzer's formulation, the state is the "hard" sphere of identity and closure, whereas the local is the "soft" sphere of "personal preference and market capacity." The state is the public sphere of coercive collective action, whereas the local is the private sphere of individual consumer choice. According to Bosniak, this scalar division is exactly how we have attempted to balance liberal and nationalist citizenship. We have "split these commitments jurisdictionally so that they do not come into direct conflict but instead are relevant in, and applicable to, different domains."[49] Federalism, in other words, is a mechanism for managing the contradictions of modern citizenship. This observation brings us full circle to the liberal-republican synthesis mentioned earlier that synthesis, as I described uses procedural institutions like federalism to separate the public from private spheres and thus reconcile liberal with republican citizenship. Hence, as the next chapter explains, it has been federalism, and particularly the relationship between the national and the local, that has mediated among the three models of citizenship. We have designated the national sphere as the *public* realm of republican and nationalist citizenship, and the local as the *private* realm of liberal citizenship. As globalization has caused the public/private distinction to collapse, those three models have come into conflict, inciting a clash between national and local governments over the meaning of citizenship.

It may be useful to chart some of the main ideas from this chapter in table form, as they provide a framework for much of the rest of the book. Table 1.1 illustrates the principal differences between the liberal, republican, and ethno-nationalist conceptions of citizenship:

TABLE 1.1 *Principal differences between the liberal, republican,*
and ethno-nationalist conceptions of citizenship

Republican	Citizen participation, civic virtue, collective decisionmaking
Liberal	Individual rights, market freedom, equality, choice, self-interest
Ethno-nationalist	Identity, organic solidarity, linked fate

[48] See Blank, *supra* note 27.
[49] LINDA BOSNIAK, THE CITIZEN AND THE ALIEN 125 (2006).

Figure 1.1 illustrates the ways in which the various conceptions have been synthesized through the public/private distinction:

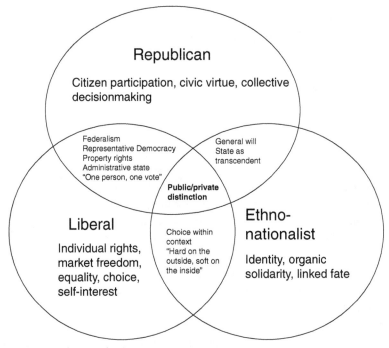

FIGURE 1.1 Synthesizing the Conceptions

Table 1.2 illustrates how the public/private distinction has been constructed so as to allocate the different conceptions of citizenship to their respective spheres:

TABLE 1.2 *Allocation of the Conceptions between the Public and Private Spheres*

Public	Government, Politics (Collective)	Republican/ethno-nationalist (identity, organic solidarity, collective decision making)
Private	Market, family (individual)	Liberal (individual rights, market freedom, equality, choice, interest)

2

Local and Federal Citizenship

One signature attribute of the modern nation-state is its jealous insistence that it alone can confer citizenship. To recognize alternative sites of citizenship is to recognize that people have multiple loyalties, an unacceptable concession for a polity rooted in the idea of a single and indivisible sovereign people. Of course, the reason this concession is unacceptable is because people *do* have multiple loyalties, and one of their primary loyalties is to their local community. The idea of citizenship itself was born in the city – the very word "citizen" literally means a resident of a city. Thus, one function of federal citizenship has been to relocate people's allegiance from the city to the nation-state. Local citizenship did not prove so easy to extinguish, however. As I explain further in the next chapter, cities were vital centers of commerce, which the state sought to encourage because commerce brought tax revenue and helped advance the centralization of power. But commerce was tied up with a liberal understanding of political membership as a matter of market choice and mobility instead of shared identity and allegiance. For that reason, reaping the advantages of commerce required the nation-state to accommodate a more liberal political culture at the local level.

As a result, modern state citizenship is divided jurisdictionally, with the federal level being the public sphere of civic identity and closure, and the local the private sphere of rational market choice and mobility. To put this in the language used in the previous chapter, national citizenship is nationalist and republican, whereas local citizenship is liberal. The federal government has the power to determine who qualifies as a citizen based on characteristics such as identity or demonstrated loyalty to the idea of the nation-state, whereas local citizenship is available to all who choose to settle in the community. In principle, there is no conflict between the two modes of citizenship because they are complementary. Local governments do not compete with the nation-state for loyalty because local citizenship is based on market choice rather than allegiance. The nation-state facilitates commerce by enabling cities to have a more open and liberal citizenship policy.

This chapter describes the current state of "citizenship federalism" and some of its implications. It details some of the principal ways in which citizenship has been divided between the federal and local levels, including voting rights, immigration and "alienage" (laws affecting the rights of aliens present in the United States), the distribution of public benefits and services, and land use regulations. In all of these cases, the distribution of power represents an effort to accommodate the republican, liberal, and ethno-nationalist visions of citizenship by allocating republican and ethno-nationalist ideas about citizenship to the federal level, and liberal ideas to the local level. However, as I also describe, this accommodation has begun to come apart as globalization has placed an enormous amount of pressure on the concept of citizenship. The result has been a heightened political conflict between the federal and local scales over what it means to be a citizen.

At the end of this chapter, I discuss the role of state citizenship. It may seem odd for a discussion of "citizenship federalism" to neglect the basic building block of federalism in the American system, the state. For many decades in the nineteenth century, citizenship was principally defined by states. Since the end of that century, however, citizenship has primarily been located at the federal and local levels, with state citizenship being a mostly passive status. In the discussion that follows, we will see that state citizenship sometimes approximates national citizenship and at other times more closely resembles local citizenship, but has few distinctive features of its own. The salient point is that, even in the United States, the federal and the local are the scales at which citizenship is being most meaningfully articulated right now.

2.1 THE RIGHT TO VOTE

A fairly straightforward example of the distinction between national and local citizenship today is the franchise. While much ink has been spilled on the question of what differentiates a citizen from a noncitizen, and I intend to spill some more on that question later, certainly the right to vote is today considered a fundamental attribute of citizenship. From the republican perspective, political participation is the *sina qua non* of citizenship. From the liberal perspective, voting is the right that is preservative of all other rights. From the nationalist perspective, the right to vote is what distinguishes the citizen from the noncitizen. If the franchise is a marker of citizenship, then it is salient that in the United States and many places around the world, the right to vote in local elections is often distinct from the right to vote in national elections. Most nation-states grant the franchise based on place of birth, lineage, or naturalization, whereas local voting rights are based on residence or interest. As I explain later, the former standard reflects a republican and nationalist conception of citizenship, whereas the latter reflects a liberal conception of citizenship.[1]

An especially interesting example of the distinction between local and national citizenship is the European Union's voting regime. Each member state establishes its own criteria for citizenship, and nations have by and large chosen some combination of birth, lineage, and naturalization.[2] Voting rights at the national level are contingent on citizenship. Citizens of each member state are entitled to travel freely to other member states, but they cannot obtain citizenship in any other member state unless they qualify under that nation's citizenship policy. However, residents of any *city* within the European Union are automatically entitled to vote in that city's elections by virtue of residence provided they are citizens of any European Union member state. A citizen of Spain who moves to Paris, for example, would automatically be entitled to vote in Parisian municipal elections, but not in French provincial or national elections. Several European countries have gone further and granted local voting rights to all residents regardless of citizenship.[3]

A similar pattern obtains in the United States. The Fourteenth Amendment of the US Constitution provides that anyone born or naturalized in the United States is a citizen of the United States and the state in which they reside. Hence, national citizenship is conferred by birth, lineage, or naturalization, which requires an extensive residency period and a demonstration of fealty to national civic ideals, whereas state and local citizenship are conferred by residence (often, but not always, combined with the prerequisite of national citizenship). This distinction is evident in the franchise. With some exceptions, all adult citizens are entitled to vote in federal elections even if they do not reside in the United States, and noncitizens may not vote in federal elections even if they do reside in the United States.[4] At the local level,

---

[1]   On the link between citizenship and voting, see Rainer Baubock, *Expansive Citizenship –
      Voting beyond Territory and Membership*, 38 PS: POLITICAL SCIENCE & POLITICS 683 (2005);
      Sanford Levinson, *Suffrage and Community: Who Should Vote?* 41 FLA. L. REV. 545 (1989).
[2]   *See* William Rogers Brubaker, *Citizenship and Naturalization: Policies and Politics*, in
      IMMIGRATION AND THE POLITICS OF CITIZENSHIP 99 (William Rogers Brubaker ed., 1989).
[3]   *See, e.g.*, Rainer Baubock, *Reinventing Urban Citizenship*, 7 CIT. STUD. 139, 148, 151 (2003).
[4]   *See* 52 U.S.C. Ch. 203 (dealing with voting in federal elections by overseas U.S. citizens); 18
      U.S.C. § 611 (prohibiting noncitizens from voting in elections for federal office). The major
      exception to citizen voting is the widespread disfranchisement of felons in many states, a
      practice that has come under increasing scrutiny and been curtailed in several states recently,
      including Virginia by executive order and Florida by a voter initiative. I discuss felon
      disfranchisement later in this chapter as it pertains to the question of state citizenship.

however, and usually the state level as well, voting rights are tied to residency. States and local governments are required to enfranchise all residents with US citizenship and are prohibited from requiring a minimum duration of residence or imposing other prerequisites on the right of local citizen residents to vote. On the other hand, they are not required to enfranchise anyone who is a nonresident.[5] All state constitutions today mirror federal law by barring noncitizen residents from voting in state elections, but local governments in many places have the authority to expand the municipal franchise to include noncitizen residents, as several cities have done.[6] In some cases, local governments have extended the franchise to others who are ineligible to vote at the state or federal level but who are deemed interested in local elections, including nonresident landowners and minors.[7]

The contrast between a birth, lineage or naturalization standard and a residency or interest standard marks an important conceptual distinction between local and federal citizenship: federal citizenship is articulated as republican, ethno-nationalist, and public, whereas local citizenship is articulated as liberal and private. Insofar as local citizenship is based on residence or interest, it is a matter of individual consumer choice, consensual and rational. According to an influential theory known as the "Tiebout" model after the economist Charles Tiebout, individuals are perceived as "consumer-voters" who have a variety of options of where to reside within a metropolitan region, and make that choice based on which community offers the most attractive package of municipal services – low taxes, quality schools, and so forth.[8] The consumer-voter is a shopper who votes with his or her feet. Local citizenship is a market commodity that people acquire the same way they would acquire any other consumer good, by purchasing or renting a home in the community. Anyone who can acquire residence can thereby acquire citizenship, regardless of birth, ethnicity, language, culture, or history. This idea of "citizenship by consent" is a thoroughly liberal one. Liberal English nationalists like John Locke considered all political associations to be artificial, created by rational

---

[5] *See* Dunn v. Blumstein, 405 U.S. 330 (1972) (holding that states and localities may not make a minimum period of residency a prerequisite to vote); Kramer v. Union Free School District No. 15, 395 U.S. 621 (1969) (holding that any limit on the ability of citizen residents to vote in state or local elections is subject to strict scrutiny); Holt Civic Club v. City of Tuscaloosa, 439 U.S. 60 (1978) (distinguishing Kramer and holding that local governments are not required to extend the franchise to non-residents).

[6] *See generally* Joshua A. Douglas, *The Right to Vote under Local Law*, 85 Geo. Wash. L. Rev. 1039 (2017). Several cities have adopted or debated the adoption of noncitizen suffrage since Douglas wrote. *See* note 6 in the Introduction.

[7] *See* Douglas, *supra* note 6, at 1052–68.

[8] *See* Charles M. Tiebout, *A Pure Theory of Local Expenditures*, 64 J. Pol. Econ. 416, 418 (1956).

individuals for their own self-protection, and therefore citizenship could only be a matter of choice.[9]

There is some uncertainty within liberal theory as to whether the idea of "citizenship by consent" requires mutual consent by both parties (the individual and the jurisdiction) or just unilateral consent by the individual.[10] Local citizenship embodies this ambiguity. While the Tiebout model views the acquisition of residency as a matter of "choice," the reality is that acquiring residency in a desired locality is often very difficult because municipalities use zoning and other land use rules to raise the cost of housing and constrain interlocal mobility.[11] Most states require municipalities to cover the costs of the services they provide out of their own revenue, which causes municipalities to compete for residents who will contribute to the fiscal bottom line, much like private business firms compete for customers.[12] In a sense, then, zoning regulations represent a way in which municipalities may choose their residents. This observation, however, is not inconsistent with seeing local citizenship as a liberal market relationship, in which those who have the ability to "purchase" citizenship may do so. Indeed, economists often use the term "choice" as a euphemism for one's ability to pay. Money and mobility, rather than nationality, are the markers of local citizenship. In our society, as Michael Walzer writes, "[t]he normal activities that enable individuals to see themselves and to be seen by others as full members, social persons, have increasingly become consumption activities; they require money."[13]

If local citizenship's foundation in residence, mobility, and interest marks it as something private and liberal, national citizenship is firmly public, republican, and nationalist. Rooted in nationality and blood rather than residence, federal citizenship reflects a primordial conception of the citizen as deeply embedded in the territory and the shared history of a

---

[9] *See, e.g.,* LIAH GREENFELD, NATIONALISM: FIVE ROADS TO MODERNITY 399–400 (1992) (English nationalism perceived the nation as a rational, voluntary chosen association, not a primordial one); PETER H. SCHUCK & ROGERS M. SMITH, CITIZENSHIP WITHOUT CONSENT: ILLEGAL ALIENS IN THE AMERICAN POLITY 22–41 (1985) (describing theory of citizenship by consent).

[10] *See, e.g.,* SCHUCK & SMITH, *supra* note 9, at 27–31 (noting "recurring, fundamental tension in liberal thought" over meaning of consent).

[11] An outstanding recent book on this topic is JESSICA TROUNSTINE, SEGREGATION BY DESIGN: LOCAL POLITICS AND INEQUALITY IN AMERICAN CITIES (2018).

[12] *See* Richard Briffault, *Our Localism: Part II–Localism and Legal Theory,* 90 COLUM. L. REV. 346, 400 (1990) (describing the "firm" theory of local governments under the Tiebout model, and contrasting it with the public-interest, or *polis* model).

[13] MICHAEL WALZER, SPHERES OF JUSTICE 106 (1983).

people. As Yael Tamir writes, where "will, choice, reflection and evaluation are ... central to the liberal idea of the person," nationalist citizenship "sees social roles and affiliations as inherent, as a matter of fate rather than choice."[14] Federal citizenship is also republican in that it rejects the Tieboutian conception of the citizen as a consumer and money as the prerequisite to citizenship. It would corrupt the very meaning of citizenship to put it up for sale. The notion that citizens can choose their state or a state can choose its citizens in the manner of a market transaction is abhorrent to both the republican and nationalist traditions.[15] According to Walzer, commodities must not be symbols of belonging because "in a democratic society, the most basic definitions and self-definitions can't be put up for purchase in this way. For citizenship entails what we might call 'belongingness ... '"[16]

Local and federal citizenship are thus distinct, the former liberal and the latter a mix of republican and ethno-nationalist. Although they are distinct, however, the two forms of citizenship are not necessarily contradictory. For example, as I have observed, local voting rights are generally based on residence *in addition to* national citizenship, not instead of national citizenship. What this demonstrates is that local citizenship is articulated as liberal, but within an overarching framework of nationalism. This construction fits within the ideology of liberal nationalism described in Chapter 1. Nationalism provides a boundary or a context within which liberalism operates, providing closure at the boundary so that people can have fuller freedom inside the boundary.[17]

This formulation is complicated a bit by the fact that local governments often have the ability to expand the franchise beyond adult US citizens to noncitizens and other groups generally not enfranchised at the state or federal level. As I will discuss further in Part II, however, this unique feature of local voting rights again marks local citizenship as thoroughly liberal. Where cities have extended the franchise beyond adult US citizens, and courts have upheld such extensions, they have typically justified doing so on the liberal grounds that those other groups share a common interest with adult US citizens in the

---

[14] YAEL TAMIR, LIBERAL NATIONALISM 20 (1993).

[15] *See, e.g.*, Ayelet Shachar, *Citizenship for Sale?*, in THE OXFORD HANDBOOK OF CITIZENSHIP 789 (Ayelet Shachar et al. eds., 2017); MICHAEL SANDEL, WHAT MONEY CAN'T BUY 200 (2013). I address the tensions between the idea of "citizenship for sale" and the republican and nationalist traditions further in Chapters 7 and 8.

[16] WALZER, *supra* note , at 106.

[17] See the discussion of liberal nationalism in Chapter 1.

conduct of local governments.[18] The notion that citizenship should be founded on interest is a feature of liberalism, in contrast to nationalism's emphasis on identity and linked fate.[19] At the same time, local governments generally cannot withdraw the franchise from US citizen residents, and expansions of the franchise are relatively rare, so what Gerald Neuman calls the "core" electorate in local elections remains US citizens, consistent with the ethno-nationalist conception.[20] Once again, this suggests that cities have some freedom to define citizenship in liberal terms but within a broader context of ethno-nationalism. Nevertheless, as I discuss later in this chapter, local governments' broader conception of citizenship does create some latent tensions with ethno-nationalism that frequently threaten to burst out into the open.

Practically speaking, the distinction in voting rights makes sense in light of the functions we typically associate with the different levels of government. The federal government is responsible for matters of national defense and political self-definition such as war, foreign policy, and immigration, so it stands to reason that voting rights would be extended to all of those, but only those, with a demonstrated loyalty to the nation. State and especially local governments are primarily responsible for affairs such as schools, sanitation, and policing which affect all residents equally, so it makes sense that the franchise should be based on residence. "Questions of ultimate allegiance," Rogers Brubaker observes, are arguably "irrelevant to local voting."[21]

There is, however, an element of circularity in this logic. One reason why the federal government has the exclusive authority over matters such as foreign affairs and immigration is *because* it is perceived as the site of ethno-nationalist and republican citizenship, whereas one reason why local governments are primarily responsible for functions such as schools and policing is because they are perceived as sites of liberal citizenship. The next section therefore elaborates how the different ideas about citizenship informed the allocation of functions between the levels of government.

---

[18] *See, e.g.*, Jamin B. Raskin, *Legal Aliens, Local Citizens: The Historical, Constitutional, and Theoretical Meanings of Alien Suffrage*, 141 U. PA. L. REV. 1391, 1468 (1993) ("At the local level, each resident's interests in good schools, public services, and transportation are very similar. If these interests diverge at all, it will be according to differences in neighborhood, income, or homeownership-not nationality or citizenship.") I discuss local noncitizen suffrage at greater length in Chapter 5.

[19] *See, e.g.*, GERALD L. NEUMAN, STRANGERS TO THE CONSTITUTION: IMMIGRANTS, BORDERS, AND FUNDAMENTAL LAW 142–43 (1996) (noting that local governments' ability to expand the franchise based on interest suggests an "instrumental" view of local membership).

[20] *See id.*

[21] *See* William Rogers Brubaker, *Introduction*, in IMMIGRATION AND THE POLITICS OF CITIZENSHIP IN EUROPE AND NORTH AMERICA 1, 21 (William Rogers Brubaker ed., 1989).

2.2 IMMIGRATION AND ALIENAGE

Over the last decade, scholars have paid increasing attention to "immigration federalism," or the roles that different scales of government play in regulating the lives of immigrants.[22] Little of this scholarship, however, has grappled with the question of "citizenship federalism," that is, how these different roles reflect divergent ideas about citizenship.[23] Scholars have generally assumed that citizenship exists solely at the level of the nation-state, at least in part because the immigration power is now often perceived as belonging exclusively to the federal government.[24] This section challenges that assumption. As we will see, the longstanding presumption that the immigration power is exclusively federal rests not on the premise that *citizenship* is exclusively federal, but that the nation is the exclusive site of ethno-nationalist citizenship, whereas the local is the primary site of liberal citizenship. That the local is the primary site of liberal citizenship is reinforced by the fact that local governments are largely responsible for providing services to immigrants and incorporating them into society.

2.2.1 *The Federal Immigration Power*

Although the Supreme Court has never ruled definitively on the matter, it is typically believed that the federal government has exclusive or "plenary" power over immigration and naturalization, meaning the entry, exclusion, removal, and naturalization of noncitizens. The idea of federal exclusivity, or

---

[22] For representative examples, see Stella Burch Elias, *The New Immigration Federalism*, 74 Ohio St. L.J. 703 (2013); Rick Su, *Local Fragmentation as Immigration Regulation*, 47 Hous. L. Rev. 367 (2010); Clare Huntington, *The Constitutional Dimension of Immigration Federalism*, 61 Vand. L. Rev. 787, 812–23 (2008); Cristina M. Rodriguez, *The Significance of the Local in Immigration Regulation*, 106 Mich. L. Rev. 567 (2008); Juliet Stumpf, *States of Confusion: The Rise of State and Local Power over Immigration*, 86 N.C. L. Rev. 1557 (2008).

[23] A notable exception, though not limited to the immigration context, is Vicki C. Jackson, *Citizenship and Federalism*, in Citizenship Today: Global Perspectives and Practices 127 (T. Alexander Aleinikoff & Douglas Klusmeyer eds., 2001). Significantly, Jackson speaks mostly about national and *state* citizenship, and concludes that national citizenship is "primary." *Id.* at 131, 136.

[24] A pair of recent articles address the question of state citizenship, but interestingly, they both see state citizenship as a dormant status that was once predominant and could potentially be revived in the future. *See* Maeve Glass, *Citizens of the State*, 85 U. Chi. L. Rev. 865 (2018); Peter L. Markowitz, *Undocumented No More: The Power of State Citizenship*, 67 Stan. L. Rev. 869 (2015). As I address at the end of this chapter, state citizenship is indeed dormant for a variety of reasons, but *local* citizenship remains an active status.

what Clare Huntington calls "structural preemption,"[25] derives largely from the nineteenth-century case of *Chy Lung* v. *Freeman*, in which the state of California sought to require that certain inbound passengers post a bond.[26] The Supreme Court struck down the law, which was a thinly veiled effort to control Chinese immigration, on the grounds that it interfered with the federal government's exclusive authority over foreign affairs. The Court stated flatly: "The passage of laws which concern the admission of citizens and subjects of foreign nations to our shores belongs to Congress, and not to the States."[27]

As Hiroshi Motomura explains, though *Chy Lung* was purportedly based on the need for the federal government to control foreign affairs and foreign commerce, its real underlying justification was to ensure that the federal government could determine the ethnic and racial character of the country, or to engage in what Motomura calls "national self-definition."[28] That is to say, the very idea of an exclusive federal power over immigration reflects an ethno-nationalist conception of citizenship. As Motomura observes, *Chy Lung* provided important precedent for the Supreme Court's notorious decision in *the Chinese Exclusion Case* one decade later, in which it upheld an act of Congress prohibiting all immigration by Chinese laborers.[29] The Chinese Exclusion Act was explicitly racial in character, and the Supreme Court found the act's underlying purpose to define the nation's membership on racial terms perfectly appropriate, holding that the act was justified by "differences of race," the refusal of the Chinese "to assimilate with our people," and the threat of "vast hordes" of Chinese overrunning the nation.[30] The federal government could legitimately use the immigration power to maintain a sense of national self-identity and the nation's existing racial composition in the face of mass immigration. The ethno-nationalist foundation of the federal immigration power was further confirmed by the adoption of the national origins system after the First World War, which was intended to maintain the country's existing racial balance by favoring immigrants from Western Europe and limiting or prohibiting immigration from most other places. Although the national origins system was largely repealed by Civil Rights-era reforms, our immigration system still reflects a nationalist

[25] *See* Huntington, *supra* note22, at 812–23.
[26] 92 U.S. 275 (1875).
[27] *Id.* at 279–80.
[28] *See* Hiroshi Motomura, *Whose Immigration Law? Citizens, Aliens and the Constitution,* 97 Colum. L. Rev. 1567, 1592–1601 (1997).
[29] 130 U.S. 581 (1889).
[30] Chae Chan Ping v. United States, 130 U.S. 581, 595, 606, 627 (1889).

ideology insofar as acquisition of citizenship by immigrants requires an extensive process of naturalization.[31]

As *Chy Lung* intimates, the ability of the federal government to engage in national self-definition requires that the immigration power be exclusively federal. National self-definition would be undermined if states or local governments could implement their own ethno-nationalist criteria for membership. Although never explicitly articulated, this view was apparently confirmed in the recent case of *Arizona* v. *United States*,[32] in which the Supreme Court struck several portions of Arizona's controversial SB 1070. The law had the stated goal to "discourage and deter the unlawful entry and presence of aliens and economic activity by persons unlawfully present in the United States."[33] The Court's decision, while not resting explicitly on structural preemption, nevertheless found several provisions of SB 1070 impliedly preempted by Congress's immigration regime, including one provision permitting state law enforcement officers to arrest individuals if they had probable cause that the individual was removable from the United States. In striking down this provision, the Court observed that vesting such power in state law enforcement officers would improperly "allow the State to achieve its own immigration policy," and went on to state that "Immigration policy shapes the destiny of the nation."[34] Implicitly, the federal government has appropriated to itself the exclusive power to shape the destiny of the nation through immigration policy.

Motomura argues that the reason the federal government has the exclusive power of national self-definition is because "American citizenship is predominantly national, not state or local."[35] This statement, however, reflects an incomplete view of American citizenship. While the cases just discussed reveal that the federal government has the apparently exclusive authority to define the character of the nation in ethno-nationalist terms, our idea of citizenship is not rooted entirely in ethno-nationalist terms. It is also founded on liberal ideas about equality and market choice, and it is that liberal approach to citizenship that largely prevails at the local level. Interestingly, Motomura's own analysis of immigration law demonstrates this distinctively local conception of citizenship. As he explains, after the Supreme Court clarified the apparently exclusive federal nature of the immigration power,

---

[31] On the national origins system and its abolition, see Moromura, *supra* note, at 1595–96.

[32] 567 U.S. 387 (2012).

[33] *Id.* at 393 (citing Ariz. Rev. Stat. Ann. § 11–1051 (West 2012)).

[34] *Id.* at 408; 415.

[35] Motomura, *supra* note 28, at 1596.

states were stripped of the ability not only to control immigration but also to control interstate population movement. In the 1941 case of *Edwards v. California*,[36] for example, the Supreme Court found that a state law prohibiting the transportation of indigent persons across state lines violated the clause in Article IV of the Constitution conferring all the "privileges and immunities" of United States citizenship on the citizens of the several states. Concurring, Justice Jackson wrote that the Privileges and Immunities Clause "was adopted to make United States citizenship the dominant and paramount allegiance among us."[37] Justice Douglas declared the right to move freely throughout the country "a right of national citizenship."[38] Since *Edwards*, the Supreme Court has subsequently clarified numerous times that citizens of the United States have the right to become citizens of whatever state or locality they choose to reside in, and that the states "do not have any right to select their citizens."[39] Indeed, the Court has gone even further and held that the constitutional right to internal migration extends to *legal noncitizen residents* of the United States as well.[40]

Taken together, these precedents clearly demonstrate that the Supreme Court sees state and local citizenship as something distinctive from federal citizenship. Consistent with the Tiebout model, state and local citizenship is fluid and liberal, the product of mobility and choice. Federal citizenship is based on identity, belonging, and "allegiance," shared fate rather than consent.

2.2.2 *Local Distribution of Services and the Incorporation of Immigrants*

It is not simply the *absence* of local immigration powers that makes local citizenship distinctive. As part of our system of immigration federalism, local governments have an affirmative responsibility to incorporate immigrants into American civic, social, and economic life. This responsibility follows from local governments' central function, which is the distribution of services such as schooling, housing, and security to local residents. The federal government has little formal policy on how admitted immigrants should be integrated into

---

[36] 314 U.S. 160 (1941).

[37] *Id.* at 182 (Jackson, J., concurring).

[38] *Id.* at 178 (Douglas, J., concurring).

[39] *See* Saenz v. Roe, 526 U.S. 489, 511 (1999); Shapiro v. Thompson, 394 U.S. 618 (1969); Motomura, *supra* note 28, at 1596–1601; *see also* Richard C. Schragger, *Cities, Economic Development, and the Free Trade Constitution*, 94 Va. L. Rev. 1091, 1110–12; 1117–18 (2008).

[40] *See* Graham v. Richardson, 403 U.S. 365 (1971).

civil life, so as a de facto matter that responsibility falls to local governments, who are generally required to provide benefits and services to all local residents regardless of immigration status. I argue that, in distributing such benefits to immigrants and residents more generally, local governments are in fact distributing incidents of local *citizenship*, and insofar as these benefits are generally allocated based on residence, local citizenship is again defined as private and liberal in contrast to the ethno-nationalist standard of federal citizenship.

Citizenship as a Bundle of Sticks

Let me begin by demonstrating that the receipt of municipal services is a benefit of citizenship. While it is often argued that the essence of citizenship is the right to vote, or perhaps immunity from immigration laws, that is not necessarily true. Many American citizens lack the right to vote due to age or incarceration, not to mention the unique voting disabilities endured by citizens living in Puerto Rico or Washington, DC. The recent controversy over a Trump administration proposal to denaturalize and deport naturalized citizens illustrates that citizens are not always immune from immigration laws either.[41] In a highly influential essay often considered the most significant modern articulation of citizenship, the British writer T. H. Marshall argued that citizenship consisted of three distinct sets of rights – political rights, such as the right to vote, civil rights, such as the right to be protected against government abuses, and social rights, such as the right to schooling, housing, and access to employment markets.[42] In the same way that property lawyers often describe property as a bundle of sticks, that is, a group of distinct rights that can be unbundled and re-grouped in different ways, we might also describe citizenship as a bundle of sticks.[43]

If citizenship is indeed a bundle of sticks rather than a single coherent set of attributes, it follows that the bundle can be broken apart, with the various sticks distributed by different jurisdictions at different scales within our federal system. In practice, while certain attributes of citizenship, such as the franchise, are conferred by both the federal and the local scale simultaneously

---

[41] Leti Volpp, *Citizenship Undone*, 75 FORDHAM L. REV. 2579, 2582–83 (2007) (naturalized citizens are considered "lesser" and more "potentially suspect" than birthright citizens, and are more legally vulnerable to having their citizenship stripped).

[42] *See* T. H. Marshall, *Citizenship and Social Class*, in CLASS, CITIZENSHIP, AND SOCIAL DEVELOPMENT 65 (1964).

[43] Rose Cuison Villazor also analogizes citizenship to a "bundle of sticks" in *American Nationals and Interstitial Citizenship*, 85 FORDHAM L. REV. 1673, 1720–23 (2017).

(albeit on different grounds), other attributes of citizenship are conferred exclusively by one scale or another. For instance, as we have seen, the exclusive nature of the immigration power means that the federal government alone has the power to naturalize citizens and bestow immunity from the immigration laws. Immunity from the immigration laws falls into what Marshall would call either a "political" or a "civil" right. But local governments are, by and large, tasked with distributing many of the social rights of citizenship, such as education, housing, and security, to local residents, generally including noncitizens. By providing such benefits, local governments are also, as a de facto matter, incorporating immigrants into American social, economic, and civic life. Ever since the landmark Supreme Court case of *Plyler* v. *Doe*[44] (discussed at length in Chapter 5), which held that cities are constitutionally required to provide free public education to *all* resident school-aged children, regardless of their immigration status, cities have been the main staging ground for the integration of immigrants. Federal civil rights laws require local officials to facilitate English literacy for nonnative English speakers, thus placing on local governments the responsibility to assimilate immigrants. Local governments are also required to provide voting material and other official information in immigrants' language of origin, are prohibited from discriminating against immigrants in matters like housing and employment, and must provide emergency medical care. All local residents, regardless of immigration status, are entitled to police protection as well. As Abigail Fisher Williamson documents extensively in a recent book, WELCOMING NEW AMERICANS?, the obligation to serve and incorporate immigrant residents induces local governments to think of immigrants as "clients." Furthermore, because local governments lack the federal government's ability to create barriers to trade or immigration, they face constant pressures to pursue economic development, which causes them to value immigrants as consumers, innovators, and laborers. As a result of all these factors, local governments often *voluntarily* adopt a welcoming attitude toward immigrants. For instance, Williamson reports that while very few cities have formally declared themselves sanctuary cities, most cities – even smaller cities outside the major metropolitan areas that we think of as friendly toward immigrants – have adopted informal law enforcement policies and practices that protect immigrants against immigration enforcement, such as "don't ask, don't tell" policies with regard to the immigration status of arrestees.[45]

[44] 457 U.S. 202 (1982).
[45] *See* Abigail Fisher Williamson, WELCOMING NEW AMERICANS? LOCAL GOVERNMENTS AND IMMIGRANT INCORPORATION (2018). In Graham v. Richardson, 403 U.S. 365 (1971), the

There is very little doubt that the distribution of benefits like housing, education and security to all local residents constitutes a form of local citizenship. Indeed, in his famous article on citizenship, T. H. Marshall argued that social rights like education and security had become the most important signifiers of citizenship in an expanding welfare state, eclipsing political and civil rights. Following the tradition of Karl Marx, Marshall believed that a right of equal participation in the political sphere was essentially hollow if stratifications within the private sphere were so severe as to create a permanent caste system. Inequalities in education, for example, could create permanent cleavages in life chances. Guaranteeing a minimum level of social rights was therefore necessary to ensure equality of opportunity and, as result, citizenship. According to Marshall, "[W]hen the state guarantees that all children shall be educated, it has the requirements and the nature of citizenship definitely in mind."[46] Today, of course, it is local governments that bear primary responsibility for providing public education, which effectively means that they are distributing an incident of citizenship to local residents. The Supreme Court recognized as much when, in holding that cities were required to educate all local residents, it observed that the public school is "the very foundation of good citizenship."[47]

Social Rights as Liberal: Local Services and Local Zoning

The distinctive feature of social rights like education and security that marks them as liberal and private in contrast to the attributes of federal citizenship is that they are tied entirely to residence. What enables people who are not

Supreme Court held that states were prohibited by the equal protection clause from discriminating against legal permanent residents in the provision of public benefits such as welfare. Since *Graham*, the law relating to public benefits has become exceedingly complex, primarily because in 1996 Congress enacted the Personal Responsibility and Work Opportunity Reconciliation Act (PRWORA), commonly known as welfare reform. The welfare reform law authorized, and in some cases required, states to bar certain classes of noncitizens from access to designated public benefits. Welfare reform has created considerable confusion as to the extent to which states can or must, consistent with *Graham* and *Plyler*, extend various types of benefits to noncitizens. The confusion was deepened by the Court's decision in *Arizona v. United States*, 567 U.S. 387 (2012), discussed previously, which held that states *withholding* certain benefits from immigrants, including unauthorized immigrants, could conflict with the federal government's immigration scheme. Despite the confusion, local governments' responsibility to provide the services discussed in the text remains unchanged. On immigrant eligibility for state public benefits, see Jenny-Brooke Condon, *The Preempting of Equal Protection for Immigrants*, 73 Wash. & Lee L. Rev. 77 (2016); Congressional Research Service, Noncitizen Eligibility for Public Benefits: Legal Issues (Sep. 9, 2013), www.everycrsreport.com/files/20130909_R43221_6b375b0965db2c6cac9515d87d8d7b4b65ebbd10.pdf

[46] *See* Marshall, *supra* note 42, at 100.
[47] Plyler, 457 U.S. at 223.

citizens at the federal level to enjoy the benefits of local citizenship is that local citizenship is a function of residence rather than nationality. Aside from its practical implications, however, the link between local citizenship and residence profoundly affects the very nature of citizenship. The politics of residence are, as Richard Briffault observes, thoroughly private and consumer-oriented. Briffault notes that most people neither live in the same municipality where they work, nor do they work with the same people near whom they live. Tying citizenship to residence thus means that issues relating to work and the nature of the economy are "off the local agenda." As a result,

> [T]he focus of local public life in most autonomous residential localities is on issues of residence – land use, schools and property taxes. These questions are usually addressed primarily in terms of their implications for the residents' private lives – their homes, families, privacy, and personal security, the preservation of personal wealth and the creation and maintenance of an atmosphere conducive to the individual consumption of consumer goods ... In this setting, public life is often focused on the protection of private life and the insulation of home and family from broader public concerns.[48]

The equation of residence with consumption, wealth, and the private sphere follows from the Tiebout conception of local government, discussed earlier. According to Tiebout, when individuals choose a municipality in which to reside, they are essentially making a consumer purchase. They are buying or renting not just a home but the entire package of municipal services that come bundled with residence – the quality of the local schools, police, utilities, the property tax burden, and so forth. Indeed, it has been widely confirmed that characteristics like these are "capitalized" into home values, meaning the price of a home reflects the quality of the local services.[49] Consumer-voters can efficiently shop for municipalities in which to settle because home prices serve as effective signals of the quality of local services. And once settled, consumer-voters' primary *political* concern, as Briffault observes, is to protect their property values and the municipal services they have paid to acquire.

---

[48] Briffault, *supra* note12, at 440.

[49] *See* WILLIAM A. FISCHEL, THE HOMEVOTER HYPOTHESIS 45–46 (2001) (describing studies detailing the extent of capitalization phenomenon). According to Fischel, impacts such as traffic congestion, high crime rates, large public housing projects, and localized air pollution have been shown to decrease property values for nearby property owners, while growth controls, high-quality local schools, and having homeowners rather than renters as neighbors have demonstrably increased property values. *See id.*

The nature of the act in which individuals engage when they rent or purchase a home is captured in Tiebout's evocative phrase "consumer-voter." As we have seen, voting is often perceived as the paradigmatic act of the citizen. Tiebout's phrase implies, however, that at the local level, people vote by consuming, as evidenced by a choice of residence. *It is therefore consumption that makes a person a citizen.* Consumption is the mark of belonging. As I quoted Michael Walzer earlier, "[t]he normal activities that enable individuals to see themselves and to be seen by others as full members, social persons, have increasingly become consumption activities; they require money."[50] And as William Fischel famously observed, homeowners tend to be "homevoters"; they participate in local politics in order to protect the value of their principal asset.[51]

In this way, local citizenship has become private and liberal, focused on individual consumption in a market setting. Indeed, an important consequence of the consumer-oriented view of local citizenship is that the goods and services municipalities provide are not "public goods" available to all, but market goods available only to those who can pay in the form of acquiring residence.[52] In the years since Tiebout wrote, economists like Fischel have observed that the Tiebout model only works as intended if municipalities have some mechanism for ensuring that eligibility for local services is limited to those with the ability to pay. For instance, if a community is known for having excellent schools (and high property values), more people may flock to the community, congesting the schools and increasing the tax burden on residents. The possibility of that event occurring would defeat the ability of consumer-voters to efficiently shop among municipalities, as home prices would no longer effectively signal the quality of local services.[53]

The principal tool municipalities use to ensure that local goods and services are provided only to those with the ability to pay is zoning. Zoning regulations allow municipalities to approve or disapprove the construction of new housing (and other land uses), as well as to determine its density,

---

[50] MICHAEL WALZER, SPHERES OF JUSTICE 106 (1983).

[51] *See* FISCHEL, *supra* note 49.

[52] *See* WILLIAM A. FISCHEL, ZONING RULES! 147 (2015) (describing how zoning converts public goods into private goods via exclusion). I use the term "public good" here in the colloquial sense of being nonexclusive rather than the technical economists' sense of a good that is both nonexcludable and nonrival. Most municipally provided goods are "rival" insofar as they are vulnerable to congestion; the combination of being rival and nonexcludable is what creates the potential for a tragedy of the commons. Goods with these two characteristics are generally referred to as common-pool resources rather than public goods.

[53] *See* FISCHEL, *supra* note 52, at 159; Bruce W. Hamilton, *Zoning and Property Taxation in a System of Local Governments*, 12 URB. STUD. 205, 206–7 (1975).

location, design, timing, and other aspects. In practice, municipalities use zoning to prevent congestion and maintain the existing tax base by limiting population growth and effectively screening new residents to ensure they will pay their fair share of the tax burden. Zoning thus effectively transforms the resources municipalities provide from public goods into private consumer goods. For this reason, zoning is often thought of as a collective private property right belonging to the community of residents, and local goods and services are conceptualized as the exclusive property of paying residents.[54] Indeed, as LaToya Baldwin Clark observes, parents who have attempted to enroll their children in schools outside the districts in which they reside have been criminally charged with "stealing" an education. According to Clark, the very idea of stealing an education presumes that taxpaying residents "regard education as a property right bearing the essential functions of property, including the right to exclude."[55]

2.3 IMMIGRATION AND ZONING IN CITIZENSHIP

That zoning is such a crucial component of the private and liberal nature of local citizenship is significant because zoning has often been considered the local analogue of federal immigration laws. Both zoning and immigration policy are mechanisms for controlling admission into the territory, and thus for determining the size and composition of the population. Further, as Rick Su has described, both zoning and immigration law have served the specific purpose of determining how immigrants are distributed in the United States.[56] But perhaps the most important similarity between immigration and zoning, through rarely discussed, is how they both help create distinctive conceptions of *citizenship* at the local and federal levels. As I discussed earlier, the immigration power enables the federal government to engage in national self-definition by applying expressly ethno-nationalist criteria for admission and naturalization. The putatively exclusive nature of the federal immigration power, however, means that local governments may *not* use their zoning laws for ethno-nationalist purposes. Indeed, during the same

---

[54] FISCHEL, *supra* note 52, at 1 ("[L]and use controls are best analyzed as collective property rights ... "); ROBERT H. NELSON, PRIVATE NEIGHBORHOODS AND THE TRANSFORMATION OF LOCAL GOVERNMENT 6 (2005) ("[Z]oning functions as a 'property right' to the collectively owned environment."); *id.* at 146–47 (arguing that by transferring the right to exclude from the individual to the community, zoning becomes a private property right belonging to the community of homeowners).

[55] *See* LaToya Baldwin Clark, *Education as Property*, 105 VA. L. REV. 397, 402 (2019).

[56] *See* Su, *supra* note 22.

period when the Supreme Court held, in *the Chinese Exclusion Case*, that the federal immigration power entailed the ability to refuse admission of Chinese immigrants on expressly nationalist grounds, the Supreme Court also struck down on equal protection grounds a zoning regulation enacted by the city of San Francisco that was enforced selectively against Chinese laundry operators, a de facto effort to regulate Chinese immigration by making it impossible for Chinese immigrants to earn a living in the city.[57] The *Yick Wo* decision was, in fact, the first case in which the Supreme Court held that noncitizens had constitutional rights, and became important precedent for the Court's decision ninety years later in *Plyler*. The Supreme Court later invalidated zoning laws in the Jim Crow south that attempted to codify racial segregation by explicitly mandating zones for different races.[58] Further, local governments have no authority to naturalize citizens or impose prerequisites to acquiring local citizenship other than residence.

On the other hand, courts have had very little difficulty upholding the constitutionality of zoning laws that effectively limit residency based on socioeconomic status, consistent with the liberal view of local citizenship embodied in the Tiebout model. In the landmark case of *Village of Euclid v. Ambler Realty*, the Court upheld a zoning law that separated multi-family apartment buildings from single-family homes. Though the lower court had denounced the ordinance as class segregation, arguing that "the result to be accomplished is to classify the population and segregate them according to their income or situation in life,"[59] the Supreme Court upheld the law, finding that apartment buildings were "parasites" in single-family districts.[60] Modern courts have upheld zoning laws that entirely prohibit multi-family housing or otherwise make it nearly impossible for people below a certain income level to acquire residency. Although the courts have been clear that state and local governments are prohibited from infringing upon the right to travel, they have consistently held that zoning regulations do not interfere with this right because they "merely make[] it more difficult for the outsider to establish his residence in the place of his choosing."[61] Although, as I discuss further in Chapter 8, there is little doubt that zoning regulations have been used to enforce class and racial segregation, courts are so entranced by the idea of free population mobility embedded in the liberal idea of local citizenship

---

[57] *See* Yick Wo v. Hopkins, 118 U.S. 356 (1886).
[58] *See* Buchanan v. Warley, 245 U.S. 60 (1917).
[59] Ambler Realty Co. v. Vill. of Euclid, 297 F. 307, 316 (N.D. Ohio 1924).
[60] Vill. of Euclid v. Ambler Realty Co., 272 U.S. 365 (1926).
[61] *See* Assoc. Homebuilders v. City of Livermore, 557 P.2d 473, 484 (1976); Vill. of Belle Terre v. Boraas, 416 U.S. 1, 7 (1973).

that they are unable to see the way that zoning inhibits mobility, and instead see it as a neutral mechanism for expressing private consumer preferences.[62]

Thus, where the immigration power enables the federal government to determine admission and citizenship on nationalist criteria such as birth, lineage, or naturalization, the zoning power enables local governments to allocate citizenship based on potential residents' ability to pay. In this way, local citizenship is constructed as liberal and private while national citizenship is constructed as public and ethno-nationalist. Because federal citizenship is about identity and belonging to a territory, the federal government has the exclusive power to determine who counts as a member of the national political community, and who is entitled to access the nation's territory. Because local citizenship is about market choice and mobility, local governments have the primary power and responsibility to distribute local services and to use the zoning power to control access to those services by restricting residency.

2.4 THE LOCAL/FEDERAL ACCOMMODATION AND THE PUBLIC/PRIVATE DISTINCTION

In principle, there is no conflict between local and federal citizenship because, per the public/private distinction, each is confined to its sphere. The federal level is the public sphere of civic virtue and collective belonging, and the local level is the private sphere of market activity and individual choice. (See Table 1.2.) In this way, the distinction between federal and local citizenship is how the state works its accommodation between liberal citizenship on one hand, and republican and ethno-nationalist citizenship on the other. The state prevents the private from corrupting the public by confining the privatized, market-oriented definition of citizenship to the local, and reserving the federal level as the sphere of civic activity. At the same time, the ascriptive citizenship of the nation-state does not interfere with the more consensual citizenship of the locality. The distinction between federal and local citizenship thus enables the state to manage the tension among the different conceptions of citizenship, essentially "delegating" liberal citizenship to the local level while not compromising its commitment to the civic values of nationalism and republicanism.

---

[62] TROUNSTINE, *supra* note 11, at 33–36, 188–89 (noting how suburban homeowners shifted from explicitly racist arguments to "colorblind" arguments of neighborhood character, property values taxes, and the like as racial arguments became less politically palatable).

Consider one telling example of how this accommodation occurs. In the Hart-Cellar Act of 1965, Congress scrapped the racist national origins system of the 1920s and replaced it with a system that prioritized admissions based on family reunification, economic prospects, and diversification of nationalities.[63] Upon admission, immigrants can obtain naturalization after a period of legal residency, a demonstration of their knowledge of civics and the English language, and evidence of their moral character and allegiance to the United States. The system is a blend of liberalism, ethno-nationalism, and republicanism – the standards for admission are liberal but the standards for citizenship are a combination of ethno-nationalist and republican. In principle, admission presupposes that we anticipate the admitted alien obtaining citizenship. In practice, the process of obtaining citizenship can take many years, and may never happen at all. This is especially the case for undocumented immigrants, of course, who enter this country outside the formal admissions process but are tacitly encouraged to enter and seek low-income work. These individuals are "admitted" under a liberal admissions standard in order to be a part of our economic and social community, but denied the ability to become a part of our political community in order to preserve our ethno-nationalist conception of citizenship.

The large number of people who have been admitted, in word or in deed, into the country but denied formal citizenship at the federal level effectively become local citizens of whatever municipality they settle in. As I have described, many of the most important "social rights" of citizenship, such as education and housing, are available to all residents regardless of immigration status. Indeed, under the authority of cases such as *Lau* v. *Nichols*,[64] local governments have a responsibility not only to educate but also to aid the assimilatory process of all resident children, including undocumented immigrant children, by expediting their English literacy. In effect, these individuals are treated as local citizens, even though they are not part of the political community at the national level, and may never be. In this way, the nation-state is preserved as the site of nationalist citizenship but our liberal aspirations are also upheld by designating the locality as the site of liberal citizenship.

Linda Bosniak has referred to this formulation of citizenship as "hard on the outside, soft on the inside."[65] Bosniak is skeptical of this formulation, however, arguing that our supposedly "hard" nationalist approach at the border is

---

[63] *See* MAE M. NGAI, IMPOSSIBLE SUBJECTS: ILLEGAL ALIENS AND THE MAKING OF MODERN AMERICA 258–64 (2004).
[64] 414 U.S. 563 (1974).
[65] LINDA BOSNIAK, THE CITIZEN AND THE ALIEN 98–100 (2006).

undermined by liberal exceptions such as a humanitarian policy of admitting refugees, and our "soft" liberal approach within the border is undermined by the fact that admitted noncitizens are constantly vulnerable to the machinations of our immigration system and, while they are here, denied political rights on nationalist grounds. In my view, however, the "hard on the outside, soft on the inside" formulation is mostly accurate as a descriptive matter, even if it is inadequate normatively. Our immigration system maintains its "hardness" on the "outside" by maintaining a nationalist standard for *citizenship*. Refugees may be *admitted* on softer liberal grounds, but they can only become *citizens* by meeting our harder nationalist standards. This distinction is relevant because, as I have just described, all those who are admitted are thereby entitled to the benefits of local citizenship wherever they reside, even if they lack citizenship at the federal level. In other words, the federal government leaves it to local governments to incorporate admitted aliens into our society under the soft standard of liberalism so that the purity of national citizenship can be maintained alongside a raft of humanitarian exceptions. Conversely, local citizenship remains soft insofar as its essence is the conferral of social benefits such as schooling, housing, and security, to which all local residents are entitled. Because local "consumer-voters" exercise citizenship by voting with their feet, the franchise is simply not as essential an aspect of local citizenship as it is of federal citizenship. That local governments have the *option* of expanding the electorate to noncitizen residents, as well as other classes of interested persons such as nonresident landowners, is consistent with a liberal understanding of the political community as flexible and instrumental, rather than determined by identity and fate. Further, as described earlier, local governments' mandate to provide security to all local residents has often induced them to adopt additional voluntary measures to reduce immigrants' vulnerability within the immigration system, such as adopting informal policies of non-cooperation with immigration authorities.

2.5 HOW GLOBALIZATION IS UNDERMINING THE LOCAL/FEDERAL ACCOMMODATION

Nevertheless, Bosniak is right to point out that liberal citizenship "will inevitably clash" with the idea of citizenship as a "bounded national community."[66] The accommodation between local and federal citizenship papers over many contradictions, and while these contradictions are ordinarily suppressed, they

---

[66] Bosniak, *supra* note 65, at 100.

emerge into full view during times when citizenship is placed under considerable stress. As described in the introduction, our present political moment is a time of such stress, as the aftermath of the Great Recession has intensified the spatial inequalities of globalization. The global economy is largely a service and knowledge based system that places less emphasis on manufacturing capacity and a premium on innovation, which is disproportionately occurring in places where creative people with diverse skills and knowledge are clustered together; that is, cities. A large number of these knowledge workers are immigrants, whose diversity of skills and knowledge boost cities' economic prospects. The flow of capital and labor into cities has been facilitated by liberal trade and immigration policies. Since the recession, almost all economic growth has been concentrated in dense urban areas that benefit from loose trade and immigration barriers. In addition, nation-states like the United States are undergoing significant demographic and cultural changes as a result of both immigration and internal factors. As I described in the introduction, cities are largely embracing those changes and with them, a more liberal conception of citizenship, while residents of rural and smaller metropolitan areas are rejecting those changes and demanding that citizenship be more sharply delineated along ethno-nationalist lines.[67] The result has been that our accommodation between liberal and ethno-nationalist ideas of citizenship is increasingly difficult to sustain. Let me give two examples:

2.5.1 *The Irvine Homeless Tent Camp*

As described in this chapter, our citizenship federalism has largely consisted of delegating liberal citizenship to the local level while reserving the federal level as the sphere of ethno-nationalist citizenship. Earlier I explained that this bifurcation is possible because citizenship, rather than being a monolithic construct, is a "bundle of sticks." Certain sticks within the citizenship bundle, such as the right to vote in most elections and freedom from immigration laws, are distributed at the federal level on ethno-nationalist criteria like birth or naturalization, whereas other sticks, such as eligibility for local benefits, are distributed locally on liberal criteria such as residence or interest. One important consequence of this system is that some people have rights of citizenship at the federal level but not the local level, while others have the reverse. For instance, in Irvine, California, where I live, a proposal to site a homeless "tent camp" near a new community of fancy homes populated largely by recent

---

[67] These trends are outlined in Kenneth Stahl, *Preemption, Federalism and Local Democracy*, 44 Fordham Urb. L.J. 133 (2017).

Asian immigrants was defeated when the immigrant community organized to fight it. Although many of these residents are not United States citizens, are ineligible to vote in Irvine, and are subject to the federal government's immigration authority, they effectively exercise a form of social citizenship at the local level because they have the ability to vote with their feet. Cities like Irvine are highly dependent on revenue from taxes and fees generated by high-end home purchases, which enables affluent homeowners to influence local officials through the threat to exit the community and depress property values. This follows from the Tiebout model, which posits that cities are essentially firms that use municipal services to lure revenue from footloose "consumer-voters." On the other hand, the homeless men and women who were denied shelter in Irvine had no effective ability to influence city hall, even though many of them are United States citizens, because they are not residents of Irvine nor do they have the economic power of the consumer. As US citizens, they are free from deportation and enjoy full rights of political participation, but have no immunity from being shunted around to various makeshift homeless camps as politicians try to dodge responsibility for homelessness.[68]

In this case, the immigrant homeowners who successfully fought the homeless shelter in Irvine have the social rights of citizenship attached to residence and financial power but not political rights, while the homeless men and women denied shelter have the political rights of citizenship without social rights. So which are the "real" citizens? The answer is that *both* groups could be considered citizens, although each group possesses different sticks in the citizenship bundle, and neither possesses all of the sticks. But this answer creates a troubling ambiguity for both liberal and nationalist political theory. Liberalism

---

[68] For perspectives on the controversy over the homeless shelter, see Anh Do, *In Fighting Homeless Camp, Irvine's Asians Win, but at a Cost*, L.A. Times (Apr. 1, 2018, 5:00 AM), https://www.latimes.com/local/lanow/la-me-homeless-asians-20180401-story.html; Nick Gerda, *OC Supervisors Back Off New Homeless Shelters, Make Promise to Work with Cities*, Voice of OC. org (Mar. 28, 2018), https://voiceofoc.org/2018/03/oc-supervisors-back-off-new-homeless-shelters-make-promise-to-work-with-cities/ ; Tomoya Shimura, *About 250 Irvine Residents Convene to Oppose Proposed Homeless Camp Next to Great Park*, O.C. Register (Mar. 23, 2018, 4:39 PM), https://www.ocregister.com/2018/03/23/about-250-irvine-residents-convene-to-oppose-proposed-homeless-camp-next-to-great-park/?fbclid=IwAR3SnvfOqsO6852AWI1cj oY8cftgtCWO8rxcHpjWzB9R79X1J4Wpt6awfjo.

Though Irvine is in southern California, about 40 miles south of Los Angeles, Aihwa Ong describes how Chinese immigrants in Northern California are similarly using their financial power to gain access to elite neighborhoods and change the meaning of citizenship, causing consternation among middle-class white Americans about the transformation of their communities and the traditional social order. *See* Aihwa Ong, Flexible Citizenship: The Cultural Logics of Transnationality 87–109 (1999).

posits an essential equality among citizens, but where two people possess two entirely different sets of rights, how can we call them both "citizen"? Nationalism posits a binary differentiation between citizens and noncitizens, but how do we make such a binary differentiation when there is no set of rights or incidents that clearly distinguish the citizen from the noncitizen?

In ordinary times, these questions do not present much difficulty, for although we treat citizenship as binary in theory, we are accustomed to various degrees of membership within the political community. In an era of globalization defined by persistently high levels of immigration, however, the ambiguity surrounding the meaning of citizenship may become intolerable. As immigrants become an increasingly common and indispensable part of social and economic life, our liberal ideology tells us that conferring social rights without political rights is an unconscionable mark of second-class citizenship. Cities like San Francisco have thus moved to give limited voting rights to noncitizens, even undocumented immigrants. Seeing the benefits of immigration and diversity, many on the left have celebrated the expansion of noncitizen rights as a step toward ending nationalist citizenship and basing it entirely on residence.[69] On the other hand, native-born citizens who believe they are losing culturally and economically from globalization see the extension of social rights to noncitizens as undermining the meaning of citizenship and threatening, as in Irvine, to exalt noncitizens with financial power over citizens without it. From their perspective, draconian immigration and trade policies that create a firm distinction between citizens and noncitizens become necessary. Further, outright discriminatory and inhumane practices like the banning of Muslims or separation of immigrant families become key symbolic means of emphasizing the nationalist component of citizenship and rejecting the long-standing accommodation with liberalism. In this way, the local definition of citizenship as open, liberal and market-oriented comes directly into conflict with the more ascriptive federal citizenship.

2.5.2 *The Sanctuary City*

Another example of the unraveling accommodation between liberal and ethno-nationalist citizenship is that the boundary between the federal sphere

---

[69] *See* Ron Hayduk, Democracy for All: Restoring Immigrant Rights in the United States (2006); Raskin, *supra* note 18, at 1468, 1469 (expressing hope that "the spread of local alien suffrage would sufficiently relax the global ideological hold of nationalism as to make people all over the world comfortable with the idea of making voting rights mobile between nation-states").

of immigration control and the local sphere of municipal service-provision, seemingly so firm in theory, has proven quite untenable when placed under the pressure of globalization. This is made clear by the controversy over sanctuary cities. During the 1990s, many local governments began innovating with what became known as "community policing." The drug war that started in the 1980s created a huge amount of antagonism between law enforcement and the communities they policed that reduced prospects for cooperation on policing objectives. Community policing was designed to reduce that antagonism by building positive relationships between the community and law enforcement. In order to create trusting relationships with predominantly immigrant communities, it was important for police to reassure members of those communities that local law enforcement would not be sharing information obtained as part of their police work with federal immigration authorities. This prompted many cities to move toward what became known as "sanctuary cities."[70]

From the local perspective, sanctuary policies were simply a common-sense policing strategy, consistent with the liberal idea of local citizenship as a right to quality public services. Indeed, sanctuary policies were championed by politically conservative law-and-order mayors like New York's Rudy Giuliani, who saw them simply as a way of making cities safer. Giuliani's administration even unsuccessfully sued the federal government for interfering with local sanctuary policies. Since that time, however, perhaps because immigration has re-emerged as a salient political issue, "sanctuary" has come to be seen by conservatives in a different light, as an effort to undermine federal immigration policy and weaken the ethno-nationalist character of American citizenship. When Giuliani ran for President in 2008, he was attacked for making New York a sanctuary city, a charge that he vehemently denied (although it was true). Giuliani has since become one of the major surrogates for the anti-immigrant Trump administration.[71]

Though it is still an open legal question whether sanctuary policies conflict with the federal government's immigration power, many people – supporters as well as critics – now view sanctuary cities not simply as an effort to provide more efficient policing but to expand the national political community. In other words, where sanctuary cities were once perceived on purely liberal

---

[70] For history and background on sanctuary cities, see, for example, Ingrid V. Eagly, *Immigrant Protective Policies in Criminal Justice*, 95 Tex. L. Rev. 245, 281–87 (2016); Bill Ong Hing, *Immigration Sanctuary Policies: Constitutional and Representative of Good Policing and Good Public Policy*, 2 U.C. Irvine L. Rev. 247, 307 (2012); Rose Cuison Villazor, *What Is a "Sanctuary"?* 61 SMU L. Rev. 133 (2008); Rodriguez, note 22, at 567.

[71] On Giuliani, see Villazor, *supra* note 70, at 134; Rodriguez, *supra* note 22, at 602–03.

terms as a way of providing local residents with security, they are now perceived on ethno-nationalist terms as a way of defining the class of citizens. A catalyst for this changing perception was that the Great Recession exacerbated the inequalities between places and intensified the economic and cultural anxieties brought on by globalization and mass immigration. Residents of metropolitan regions neglected by globalization latched onto a primordial meaning of citizenship as a bulwark against the demographic tide of globalization, while people in those areas benefitted by globalization saw it heralding a more liberal and less tribal understanding of citizenship. The sanctuary city became a litmus test for the meaning of citizenship, with some using it as a talking point to call for tighter immigration standards and a firmer distinction between citizens and noncitizens based on ethno-nationalist criteria, and others, like San Francisco, using it to call for a liberal expansion of the rights of citizenship. In this way, the liberal idea of citizenship prevalent at the local level and the ethno-nationalist idea of citizenship prevalent at the federal level have come directly into conflict.

2.6 THE DIMINISHING IMPORTANCE OF STATE CITIZENSHIP

In focusing on federal and local citizenship, I have deliberately de-emphasized citizenship at the *state* level in the United States. This may seem an odd choice given that, in our system, states are considered the building blocks of federalism. Today, in fact, we are seeing states like California and Texas wading into the citizenship debate by taking sides on the "sanctuary" question, with California's SB 54 declaring the entire state a sanctuary and Texas's SB 4 prohibiting sanctuary cities. In practice, however, state citizenship is largely passive and reactive. As the California and Texas approaches to the sanctuary question both illustrate, these states are not articulating a distinctive "state" version of citizenship, but either taking the side of sanctuary *cities* within their state against the federal government, or siding with the federal government's definition of citizenship against sanctuary cities.[72] Only very recently have states begun thinking about re-creating the sort of distinctive state citizenship that existed before the late nineteenth century. In the past few years, for example, the state of New York has considered a bill that would grant state citizenship to undocumented immigrants, which would include

---

[72] Markowitz, *supra* note 24, at 873 (state efforts to incorporate immigrants have not been "aggressive" in asserting "a new role for states in defining who does and does not belong," but have mostly been "playing defense").

rights such as the vote, access to public benefits, and anti-discrimination protections.[73] The bill has failed to pass since being introduced in 2015, and even if it were to pass, the state of New York would only be catching up with the many municipalities that already offer similar rights to all local residents. In summary, the local and the federal scales are where the contours of modern citizenship are being meaningfully articulated, and the state is largely reacting to developments at those scales.

The secondary status of state citizenship is largely the result of a historical process, much of which is discussed in subsequent chapters but I briefly sketch here. At the time of the founding, states played a primary role in defining citizenship. States determined who could vote not only in state and local elections but also elections to the federal House of Representatives. For many decades, states naturalized aliens as state citizens, giving them the right of suffrage and other incidents of citizenship. State courts agreed that states could confer citizenship on people who were not citizens of the United States. States also had the power to control the movement of people into their jurisdictions, which they used especially vigorously against the poor and free blacks.[74] After the enactment of the Fourteenth Amendment, however, which declared that all citizens of the United States are also citizens of the state in which they reside, the states lost a considerable amount of their power to define state citizenship. Citizenship became "a matter of national law and national concern."[75] The Supreme Court stripped states of the power to regulate inter- and intrastate population movement, and later articulated a voting rights doctrine that largely controls both state and federal elections. During the surge of immigration in the late nineteenth century, every state eliminated suffrage rights for aliens, essentially causing state citizenship to align with federal citizenship.[76]

At the same time states were losing their distinctive conception of citizenship, however, municipalities were imbued with a degree of autonomy to define *local* citizenship. Progressive reformers conceptualized cities as distinct from states in that they were primarily administrative rather than political bodies, and therefore could have distinctive suffrage rules (see Part II). Local

---

[73] *See id.* at 906–12; Glass, *supra* note 24, at 929–30.

[74] On state citizenship prior to the Fourteenth Amendment, see NEUMAN, *supra* note 19, at 19–43 (on state mobility restrictions); 63–71 (on state suffrage and naturalization rules); *see also* KUNAL M. PARKER, MAKING FOREIGNERS: IMMIGRATION AND CITIZENSHIP LAW IN AMERICA, 1600–2000, at 81–115 (2015).

[75] BOSNIAK, *supra* note 65, at 82.

[76] *See* ALEXANDER KEYSSAR, THE RIGHT TO VOTE: THE CONTESTED HISTORY OF DEMOCRACY IN THE UNITED STATES, at 136–41 (2000).

governments were allowed freely to incorporate and given the power to enact zoning laws, which enabled them as a de facto matter to control population movement and set barriers to entry. It has long been the practice for states to delegate to local governments the primary responsibility over the provision of many governmental services, including land use, health care, policing, sanitation, education, and others. By the 1960s many of these services were coming to be seen as essential social rights of citizenship, and local governments could largely determine eligibility for such services – and thus local citizenship – based on how strict or loose their zoning laws were. As a practical matter, local governments have been induced to articulate a distinctive and strategic conception of citizenship by state fiscal structures that force cities to vie against other municipalities for a share of a shrinking pie of revenue. Where frontier states once dangled the prospect of citizenship for immigrants in order to lure new settlers, today cities must do the same to entice the highly skilled immigrants or mobile capital their budgets often depend on (explaining why some cities have extended the franchise to noncitizen residents or nonresident landowners).

None of this is to say that state citizenship is unimportant. States play a principal role in determining access to public benefits like Medicaid and in-state tuition discounts, benefits that are surely among the "social rights" of citizenship.[77] States still have some distinctive suffrage rules, particularly as they relate to the voting rights of convicted felons. Though states are barred from enacting immigration legislation, state efforts to regulate immigration can still influence the immigration debate even if they fail in the courts, as was the case with Arizona's SB 1070 and, before that, California's draconian Proposition 187. The point, however, is that state citizenship does not have a *distinctive character* in the way that local and federal citizenship do. States' policies regarding access to public benefits and felon enfranchisement are extremely disparate, and there is no consistent rationale for these policies that evidences any theory of citizenship or marks state citizenship as distinct in principle from either federal or local citizenship.[78]

---

[77] An important recent book on state variations regarding Medicaid policies, describing Medicaid as among the "social rights" of citizenship, is JAMILA MICHENER, FRAGMENTED DEMOCRACY: MEDICAID, FEDERALISM, AND UNEQUAL POLITICS 57 (2018).

[78] S. Karthick Ramakrishnan & Allan Colbern, *The California Package: Immigrant Integration and the Evolving Nature of State Citizenship* 6 POL. MATTERS 1, 5–6 (2015) argues that California's unique "package" of benefits that it accords to undocumented immigrants represents a "de facto state citizenship." I agree, but the fact that California's approach is unique among the states proves my point that there is not at the moment a distinctive conception of what state citizenship means.

On reflection, the secondary character of state citizenship is not altogether surprising. Throughout much of history, the city and the nation-state have been the primary contestants over the meaning of citizenship, leading ultimately to the tenuous accommodation that we now see fraying. The next chapter examines how our multi-faceted and multi-scalar conception of citizenship came to be.

3

A Short History of Local Citizenship

Chapter 2 described the way American law has divided citizenship among different scales. We have largely conceptualized the federal government as the "public" sphere of republican and ethno-nationalist citizenship, meaning that it is defined by collective civic identity and linked fate, whereas we have largely defined local citizenship as the "private" sphere of liberal citizenship, meaning that it is defined by residence, interest, and individual consumer choice. This dichotomy enables us to balance our disparate and often conflicting commitments to the primordial conception of the nation, the civic ideal of the republic, the exigent needs of a commercial society, and liberal aspirations for equality. But how exactly did we come to divide citizenship in this way? This structure did not spring forth overnight or by the conscious hand of any one individual. Instead, it emerged as part of the long process by which the nation-state evolved out of the city-state. This chapter provides a brief historical overview of that process.

3.1 CITIZENSHIP IN THE ANCIENT AND MEDIEVAL CITY

Citizenship was born in the ancient Greek city-state. The city-states were constantly at war, either with each other or the hated Persians, so politics was literally a matter of life and death. For that reason, the Greeks understood citizenship primarily as an obligation to engage in the civic life of the city. In addition, since war with foreign powers was the main item on the political agenda, it was critically important to maintain a distinction between citizens and foreigners, whose loyalty to the city-state was uncertain. In Athens, foreign guest-workers were given the special status of *metic*, which enabled them to live and work freely in the city but forbade them or their descendants from ever becoming citizens.[1]

The fact that the Athenians saw a need to create a status for foreigners at all, however, shows that despite the strains of war they still needed to have friendly relations with outsiders. Indeed, Athens rose to power through commerce, trading wine, olive oil, spices, and papyrus with neighboring cities.[2] To balance its need for commerce with its preparations for war – two distinct modes of dealing with foreigners – the Athenians used citizenship to distinguish between the public realm of war, from which foreigners were excluded, and the private realm of commerce, in which they were included. As Arlene Saxonhouse writes, the Greeks invented the public/private distinction to manage the problem of diversity.[3]

As the era of city-state warfare drew to a close with the dawn of empire, this distinction diminished in importance. Commerce became the lifeblood of cities, and cities grew to be far more dynamic and cosmopolitan than ancient Athens had ever been. Accordingly, cities' membership policies became more open and accepting. The Islamic scholar Al-Farabi approvingly contrasted tenth-century Baghdad with ancient Athens by noting that in cosmopolitan Baghdad, anyone could become a citizen, and "strangers cannot be distinguished from residents."[4] The cities of medieval Europe, largely freed from the concerns of warfare in a feudal society, became full-fledged business enterprises that devoted almost all of their resources to controlling commerce.[5] Unlike the oppressive feudal society outside the urban walls, where land ownership was the sole determinant of one's social, economic, and political status, anyone who participated in the commercial activity of the city could become a "freeman" after residing in the city for a year and a day. Cities became synonymous with the freedom that commerce provided, as epitomized in the famous expression *Stadtluft macht frei* ("City air makes you free.")[6]

---

[1]　*See, e.g.,* J. G. A. Pocock, *The Ideal of Citizenship since Classical Times,* in The Citizenship Debates 32 (Gershon Shafir ed., 1998); Arlene W. Saxonhouse, Fear of Diversity: The Birth of Political Science in Ancient Greek Thought (1992); Robert Dahl, Democracy and Its Critics 14–23 (1989).

[2]　*See* Edward Glaeser, Triumph of the City 19–20 (2011).

[3]　*See* Saxonhouse, *supra* note 1.

[4]　See Muhammad Ali Khalidi, *Al-Farabi on the Democratic City,* 11 Brit. J. Hist. Phil. 379, 386 (2003).

[5]　*See* Max Weber, *Citizenship in Ancient and Medieval Cities,* in The Citizenship Debates, *supra* Note 1, at 43.

[6]　*See generally* Harold J. Berman, Law and Revolution: The Formation of the Western Legal Tradition 357–403 (1983); Lewis Mumford, The City in History: Its Origins, Its Transformations, and Its Prospects 248–65, 269–77, 335–43, 410–19 (1961).

Urban citizenship was, at this point, decidedly shifting away from the ancient republican tradition of civic activity and a fixed notion of membership toward the modern liberal idea of citizenship rooted in commerce and a more fluid notion of membership. However, citizenship was not yet liberal in the sense of a firm distinction between the public sphere of the state and the private sphere of civil society. The politics of the medieval city blended the public and private realms in a way that was unimaginable to both the ancient republican world and modern liberal societies. The purpose of city government was to advance the economic interests of the freemen. At the same time, the freemen's economic interests were not considered distinct from the interest of the city as a whole. Merchants had no individual rights to own property or to engage in commercial transactions in a "free" market. As Jerry Frug writes, "[t]he town association controlled individual commercial conduct with a thoroughness unmatched in history." The town "protected the worker from competition and exploitation, regulated labor conditions, wages, prices and apprenticeships, punished fraud, and asserted the town's interests against neighboring competitors."[7]

Though not yet liberal, the medieval city paved the way for the emergence of the liberal state and a liberal idea of citizenship. At least initially, it was mutually beneficial for cities to form relations with ambitious monarchs who sought to centralize power. Kings sheltered cities from piracy and competition while using their military power to open up overseas trade routes, which boosted city economic fortunes and provided kings with a reliable source of tax revenue.[8] Gradually, the older decentralized feudal regime that featured a personal relationship between lord and vassal was displaced by a new era of centralized authority and a more abstract relationship between the sovereign and the residents of a specific territory. Cities that had long prized their independence found this new power arrangement uncomfortable, and they used their economic leverage to wring the maximum amount of autonomy from the sovereign, which was usually formalized in a city charter. In asserting their demands against the sovereign and embodying them in the charter, the cities pioneered the liberal idea that citizens were rights-bearing individuals with claims against the state that could be set down in binding legal instruments. At the same time, kings sought to subject cities to royal control by asserting a direct relationship between the monarch and the individual citizen, undermining the status of intermediate organizations like the city and

---

[7] See Gerald E. Frug, *The City as a Legal Concept*, 93 HARV. L. REV. 1057, 1084 (1980).
[8] See *id.* at 1091.

planting the seeds for a revitalized distinction between the public realm of the
state and the private realm of individual striving.[9]

These same trends paved the way for the emergence of nationalism and the
ethno-nationalist conception of citizenship. As I explained in Chapter 1,
liberalism and nationalism emerged together out of the rubble of feudalism
to form a liberal-nationalist vision of the state. The decline of feudalism,
hastened by the rise of cities and commerce, broke the lines of allegiance
binding subjects to their king. Monarchs relied on the abstract notion of a
unitary "nation" rooted in a territory to recreate those ties. The idea of an
unmediated relationship between the sovereign and the people, which was a
critical part of the emergence of liberalism and the revival of the public/private
distinction, served also to cement the bonds of national allegiance. Nationalism had the additional benefit of creating an imagined form of equality among
citizens at a time when feudalism's decline was causing massive social
upheaval and economic inequality.[10] The "imagined community" of nationalist citizenship was predicated, however, on the liberalizing economic system
that cities were then creating. Money was the mediating device that substituted impersonal relations for personal ones and created a unified economic
community on which a cultural community could also be built. So monarchs
had to make their peace with the cities and allow a more liberal, urban form of
citizenship to coexist alongside the nationalist form of citizenship then
coming into being.[11]

3.2 LOCAL CITIZENSHIP IN EARLY AMERICA

Cities' commitment to commerce and a liberalizing idea of citizenship
followed them across the Atlantic when the Dutch West India Company
founded the city of New Amsterdam as a company town in 1624. Twenty years
later, the city had become a hub of religious tolerance and ethnic diversity in
which at least eighteen different languages were already spoken. When Jews

---

[9]   See SASKIA SASSEN, TERRITORY, AUTHORITY, RIGHTS 36, 40–54, 64–67 (updated ed. 2008);
      BENJAMIN R. BARBER, JIHAD V. McWORLD 166 (1995) (displacement of feudalism by
      nationalism transformed people "from individual subjects into individual freemen whose
      obedience to the crown and responsibility to others grew out of rights they now understood
      themselves as possessing by birth and liberties they conceived as belonging to them by nature").
[10] See LIAH GREENFELD, NATIONALISM: FIVE ROADS TO MODERNITY 48–51 (1992) (describing
      origins of English nationalism).
[11] See SASSEN, *supra* note 9, at 76–110; JAMES C. SCOTT, SEEING LIKE A STATE 30–52 (1998)
      (describing how rise of market economy was linked to state centralization and emergence of
      "uniform, homogenous citizenship").

and Quakers began arriving on the shores of New Amsterdam, however, the Dutch governor Peter Stuyvesant sought to turn them away from the city. His superiors rejected Stuyvesant's request, reminding him that he was running a business, not a religious commune.[12]

American cities continued to blend commerce with politics into the colonial period, and so membership in the political community remained largely indistinguishable from membership in the economic community. According to Jon Teaford, American cities like Philadelphia were chiefly occupied with the regulation of commerce. As in the feudal city, colonial Philadelphia strictly controlled wages, prices, the management of public markets, and entry to trades. Anyone with an economic interest could vote and participate in the commercial life of the city, though elections were usually sleepy affairs since city aldermen generally had life tenure and elections were rarely contested. There was no distinction between city politics and the economic affairs of the city. Colonial New York City was less involved in regulating commerce than Philadelphia, focused instead on the management and disposition of its vast real estate holdings, but in this, as well, the city's property decisions were somewhere between private real estate transactions and a "mode of public planning and governance."[13]

The blending of public and private in city government and the dominance of economic interests in local political affairs were just the sort of problems that our founders were especially worried about – the corruption of the public realm by the private. As discussed in Chapter 1, the founding generation was deeply influenced by the civic republican tradition and heavily preoccupied with corruption. Thus, it should come as no surprise that the founders were very suspicious of cities. Associating cities (correctly) with the rise of money and commerce, and the declining importance of real property ownership, they worried that a landless urban population would encourage dependence and self-seeking, rather than the civic virtue they believed resided in a stable population of independent landowners. Thomas Jefferson, for example, saw in the cities of Europe "a depravity of morals, a dependence and corruption, which renders them an undesirable accession to a country whose morals are sound."[14] In addition to republican concerns about corruption, the founding

---

[12] See Remonstrance of the Inhabitants of the Town of Flushing (1657), reprinted in EMPIRE CITY: NEW YORK THROUGH THE CENTURIES 33 (Kenneth T. Jackson & David S. Dunbar eds., 2002).

[13] See HENDRIK HARTOG, PUBLIC PROPERTY AND PRIVATE POWER: THE CORPORATION OF THE CITY OF NEW YORK IN AMERICAN LAW, 1730–1870, at 36–40 (1983); JON C. TEAFORD, THE MUNICIPAL REVOLUTION IN AMERICA 4–35 (1975).

[14] See MORTON WHITE & LUCIA PERRY WHITE, THE INTELLECTUAL VERSUS THE CITY: FROM THOMAS JEFFERSON TO FRANK LLOYD WRIGHT 14 (1962) (quoting Jefferson's Notes on Virginia).

generation's fears of the city were also animated by liberal Lockean concerns about public power threatening private property rights. Where the city was once perceived as an organic entity that exercised what we would today consider both property rights and sovereign power, and inseparable from the people contained within it, it was now perceived as wielding an exclusively public power that could only threaten the private property rights of individuals.[15] In 1784, a governing body of the state of New York rejected a bill that would confer the power of taxation on New York City, noting that such power was inappropriate for "a commercial city, where selfish views may stimulate assessors to oppress their rivals in trade, and destroy that security which makes the basis of commerce."[16] Finally, the rise of commercial cities was hostile to the emerging nationalist ethos that also motivated the founders. The founders saw a country riven by ethnic and religious discord and were insistent on knitting the people into a single nation. It was a staple of American nationalism that the republic needed to be "one moral whole," and was dependent on "a population homogenous in its customs and concerns." There was little room for "fragmentary and discordant local governments" within this ideology.[17]

Many of these concerns were embodied in James Madison's FEDERALIST 10. Madison was very worried about the growth of the landless population in cities, so much so that he (unsuccessfully) attempted to introduce a national property qualification for the franchise into the federal Constitution.[18] FEDERALIST 10 is, as much as anything else, a polemic against cities and the commercial society they had begotten. The self-interested "factions" that Madison famously describes in the tract are mostly associated with the rise of commerce and cities – he warns that faction arises "of necessity in civilized nations" when those nations split into "a landed interest, a manufacturing interest, a mercantile interest, a monied interest," the last three all associated with cities and commerce.[19] He further warns about "a rage for paper money" and "an abolition of debts," both of which were critical aspects of the rise of commerce.[20] And, finally, he sees faction far more likely to arise in small city-states than in larger nation-states because "the smaller the number of individuals composing a majority, and the smaller the compass within which

---

[15] See Frug, *supra* note 7, at 1089, 1101–05.

[16] See HARTOG, *supra* note 13, at 88.

[17] See *id.* at 86; *see also* GREENFELD, *supra* note 10, at 423–31.

[18] See ALEXANDER KEYSSAR, THE RIGHT TO VOTE: THE CONTESTED HISTORY OF DEMOCRACY IN THE UNITED STATES 9–10 (2000).

[19] See THE FEDERALIST No. 10, at 59 (James Madison) (Jacob E. Cooke ed., 1961).

[20] *Id.* at 65.

they are placed, the more easily they will concert and execute their plan of oppression."[21] Hence, he notes that city-states historically "have ever been spectacles of turbulence and contention, have ever been found incompatible with personal security, or the rights of property; and have in general been as short in their lives, as they have been violent in their deaths."[22]

As described in Chapter 1, however, the liberal/republican solution to the problem of self-interest in politics was not to eradicate it but to structurally mitigate it so that public and private interest would coincide. Hence, Madison proposed to remove power from smaller governments like cities and vest it in the nation-state, to "extend the sphere" of government to "take in a greater variety of parties and interests."[23] He also proposed to displace the republican tradition of direct democracy with representative democracy, expressing confidence that representation could ensure a virtuous civic realm because "representatives, whose enlightened views and virtuous sentiments render them superior to local prejudices" would counteract the self-interest of their constituents.[24] Finally, FEDERALIST 10 reflects the liberal/nationalist desire to subsume intermediate organizations like cities to the state, so as to create a direct relation between the state and its citizens and a firm distinction between the public sphere of the state and the private sphere of individual freedom.

In short, what FEDERALIST 10 proposed was that citizenship, associated with the local since antiquity, would now be a status exclusively conferred by the state. The local would no longer be a meaningful site of citizenship. This was a potentially explosive idea at a time when cities like Philadelphia and New York were engines of the nation's economic growth. For the time being, though, questions of city power and local citizenship remained largely unexplored. THE FEDERALIST was a work of propaganda designed to convince the voters of New York to ratify the new Constitution, which vested far more power in the national government than the old Articles of Confederation. The city-state was a convenient foil to make that argument, but it does not appear that constraining city power was one of the framers' top concerns. Most American cities were small at this time, and the framers largely assumed that America would continue to be an agricultural society for the foreseeable future. As a result, the Constitution said nothing specific about local governments.[25]

---

[21] *Id.* at 64.
[22] *Id.* at 61.
[23] *Id.* at 64.
[24] *Id.* at 64.
[25] *See* KEYSSAR, *supra* note 18, at 8–10; 18–19, 37–40.

Nevertheless, as an industrializing economy caused cities to grow in size and power after the Constitution's ratification, the implications of FEDERAL-IST 10 became clearer. The threat of local "factionalism," it seemed, could only be contained by conceptualizing cities as "public" entities subject to state control and thus incapable of formulating any conception of citizenship distinct from the state. For a time, it appeared indeed that local citizenship was dead.

3.3 CITIZENSHIP IN THE PUBLIC CITY: THE JACKSONIAN ERA AND THE GILDED AGE

Local governments initially began becoming public, and shedding their unique approach to citizenship, almost by happenstance. As industrialization advanced, cities became less concerned about regulating trade and more about protecting the health, safety, and welfare of their residents. The Jacksonian age was gripped by an anti-corporate sentiment in which monopolistic entities like cities were frequently denounced for putting their own private interests ahead of the public good. Driven by the spirit of the age, many cities abolished the closed-corporation, in which aldermen had life tenure, and held regular elections. The franchise was extended to all residents. As Jerry Frug explains, this movement "helped confirm the emerging public character of city corporations."[26] The city was becoming a public institution, distinct from the private sector of the marketplace, and as such citizenship was being decoupled from business interests. The city charter, which had emerged during the middle ages as a means for cities to assert a unique form of urban citizenship against the state, was blamed for conferring unearned privileges on cities. States asserted the power to unilaterally re-define city charters, which courts liberally upheld.[27]

This trend toward seeing cities as public and local citizenship as irrelevant intensified during the gilded age, as the rise of urban political machines raised both liberal concerns about government interfering in the private marketplace and republican concerns about private interests invading the public sphere. Because the political machines were fueled by an influx of immigrants from southern and eastern Europe, the traditional liberal/republican anxieties about the city mingling public and private were now mixed with ethno-nationalist worries about the changing demographic composition of the

---

[26] Frug, *supra* note 7, at 1101.
[27] On the many changes to the city's legal character during the Jacksonian period, *see* HARTOG, *supra* note 13, at 71–175; TEAFORD, *supra* note 13, at 70–100.

country. Progressive reformers introduced a variety of innovations designed to professionalize and bureaucratize city government so that the private and the public would be kept separate and, not coincidentally, the influence of the machines and their immigrant constituents would be minimized. The movement to introduce the public/private distinction into city government peaked with the codification of a new legal status for cities, called "Dillon's Rule." John Dillon, the Iowa judge and treatise author who formulated the eponymous rule, shared the fears of his contemporaries about the Progressive-era city. He worried that the mingling of the public and private spheres caused cities to imperil private property rights, as cities engaged in wasteful spending that led to excessive taxation on property owners. Dillon's solution, much like Madison's, was not to instill civic virtue at the municipal level but to remove power from the local to the state level. In true liberal/republican fashion, Dillon trusted that the vertical structure of power would be the best protection against municipal extravagance. Dillon's rule, accordingly, provides that municipalities have only the powers delegated to them by their states, and any powers so delegated must be strictly construed against the municipality. The local government was now decisively associated with the public realm, differentiated from the private sphere of the market, and subordinated to the state.[28]

Under Dillon's rule, local citizenship continued to diminish in significance. As I describe further in Chapter 5, the ethno-nationalist concerns about the immigrant base of the political machine that led to Dillon's rule also led the federal government to centralize immigration control and take away the power state and local governments had once enjoyed to naturalize immigrants. At the same time, as we saw in Chapter 2, the Supreme Court affirmed that the federal government had the exclusive authority to control immigration. Local control over the composition of the electorate, already diminished by the assault on city charters during the Jacksonian period, was further eroded as states used Dillon's rule to mandate that cities adopt state voting rules.[29]

3.4 CITIZENSHIP IN THE PRIVATE CITY: THE PROGRESSIVE ERA AND THE RISE OF HOME RULE

Local citizenship did not prove so easy to eradicate, however, because Dillon's rule was not the last word on local government's place within the

---

[28] Jerry Frug's classic article *The City as a Legal Concept* describes how Dillon's Rule solidified cities' status as "public" and thus subordinate to the state. *See* Frug, *supra* note 7, at 1109–13.

[29] *See* KEYSSAR, *supra* note 18, at 23–26.

public/private distinction. Urban reformers in the early twentieth century became deeply concerned about what they saw as excessive meddling by corrupt state legislators into the business of city government, and they attributed this state of affairs in part to Dillon's rule, which placed cities at the mercy of state legislatures.[30] The reformers envisioned local government as an *imperium in imperio*, or a "state within a state," and they successfully pushed to give local governments what became known as "imperio" home rule, which conferred on municipalities the independent authority to initiate legislation without an express delegation from the state, as well as immunity against state interference into local prerogatives.[31] The city charter, which had been an instrument of city independence since medieval times but rendered moot as states centralized control over local governments, was now revived as an instrument for municipalities to enact legislation. Unlike Dillon's rule, which subjected local governments to state control, imperio home rule provides that states and local governments have distinct and mutually exclusive spheres of activity: local governments may only regulate in matters of "local" or "municipal" concern, and the state can only legislate in matters of greater than local concern, often called "statewide" matters.[32]

Although home rule never quite lived up to its promise to give local governments a sphere of autonomy, it marked an important conceptual shift away from Dillon's rule in that where Dillon's rule assimilated local governments entirely to the public sphere of the state, home rule conceptualizes them as operating within a distinct, and distinctly private, sphere of local activity. As David Barron observes, home rule advocates disliked Dillon's rule because it failed to mark off a private sphere for locals that was distinct from the public sphere of the state: "With the city understood as a creature of the state, no practicable way had been devised to cordon off the local realm – and with it the privatism that many believed it should reflect – from the influence of higher politics."[33] Home rule promised to create such a privatized "local realm," but Barron is careful to note that home rule was *not* intended solely to empower cities. Rather, it was intended to limit cities' freedom of action by circumscribing it to a privatized realm. Home rule, according to Barron,

---

[30] *See, e.g.*, Kenneth A. Stahl, *Local Home Rule in the Time of Globalization*, 2016 BYU L. Rev. 177, 179–86, 252–53 (2016); Dale Krane et al., Home Rule in America: A Fifty-State Handbook 10–11 (2001); David J. Barron, *Reclaiming Home Rule*, 116 Harv. L. Rev. 2257, 2285–88 (2003).

[31] *See* Krane et al., *supra* note 30, at 11–12.

[32] *See* Stahl, *supra* note 30 at 203–05; *See* Lynn A. Baker & Daniel B. Rodriguez, *Constitutional Home Rule and Judicial Scrutiny*, 86 Denv. U. L. Rev. 1337, 1341, 1349–55 (2009).

[33] Barron, *supra* note 30, at 2286–88.

"promised to confine local power to a quasi-private sphere even more than Dillon's rule of strict statutory construction."[34]

With local governments now secure in a private sphere sealed off from the public sphere of state and federal government, a distinctly local idea of citizenship re-emerged. Under the authority of home rule, as I describe in Part II, cities once again began creating unique standards for suffrage. Initially, many cities extended the franchise to women, who were not yet entitled to vote in most state or federal elections, and then, later, to nonresident landowners, minors, and even noncitizens. In each case, the franchise was extended to groups deemed to have a sufficient interest in local government, reflecting the liberal view that local politics is rational, consensual, and instrumental. The movement toward perceiving local citizenship this way was triggered by an important demographic trend that emerged contemporaneously with home rule. During the 1920s, it became feasible for middle-class residents to leave the city for incorporated suburbs outside the city where they could obtain higher quality municipal services for cheaper prices. Prior to the 1920s, according to the historian Olivier Zunz, most people chose communities based on ethnic groupings; after the 1920s they selected based on occupation and common demand for municipal services. Suburbanites were becoming what Charles Tiebout would later call "consumer- voters" who selected where to live based on rational consumer self-interest rather than ethnicity and identity.[35] Residence and interest became the hallmarks of local citizenship, and as such, local citizenship became centered on the delivery of municipal services to families. As Richard Briffault observes, "[t]he central function of local government is to protect the home and family – enabling residents to raise their children in 'decent' surroundings, servicing home and family needs, and insulating home and family from undesirable changes in the surrounding area." The locality is effectively "an agent not of the state but of local families, acting to defend the private sphere surrounding home and family."[36]

Interestingly, this move toward seeing local citizenship as liberal, private, and rooted in interest and residence began occurring at the same time federal

---

[34] *Id.* at 2294.

[35] *See* OLIVIER ZUNZ, THE CHANGING FACE OF INEQUALITY: URBANIZATION, INDUSTRIAL DEVELOPMENT, AND IMMIGRANTS IN DETROIT, 1880–1920 (1982). As Zunz notes, one major exception to this trend was the continued racial segregation that became a defining pattern in American life beginning in this period. As I discuss further in Part III, the liberal idea of local citizenship as rooted in consumer choice and mobility has often worked to disguise the reality of entrenched racial segregation.

[36] Richard Briffault, *Our Localism: Part II: Localism and Legal Theory*, 90 COLUM. L. REV. 346, 382 (1990).

citizenship was moving in the opposite direction. A backlash against mass immigration led the federal and state governments to expressly limit the franchise to American citizens, while the federal government asserted the exclusive power to shape the nation's demography through immigration. National citizenship was increasingly articulated as a matter of identity and shared fate, in contrast to local citizenship's focus on residence and interest. As I describe further in Chapter 5, the divergence between federal and local citizenship was part of a larger ideological movement to sharpen the distinction between the public and private and between federal and local spheres of activity. Jurists of the Progressive age were in thrall to the ideology of "dual federalism," which held that national and state governments had distinct realms, within which their power was absolute and outside of which each was powerless.[37] For a long period, dual federalism animated the courts' interpretation of the Constitution's Interstate Commerce Clause, as courts attempted to draw the line between the "national" sphere of interstate commerce and the "local" sphere of intrastate commerce. In *Chy Lung v. Freeman*,[38] the Supreme Court similarly held that, under the Constitution's *foreign* commerce clause, the federal government had the exclusive power to regulate immigration, reflecting the dual federalist idea that national and local governments have distinct spheres of authority.[39] Home rule, likewise, sought to divide the world of government activity by strictly separating statewide from municipal affairs, designating the state as the appropriate realm for politics and the local as the realm for administration. Thus, demographic factors combined with ideology to craft a rigid distinction between a public sphere of federal citizenship rooted in ethno-nationalism and a private sphere of local citizenship rooted in liberalism.

By and large, as described in the previous chapter, the bifurcated approach to citizenship contrived during this era remains in force. This is not to say that the development of local citizenship ended in the 1920s. Far from it. Subsequent demographic, political, and ideological changes during the twentieth

---

[37] *See* Ernest A. Young, *Dual Federalism, Concurrent Jurisdiction, and the Foreign Affairs Exception*, 69 Geo. Wash. L. Rev. 139, 143 (2001) (quoting Alpheus Thomas Mason, *The Role of the Court, in* Federalism: Infinite Variety in Theory and Practice 8, 24–25 (Valerie Earle ed., 1968)) ("'[D]ual federalism' contemplates 'two mutually exclusive, reciprocally limiting fields of power – that of the national government and of the States. The two authorities confront each other as equals across a precise constitutional line, defining their respective jurisdictions.'"); Stahl, *supra* note 30, at 201–6.

[38] 92 U.S. 275 (1875).

[39] *See* Jennifer Gordon, *Immigration as Commerce: A New Look at the Federal Immigration Power and the Constitution*, 93 Ind. L.J. 653, 674–75 (2018) (describing roots of exclusive federal immigration power in the foreign commerce clause).

century contributed to new and different understandings of local citizenship. In particular, the neighborhood organizing movement that arose in many cities in the late 1960s and early 1970s in response to urban renewal brought with it a new, collectivist vision of local citizenship reminiscent of the ancient Greek city-states. However, for the most part the *law* regarding local citizenship has remained stuck in the progressive era. Within our legal and political tradition, local citizenship is still conceptualized as private and liberal.

On that note, the next part discusses three case studies of how local citizenship has been constructed in the legal imagination as liberal, in contrast to the nationalist character of federal citizenship – women, noncitizens, and landowners. It concludes in Chapter 7 by demonstrating, with respect to each of the case studies, how globalization has broken down the distinction between local and federal citizenship and caused a crisis in the meaning of citizenship. Subsequently, in Part III, I revisit the neglected alternative history of local citizenship embodied in the neighborhood organizing movement, and ask whether, as globalization causes our current model of local citizenship to erode, we could find a worthy substitute elsewhere in the history of local citizenship.

PART II

"Noncitizen Citizens"

Three Case Studies of Local and Federal Citizenship

This part discusses three case studies that illustrate the distinction between local and federal citizenship: women, noncitizen residents, and landowners. These groups have all at some time had the status of "noncitizen citizens," to use Linda Bosniak's apt term.[1] Specifically, they have been treated as citizens at the local level but not at the federal level. In each case, the republican, ethno-nationalist, and liberal conceptions of citizenship have been reconciled by using the public/private distinction to simultaneously maintain two overlapping forms of citizenship: a local citizenship that is private and liberal alongside a federal citizenship that is public, republican, and ethno-nationalist. In articulating the contours of local citizenship, courts and advocates have frequently emphasized the ways in which local and federal citizenship are distinctive and complementary.

Each case study described in Chapters 4 through 6 demonstrates the promises and perils of conceptualizing local citizenship in liberal terms, and also reveals the seeds of an eventual conflict between local and federal citizenship. On one hand, liberalism has allowed and often required local governments to embrace a vision of citizenship that is cosmopolitan, welcoming, and open to the world, and therefore offers a possible antidote to the xenophobia and provincialism now affecting our national politics. On the other hand, it has also truncated the local sphere to consumption and market participation, eschewing the robust tradition stretching back to the ancient Greeks in which cities served as hubs of civic activity. As Chapter 7 then describes, the double-edged nature of local citizenship has become starkly evident during our era of globalization, causing local and federal citizenship to clash. As globalization has weakened the public/private distinction, the

---

[1] LINDA BOSNIAK, THE CITIZEN AND THE ALIEN 4–5, 81, 100 (2006).

liberal conception of citizenship that long prevailed at the local level now threatens to invade the sphere of federal citizenship, which is increasingly defined by consumption and mobility. The sense that an affective and primordial conception of citizenship is being corrupted has caused a reinvigorated ethno-nationalism to emerge, with its sights set firmly on the local as the agent of that corruption.

4

Local Citizenship and Woman Suffrage

The question of what it means to be a citizen has perhaps been most starkly presented by the political status of women. This chapter presents an interesting historical puzzle: women were enfranchised in many municipal elections prior to the Nineteenth Amendment, which prohibited any discrimination in voting on the basis of sex. I argue that during this time women were "noncitizen citizens" who enjoyed citizenship at the local but not the federal level. Moreover, women's status as noncitizen citizens illustrates that local and federal citizenship were seen as distinct and complementary.

4.1 THE RIGHT TO VOTE

In the 1874 case of *Minor v. Happersett*,[1] a woman who had been denied the right to vote in her home state claimed that the newly enacted Fourteenth Amendment, which conferred citizenship on every person born in the United States, thereby also gave such persons the right to vote. The Supreme Court acknowledged that women born in the United States were citizens, but at the same time denied that the status of citizen entailed political rights such as the franchise. The Court observed that women had been considered citizens since the founding of the republic, but had always been denied the right to vote, and also noted that many states enfranchised noncitizens. On that basis, the Court reasoned that there was no necessary connection between citizenship and voting.

The Court's conclusion rested on a doubly weak foundation, however. First, women had never been considered true or full citizens. Women could be naturalized, were subject to the laws, and could, if they were single, be

[1]   88 U.S. 162 (1875).

taxed, but they lacked many of the rights of citizens. Aside from having no right to vote, hold office, or otherwise participate in politics, under the law of "coverture" women who were married could also not hold or dispose of their own property. Coverture, as Linda Kerber expertly describes, was often used as a pretext to deny that women were citizens because it made them financially dependent on their husbands and thus incapable of exercising independent political judgment.[2] A married woman, or *feme covert*, could not take an oath of loyalty to the state because her ultimate allegiance was to her husband. In the early case of *Martin* v. *Commonwealth of Massachusetts*,[3] the Massachusetts Supreme Judicial Court held that a married woman could not have her property confiscated for participation in her husband's rebellion against the United States because she was incapable of disobeying her husband; as the winning lawyer successfully argued, a *feme covert* cannot commit treason because she is "not a member" of the political community and "has no political relation to the state any more than an alien."[4] Into the twentieth century, courts held that women who married noncitizens thereby lost their citizenship.[5]

Second, even at the time of the *Minor* decision it was already clear that there was a strong link between citizenship and voting. As Gerald Neuman points out, prior to *Minor* several state courts and state constitutions had determined that conferring suffrage on noncitizens necessarily made them into citizens of the *state*.[6] Even the federal courts acknowledged the link between citizenship and voting by holding that Congress's authorization of noncitizen voting on the formation of constitutions for new states transformed those noncitizens into citizens of the state on its admission to the union.[7] Thus, although *Minor* was not yet ready to confront this reality, the denial of woman suffrage was effectively an acknowledgment that women were not really citizens.

Women did eventually gain the right to vote in state and federal elections through the Nineteenth Amendment in 1920. Long before the Nineteenth Amendment, however, women were already enfranchised in many municipal elections, either through state legislation or municipal home rule charters.

---

[2] See Linda K. Kerber, *The Paradox of Women's Citizenship in the Early Republic: The Case of Martin v. Massachusetts, 1805,* in 97 AMER. HIST. REV. 349 (1992).

[3] 1 Mass. Reports 348 (1805).

[4] *Id.* at 362–63.

[5] See Kerber, *Supra* note 2, at 377–78.

[6] See GERALD L. NEUMAN, STRANGERS TO THE CONSTITUTION: IMMIGRANTS, BORDERS, AND FUNDAMENTAL LAW 66–70 (1996).

[7] See id.

As early as 1838, Kentucky women were given the right to vote in school board elections, and soon after women were enfranchised elsewhere not just in school board elections but in liquor licensing, bond referenda, and general municipal elections as well. Though there was some disagreement among the courts about the authority of states and local governments to grant women the right to vote in municipal elections, considering that many state constitutions expressly conferred the franchise only on men, courts frequently upheld the expansion of the municipal franchise to women.[8]

Why were women simultaneously denied the franchise at the state and federal levels but granted it at the municipal level? If, as I think is fairly clear, the right to vote is an important marker of citizenship, then one explanation is that women were effectively considered citizens at the local level but not at the state and federal level. As described in the previous part, local citizenship is fundamentally distinct from federal citizenship, and often conferred on different grounds. Federal citizenship is republican, nationalist, and public, meaning that it is generally conferred based on civic allegiance and identity, whereas local citizenship is liberal and private, meaning that it is based on mobility, self-interest, and rational individual choice. The case of woman suffrage provides another illustration of this pattern, and is thus additional historical evidence of the distinctive characters of local and federal citizenship. At the same time, the significance of the woman suffrage debate is not entirely historical. It illuminates several contemporary problems in our thinking about citizenship.[9]

---

[8]   *See* ALEXANDER KEYSSAR, THE RIGHT TO VOTE: THE CONTESTED HISTORY OF DEMOCRACY IN THE UNITED STATES 167–68; 185–87 (2000). Keyssar comprehensively charts the state of woman suffrage prior to the Nineteenth Amendment in the appendix, tables A.17 through A.20. *See also* Joshua A. Douglas, *The Right to Vote under Local Law*, 85 GEO. WASH. L. REV. 1039, 1048–51 (2017). I discuss the relevant case law further later.

[9]   There is of course a voluminous literature on the woman suffrage movement, and I can only give it limited attention here. Some important recent sources include CORRINE M. MCCONNAUGHY, THE WOMAN SUFFRAGE MOVEMENT IN AMERICA: A REASSESSMENT (2013); REBECCA J. MEAD, HOW THE VOTE WAS WON: WOMAN SUFFRAGE IN THE UNITED STATES, 1868–1914 (2004). There are a wide range of perspectives on how woman suffrage was achieved. For example, some sources stress ideological arguments like changing ideas about the role of women in society, while others stress instrumental arguments like the perceived advantages that parties or interest groups would attain from enfranchising women. For a good overview, see MCCONNAUGHY, this note, at 4–8. While this chapter stresses the ideological arguments for enfranchising or refusing to enfranchise women, I recognize that ideological arguments may have been advanced as pretexts for purely instrumental ends. Nevertheless, the trajectory of woman suffrage outlined here is consistent with my argument that local and federal citizenship have been conceptualized in distinct terms.

4.2 FEDERAL CITIZENSHIP

Prior to the enactment of the Nineteenth Amendment, the question of woman suffrage in state and national elections cropped up periodically, but was dismissed each time with a litany of anti-suffrage arguments. These arguments were often informed by republican, liberal, and ethno-nationalist ideas about citizenship.[10] According to republican ideology, women lacked the requisite independence to vote because they were creatures of the home, not the political community. Women belonged to the private sphere of necessity and struggle, not the public sphere of citizenship. Their entry into the public sphere would necessarily corrupt it by bringing the affairs of the household into the state.[11] Women's privateness was confirmed by liberal ideology, which stressed the distinction between the "natural" sphere of private rights and the artificial realm of the state, thereby reinforcing the idea that the existing sexual division of labor and the larger public/private distinction represented the natural order of things. As industrialization advanced during the nineteenth century, liberalism gave birth to the "separate spheres" ideology, which exaggerated the sexual division of labor by crafting a distinction between the harsh male sphere of the industrial workplace and the affective female realm of the home. The separate spheres ideology served to depoliticize and devalue the labor performed by women in the home while also rationalizing the dehumanizing impacts of the new industrial economy by offering working men the sanctuary of the home. At the same time, the separate spheres ideology also confirmed that women had no place in the hardscrabble political world. The woman's domain was the home, her kingdom "the empire of softness," not the cruel world of politics.[12]

---

[10]   Many of these arguments are discussed in Rogers M. Smith, *"One United People:" Second-Class Female Citizenship and the American Quest for Community*, 1 YALE J. L. & HUM. 229, 236–39 (1989).

[11]   *See* J. G. A. Pocock, *The Ideal of Citizenship since Classical Times*, in THE CITIZENSHIP DEBATES 32, 34 (Gershon Shafir ed., 1998); ARLENE W. SAXONHOUSE, FEAR OF DIVERSITY: THE BIRTH OF POLITICAL SCIENCE IN ANCIENT GREEK THOUGHT (1992); HANNA FENICHEL PITKIN, FORTUNE IS A WOMAN: GENDER AND POLITICS IN THE THOUGHT OF NICCOLO MACHIAVELLI (1984); HANNAH ARENDT, THE HUMAN CONDITION 27 (1958).

[12]   *See* MARY P. RYAN, WOMANHOOD IN AMERICA 113–65 (1983); Kenneth A. Stahl, *The Suburb as a Legal Concept: The Problem of Organization and the Fate of Municipalities in American Law*, 29 CARDOZO L. REV. 1193, 1245–51 (2008); Smith, *supra* note 10, at 233–36; Reva B. Siegel, *"The Rule of Love": Wife Beating as Prerogative and Privacy*, 105 YALE L.J. 2117, 2142–50 (1996); Linda K. Kerber, *Separate Spheres, Female Worlds, Woman's Place: The Rhetoric of Women's History*, 75 J. AMER. HIST. 9 (1988); Frances E. Olsen, *The Family and the Market: A Study of Ideology and Legal Reform*, 96 HARV. L. REV. 1497 (1983). Jean-Jacques Rousseau described the woman's "empire of softness" in III EMILIUS, OR, A TREATISE ON EDUCATION 10 (1768).

Finally, ethno-nationalism also undergirded the resistance to woman suffrage. Denying the franchise to women – not to mention blacks and foreigners – created a sense of common identity among white men by defining them in contrast to those who were excluded from the full benefits of citizenship. According to Kerber, "adult men who were differently situated in terms of class – as artisans, farmers, merchants, planters – were similarly situated in regard to gender."[13] As Paula Baker observes, the separate spheres ideology re-emerged "with a vengeance" after states abolished property qualifications for voting, because the demise of the property qualification left citizens with little to provide a sense of shared identity other than their common maleness.[14]

From the ethno-nationalist perspective, furthermore, woman suffrage was seen as a threat to the permanence and sanctity of the union because it eroded the essential foundation of Anglo-Saxon citizenship: the marriage. According to Sarah Barringer Gordon, in the anxious period after Reconstruction, anti-suffragists worried that giving women a separate political identity would reduce marriage – and therefore the union itself – into a mere partnership, a contractual and therefore dissolvable relationship rather than something permanent and transcendent.[15] They openly expressed their belief that marriage was "one of the pre-existing conditions of our existence as civilized white men."[16] Concerns about how the decline of marriage would dissipate the bonds of the union were amplified by the postwar western expansion, which created a migratory and transient culture in which divorce was commonplace. Not coincidentally in the minds of anti-suffragists, newly created western states like Indiana, Wyoming, and Utah freely granted the franchise to women (the latter being special cause for concern because of its association with polygamy).[17] The worry in short was that woman suffrage would cause marriage – and therefore citizenship – to become a matter of rational choice and self-interest rather than shared fate.

4.3 LOCAL CITIZENSHIP

Despite these concerns, women were permitted to vote in many local and some state elections prior to the Nineteenth Amendment.[18] The claim that

---

[13] See Kerber, *supra* note 12, at 352–53.
[14] Paula Baker, *The Domestication of Politics: Women and American Political Society, 1780–1920,* 89 AMER. HIST. REV. 620, 629 (1984); *see also* Smith, *supra* note 10, at 239–41.
[15] Sarah Barringer Gordon, *"The Liberty of Self-Degradation": Polygamy, Woman Suffrage, and Consent in Nineteenth-Century America,* 83 J. AMER. HIST. 815, 832–33, 838, 840–41 (1996).
[16] *See id.* at 840–41.
[17] *See id.* at 842 (observing that ease of divorce in a transient culture was a constant theme of critics who saw breakdown of marriage in the west).
[18] *See* KEYSSAR, *supra* note 8, at tables A.17 through A.20.

women could not participate in politics because they belonged in the purely private sphere of the home had little force with regard to local elections, because local government was increasingly coming to be seen as itself part of the private sphere of the home, in contrast to the public sphere of the state. During the age of industrialization, municipal governments began regulating in many areas that had previously been associated with the home, including the improvement of housing, child labor, public health, education, land use, temperance, and the like.[19] Middle-class women, many of whom were active in these causes under the banner of the Progressive reform movement, pressed for access to the ballot in municipal elections on the grounds that municipal government was essentially a form of housekeeping, and that the association between women and the home made women ideally suited to tackle the homelike problems of the modern industrial city. One suffrage advocate, for example, argued that women should be given a voice in such issues as "garbage disposal, cleanliness of the streets, [and] the care and education of children,"[20] issues that were now central items on the municipal regulatory agenda, because "[i]f a woman is a good housekeeper in her own home, she will be able to do well that larger housekeeping."[21] According to one historian, "the statement that the home was woman's sphere was now an argument not against woman suffrage but in favor of it, for government was now 'enlarged housekeeping.'"[22]

The republican concern about household affairs corrupting the political sphere was inapplicable in the local context, because municipal government was not "political" at all. The doctrine of home rule, discussed in Chapter 3, divided government into analytically distinct spheres for "local" and "general" or "statewide" matters. Local government was understood primarily as a matter of corporate administration, entirely separate from the "general" sphere of civic activity. Reformers saw home rule as a means of removing politics from local government so that local government could be run like a business, or on administrative principles of expertise and efficiency. For many advocates, indeed, home rule meant that cities would be governed by an inflexible charter designed and approved by a super-legislature of experts or businessmen and immunized from ordinary legislative politics.[23] Home rule was part of a

---

[19] See RYAN, *supra* note 12, at 150–54; AILEEN KRADITOR, THE IDEAS OF THE WOMAN SUFFRAGE MOVEMENT, 1890–1920, at 65–71 (1965).

[20] GWENDOLYN WRIGHT, MORALISM AND THE MODEL HOME: DOMESTIC ARCHITECTURE AND CULTURAL CONFLICT IN CHICAGO, 1873–1913, at 109 (1980) (quoting Louise de Koven Bowen).

[21] *Id.*

[22] KRADITOR, *supra* note 19, at 67.

[23] See David J. Barron, *Reclaiming Home Rule*, 116 HARV. L. REV. 2257, 2297–98 (2003),

more general Progressive movement to take the politics out of local government by transferring powers from elected city councils to appointed city
managers, vesting significant authority in expert commissions, and instituting
non-partisan, at-large elections.[24] At the same time, however, home rule's
devolution of local affairs to municipal control also empowered municipalities
to articulate distinctive suffrage rules on matters like schooling that were
considered paradigmatically local in nature.[25] Ironically, home rule thus
permitted the expansion of the electorate at the same time that it was contracting the scope of the matters the electorate actually decided. Indeed, that
may have been exactly the point – women were allowed to vote precisely
because the scope of municipal politics had been so radically constricted.[26]
Likewise, in Dillon's Rule states where municipalities required a specific
authorization from state legislatures to expand the franchise, legislatures
authorized women to vote on local issues like schooling, on the grounds "that
school matters were distinct from 'politics.'"[27]

Another reason why municipal suffrage for women was more palatable than
suffrage at the state or federal level was that it did not threaten ethno-
nationalist ideas about identity. In the age of industrialization, municipal
politics became less about shared identity and partisanship and more about
common economic interests.[28] Where political participation had once
appeared to be a signal of one's manhood, it was now an instrumental tool
to obtain economic or consumer goals. The famed Chicago School of Urban
Sociology observed that the anonymity of the great city and the mobility
within it broke down ethnic ties and recombined people into new groupings
based on shared economic interests. According to Robert Park, one of the
Chicago school's leading lights, "Personal tastes and convenience, vocational
and economic interests, infallibly tend to segregate and thus to classify the

---

[24] See KEYSSAR, *supra* note 8, at 232 (discussing various methods for depoliticizing and
professionalizing local government).
[25] See State ex rel. Taylor v. French, 117 N.E. 173, 184 (Ohio 1917) (upholding a home rule charter
granting women the right to vote on the grounds the charter was "limited to matters of purely
local and municipal concern").
[26] See KEYSSAR, *supra* note 8, at 232 (noting that restrictions on the franchise slowed down during
the 1920s because political reforms had removed many matters from democratic control);
Thomas Bender, *Intellectuals, Cities, and Citizenship in the United States: The 1890s and
1990s*, in CITIES AND CITIZENSHIP 21, 32 (James Holston ed. 1999) (noting that Frank
Goodnow, one of the architects of the home rule doctrine, sought to circumscribe municipal
power because he "held a dim view of the capacity of ethnic and racial minorities").
[27] KEYSSAR, *supra* note 8, at 186; *see also id.* at 167–68 (explaining how Dillon's Rule enabled
distinctive municipal suffrage standards).
[28] See Baker, *supra* note 14, at 639.

populations of great cities."[29] Where the nation was perhaps intended to be permanent and sacrosanct, the industrial city and its suburban satellites were almost defined by their transitory character. A proliferation of suburban communities on the urban outskirts, the improvement of suburban infrastructure, and the popularization of the streetcar and the automobile gave residents increasing freedom of movement and the ability to choose where to settle.[30] In that light, the traditional nationalist concern that woman suffrage would undermine marriage and threaten the permanence of the union was inapplicable at the municipal level. In fact, suffragists' emphasis on the association between women and the home provided reassurance for reformers who were worried about women's increasing economic and sexual freedom that they were still fundamentally creatures of the home.[31]

To summarize, woman suffrage at the municipal level was appropriate because, and only insofar as, municipal citizenship was perceived as qualitatively distinct from federal citizenship. Local citizenship was fundamentally liberal, based on mobility, interest, and individual choice, firmly located within the private sphere of the home, the family, and the marketplace. As such, it was strictly differentiated from the public sphere of national citizenship, which was fundamentally republican and ethno-nationalist in character, predicated on identity, permanence, and civic-minded independence from the market. Accordingly, woman suffrage posed no threat to republican or nationalist conceptions of citizenship as long as it was confined to the municipal sphere.

In upholding the extension of the municipal franchise to women, courts stressed the conceptual distinction between local and federal citizenship. The Ohio Supreme Court upheld a home rule charter granting women the right to vote on the grounds that the charter was "limited to matters of purely local and municipal concern. No power is thereby granted to legislate upon or interfere

---

[29] Robert E. Park, *The City: Suggestions for the Investigation of Human Behavior in the Urban Environment*, in The City 1, 5 (Robert E. Park et al. eds., 1925).

[30] *See, e.g.,* Eric H. Monkkonen, America Becomes Urban: The Development of U.S. Cities & Towns 1780–1980, at 194–97 (1988) (discussing increasing residential mobility in the 1920s); Kenneth T. Jackson, Crabgrass Frontier: The Suburbanization of the United States 148–56 (1985) (discussing improved suburban infrastructure); 157–71 (discussing rise of the automobile and its role in suburbanization).

[31] *See* Baker, *supra* note 14, at 642 (suffragists stressed that "the vote would not remove women from the home"); *see* Mona Domosh & Joni Seager, Putting Women in Place: Feminist Geographers Make Sense of the World 69–109 (2001) (social anxieties caused by women's increasing freedom were resolved by limiting their mobility, especially by confining them to the home). I pursue the theme of women's mobility in the city further in Chapter 10.

in any way with the affairs of the state government."[32] Courts made clear that women were authorized to vote in local elections because such elections were primarily about interest rather than identity, liberalism rather than nationalism. One court upheld a state law permitting women to vote for local elected officials, despite a Constitutional provision expressly granting the franchise only to men, on the grounds that the constitutional provision did not apply to "the determination of local matters in which they [women] may have a legitimate interest in common with men."[33] A few courts also upheld state laws permitting women who owned property to vote in local elections to authorize the issuance of bonds, presumably on the grounds that property ownership provided the requisite interest to warrant the right to vote.[34]

4.4 THE AMBIGUITY OF LOCAL CITIZENSHIP FOR WOMEN

While the liberal nature of local citizenship facilitated expanding the franchise to women, it also had two more ominous implications that will prove relevant for the discussion that follows. First, local woman suffrage was based on a cramped view of the municipality as an essentially administrative body preoccupied with "homelike" matters such as schools and garbage collection, rather than the civic affairs of state. This was not an inevitable development. Prior to the Progressive age, municipal services like schools and sanitation were themselves perceived as civic in nature. Municipal sanitation, for example, was part of a campaign to beautify and instill civic pride in the city, an invitation to all municipal dwellers to participate "in the collective task of making city living desirable."[35] Reconceptualizing these public services as part of the "woman's sphere," the private realm of the home and family, transformed them from collective civic affairs into individualized consumer goods, and transformed the city itself from a forum for civic activity into a provider of cheap consumer services. Sanitation and schools are no longer

---

[32] State ex rel. Taylor v. French, 117 N.E. 173, 184 (Ohio 1917).

[33] Spatgen v. O'Neil, 169 N.W. 491, 493 (N.D. 1918); *see also* Coggeshall v. City of Des Moines, 117 N.W. 309 (Iowa 1908) (upholding Iowa statute allowing women to vote in local bond elections). Some courts held, however, that state constitutions defining qualified electors as "male" barred legislatures from extending the franchise to women. *See* Bd. Of Election Commissioners of Indianapolis v. Knight, 117 N.E. 565 (Ind. 1917); Coffin v. Bd. Of Election Commissioners of Detroit, 56 N.W. 567 (Mich. 1893).

[34] Village of Waverly v. Waverly Waterworks, 125 N.Y.S. 339 (Sup. Ct. Tioga Cty. 1910); Gould v. Village of Seneca Falls, 118 N.Y.S. 648 (Sup. Ct. Seneca Cty. 1909). One published court decision upheld a state law extending the franchise to women in school board elections. People ex rel. Ahrens v. English, 29 N.E. 678 (Ill. 1892).

[35] Gerald E. Frug, *City Services*, 73 N.Y.U. L. REV. 23, 86–87 (1998).

perceived as ways of bringing people together, but as commodities people acquire by buying or renting a home in a community. This transformation was consistent with the emerging character of local citizenship as thoroughly private and liberal.

Second, municipal woman suffrage was also predicated on a very narrow view of women's role in society, reinforcing their historical and "natural" role as homemakers at the very moment that urbanization was challenging that traditional role. As we will see in Chapter 7, once women achieved full suffrage through the Nineteenth Amendment, it heralded that citizenship itself was increasingly becoming synonymous with household consumption, and women were expected to practice citizenship by acquiring consumer goods in the isolation of the detached single-family home and the suburban shopping mall. In short, women became citizens at the same time that the meaning of citizenship was being diminished and women's role in society was being codified.

Nevertheless, the example of woman suffrage also demonstrates the promise of reconceptualizing citizenship in accordance with liberal principles. Woman suffrage confirmed and advanced an emerging new political and economic status for women. The transitory nature of city life that weakened the pull of ethno-nationalism and led to woman suffrage also loosened many of the traditional constraints on women's freedom. Women were increasingly economically independent as they began participating in greater numbers in the workforce. Women also played a critical role in the labor and consumer rights movements.[36] Many of the most significant Progressive reformers were women. And, with their increasing economic and political independence came increased freedom in gender relations. Incidences of divorce markedly increased as women became more economically independent.[37] Indeed, as I have just noted, the reason suffrage advocates were so careful to emphasize women's domestic roles was because women were increasingly moving beyond those roles. Suffrage emboldened women to continue pressing for more freedoms – and the suffrage movement, of course, did not end at the municipal level.

---

[36] On women's role in the consumer movement, see Lizabeth Cohen, A Consumers' Republic: The Politics of Mass Consumption in Postwar America 31–41; 75–83 (2003). On the labor movement, see Elizabeth Ewen, Immigrant Women in the Land of Dollars: Life and Culture on the Lower East Side, 1890–1925, at 25, 252–56 (1985); Kathie Friedman-Kasaba, Memories of Migration: Gender, Ethnicity and Work in the Lives of Jewish and Italian Women in New York, 1870–1924, at 120–36 (1996).

[37] See Wright, *supra* note 20, at 109 (noting increased incidents of divorce and its relationship with women's increasing economic freedom).

I return to the subject of the Nineteenth Amendment in Chapter 7. I note here, though, that the enactment of the Nineteenth Amendment signaled an erosion in the separation between the public sphere of federal citizenship and the private sphere of municipal citizenship. As that dividing line eroded, the liberal view of government and the citizen embodied in municipal citizenship invaded the public sphere of ethno-nationalist and republican citizenship at the federal level; at the same time, it became increasingly clear that women would no longer be contained within the private sphere of the home. What had been considered private became public, the personal became political, and it forever changed our politics. Likewise, in our current era of globalization, during which the public/private distinction is under constant stress, the liberal model of local citizenship persistently threatens to burst out of its boundaries and fundamentally alter the nature of federal citizenship.

5

Local Citizenship for Noncitizen Residents

The previous chapter showed that, prior to the Nineteenth Amendment, women sometimes had incidents of citizenship (particularly the right to vote) at the local level but not at the state or federal level. This divergent treatment illustrated that courts and policymakers perceived federal and local citizenship as conceptually distinct. Federal citizenship is envisioned as republican, ethno-nationalist, and public in character, meaning that it is conferred based on identity and a primordial identification with territory, whereas local citizenship is envisioned as liberal and private, meaning that it is conferred based on mobility and individual consumer choice. A similar distinction is evident today in the status of noncitizen residents of the United States. They have many of the incidents of citizenship at the municipal level but very few, if any, at the federal level. They are "noncitizen citizens."[1] And, as was the case with woman suffrage, this difference reflects distinct conceptions of citizenship at the local and federal scales.

The right to vote presents the most obvious analogue with the previous status of women. Noncitizens are prohibited from voting in federal and state elections in every state. The arguments against noncitizen suffrage tend to proceed from ethno-nationalist premises; specifically, the need to firmly differentiate citizens from noncitizens so as to create a unity of identity among citizens, aid the assimilation of immigrants, and ensure that the electorate has undivided loyalty to the United States. According to one opponent of noncitizen suffrage: "Voting is one of the few, and doubtlessly the major, difference between citizens and non-citizens. Citizenship itself, and open access to it, is one of the major unifying mechanisms of *E Pluribus Unum*."[2]

---

[1] LINDA BOSNIAK, THE CITIZEN AND THE ALIEN 4–5, 81, 100 (2006).
[2] Stanley Renshon, *The Value of Citizenship*, N.Y. SUN (Sep. 15, 2003); *see also* RON HAYDUK, DEMOCRACY FOR ALL: RESTORING IMMIGRANT VOTING RIGHTS IN THE UNITED STATES 72–85 (2006) (discussing this and several other objections to noncitizen suffrage).

Another critic, a former head of the Immigration and Naturalization Service (since replaced by Immigration and Customs Enforcement) wrote that noncitizen suffrage "could seriously affect the assimilation process immigrants have pursued in this nation for 200 years."[3] A third critic, echoing the historical argument against woman suffrage that it would threaten the sanctity and permanence of marriage, wrote that immigrants should earn the right to vote "by getting married to America, if you will, by way of citizenship, rather than just living together, which is essentially what a green card holder is doing."[4] For its part, the US Supreme Court has upheld the constitutionality of excluding noncitizens from the franchise and other forms of participation, holding that "[t]he exclusion of aliens from basic governmental processes is not a deficiency in the democratic process but a necessary consequence of the community's process of political self-definition."[5]

Nevertheless, a number of municipalities have chosen to extend the franchise to noncitizens, and that number has grown in just the last few years.[6] These municipalities have emphasized, as advocates for enfranchising women in municipal elections once did, that issues about loyalty, assimilation, and identity are irrelevant at the local level because local governments are concerned mostly with matters of daily life in which all residents share a common interest. For example, just as woman suffrage advocates stressed that municipal government was principally concerned with home-like matters such as "garbage disposal, cleanliness of the streets, [and] the care and education of children,"[7] advocates for extending the municipal franchise to noncitizens have argued that "[i]ncorporated municipalities such as ours are concerned with the necessities of daily life – garbage collection, recycling, paving streets, snow removal, tree maintenance, building permits-and for the larger ones, crime prevention. As a municipality, our powers do not extend to national or

---

3 Former INS Commissioner Alan C. Nelson *quoted in* HAYDUK, supra note 2, at 91.
4 Mark Krikorian *quoted in* HAYDUK, *supra* note 2, at 125.
5 Cabell v. Chavez-Salido 454 U.S. 432, 439–40 (1982) (excluding aliens from serving as probation officers). In *Cabell* and several other cases, the Court has also upheld prohibitions on noncitizens serving in public office and holding jobs in the public sector, which the Court has characterized as "political" in nature. In addition to Cabell, see Foley v. Connelie, 435 U.S. 291 (1978) (police officers); Ambach v. Norwick, 441 U.S. 68 (1979) (schoolteachers). I discuss these cases in somewhat more detail later.
6 *See* Introduction Note 6.
7 GWENDOLYN WRIGHT, MORALISM AND THE MODEL HOME: DOMESTIC ARCHITECTURE AND CULTURAL CONFLICT IN CHICAGO, 1873–1913, at 109 (1980) (quoting Louise de Koven Bowen).

state-wide policies."[8] One noncitizen resident of Takoma Park, Maryland, made the case for his enfranchisement (successfully) as follows, "I have as much interest in the community as anyone ... We're not asking for a voice at the national level or in foreign policy ... But in local matters, we're no different than somebody who has moved to Takoma Park from California."[9]

While to date very few municipalities have extended the franchise to noncitizens, I contend that the extension of suffrage to noncitizens is a logical culmination of a long-term trend in which many of the benefits of local citizenship are being conferred on all local residents regardless of immigration status. For example, while the federal government strictly controls the movement of noncitizens across international borders, subjects noncitizens to the vicissitudes of the immigration system, and withholds from many noncitizen residents access to federal public benefits such as federally funded Medicaid, municipalities are *required* to provide all local residents, regardless of immigration status, with freedom of movement and access to benefits such as education, housing, emergency health care, and public safety. As I discussed in Chapter 2, and revisit further later, these benefits are the sort of "social rights" that have increasingly become defining aspects of citizenship in the modern welfare state, arguably surpassing the right to vote in importance. In effect, then, by holding that eligibility for local services is established by residence, the courts have held that all local residents are local citizens. The judicial recognition of noncitizen residents as local citizens has, in turn, often induced municipalities to *voluntarily* extend additional incidents of citizenship, such as municipal identification cards, access to health care and banking institutions, creation and funding for day laborer sites, "sanctuary" policies that offer noncitizen residents some protection from the immigration authorities, and, more recently, the franchise. (As described in Chapter 2, many states have also opted to extend benefits to immigrants like in-state tuition discounts, state-funded Medicaid, drivers' licenses, and so forth, but state policies vary

---

[8] *See* Jamin B. Raskin, *Legal Aliens, Local Citizens: The Historical, Constitutional, and Theoretical Meanings of Alien Suffrage,* 141 U. Pa. L. Rev. 1391, 1452, & n.320 (1993) (quoting *Testimony by the Village of Martin's Additions Regarding Maryland Assembly Bill 665,* at 2 (presented by Sharon Hadary Coyle, Chairperson, Village Council)). Ms. Coyle went on to say: "We believe every resident in our community-regardless of ultimate national or state citizenship-is entitled as a fundamental right to participate in governing our municipal affairs-to have a say in whether we will pave the street in front of his or her house-to influence garbage collection and recycling-and to ensure that the streets are plowed in the winter." *See id.* at n.373.

[9] *See id.* at 1464, *quoting* Beth Kaiman, *Takoma Park Weighs Noncitizen Vote,* Wash. Post, Oct. 31, 1991, at M2; *see also id.* at 1464 n.379 (quoting local resident stating "[a] non-citizen is just as affected by the decisions of the City Council as anyone else.")

considerably and so "state citizenship" does not appear to have a consistent character in the way local citizenship does).

The increasing recognition of noncitizen residents as local citizens, at the same time they are denied many of the rights of federal citizenship, again reflects a distinction between a private, liberal idea of citizenship based on residence and individual self-interest, and a public, ethno-nationalist conception of citizenship based on collective identity and loyalty. This chapter elaborates on that point in two parts. The first part explores the historical process by which, as local and federal citizenship evolved into distinct statuses, noncitizen residents came to be perceived simultaneously as citizens at the local level and aliens at the federal level. The second part examines in closer detail two particular rights of local citizenship enjoyed by noncitizens: the right to education secured by the Supreme Court's landmark decision in *Plyler* v. *Doe*[10] and the right to security embodied in the decisions of many cities and states to become "sanctuaries" for unauthorized immigrants. These two rights embody both the promise and the limits of liberal local citizenship for immigrants. Although holding out the possibility of a capacious understanding of membership in the political community, they also make clear that local citizenship is a "right" to be enjoyed only by those with the privilege of money and mobility. In that light, this discussion has relevance far beyond the immigration context; it reveals the very nature of local citizenship and the reasons why we are now seeing so much discontentment with it.

5.1 HOW NONCITIZENS BECAME LOCAL CITIZENS

5.1.1 *Federal Citizenship*

The process by which alien residents came to be perceived as noncitizens at the federal level and citizens at the local level was long and tortuous. A good starting point, naturally, is the franchise. Today, every state disfranchises noncitizens in state elections, and federal law bars them from participating in federal elections as well. As illustrated previously, it is often taken for granted in our political discourse that limiting suffrage to citizens is essential for differentiating citizens from noncitizens. It took some time to arrive at the point where suffrage was confined to US citizens, however.[11] In fact, noncitizen suffrage was

---

[10] 457 U.S. 202 (1982).

[11] This observation is not in conflict with my observation in Chapter 4 that voting was historically equated with citizenship. As described further later, enfranchised noncitizens were often considered citizens of the *state* but not national citizens. *Cabell's* statement that excluding

quite common in many states and localities at the time of the founding and for many decades thereafter. As it turns out, republican and liberal ideologies were both somewhat ambiguous on the question of noncitizen suffrage. Eventually, however, ethno-nationalist ideology won out as anti-immigrant sentiment led the franchise to be restricted to citizens and federal citizenship to be conceptualized predominantly in ethno-nationalist terms.

In the early republic, there was no consistent ideological position on the status of noncitizens. The Constitution itself said little about citizenship or the rights of citizens. Its only references to citizenship were, as Martha Jones observes, "fragmentary and implicit."[12] There were republican and liberal arguments both for and against noncitizen involvement in politics. The republican case against noncitizen suffrage echoes many of the arguments from a century ago against woman suffrage. Under the republican conception of citizenship, foreigners were grouped together with women as being unsuited for political participation. Although not necessarily creatures of the home like women, noncitizens also lacked the requisite "independence" to participate in politics. Just as a married woman was deemed incapable of taking an oath of loyalty because her true allegiance was to her husband, noncitizens were likewise thought incapable of citizenship because their loyalty might lie with a foreign nation. The republican solution was to consign foreigners to the private sphere of dependence alongside women. As we recall, the Athenians devised a special status for foreigners that enabled them to participate in economic matters but not in the public affairs of the state.[13]

Motivated in part by republican ideology, the framers of our Constitution worried that public officials would be corrupted by foreign influence. In order to stem that concern, they required that legislators in the House of Representatives have seven years of residence in the United States. George Mason, who introduced the provision, stated that he supported "opening a wide door for emigrants; but did not chose to let foreigners and adventurers make laws for us and govern us."[14]

---

aliens from the political process is essential to national self-definition is a relatively recent development.

[12] MARTHA S. JONES, BIRTHRIGHT CITIZENS: A HISTORY OF RACE AND RIGHTS IN ANTEBELLUM AMERICA 24 (2018).

[13] *See, e.g.,* J. G. A. Pocock, *The Ideal of Citizenship since Classical Times,* in THE CITIZENSHIP DEBATES 32, 33–35 (Gershon Shafir ed., 1998); Arlene W. Saxonhouse, FEAR OF DIVERSITY: THE BIRTH OF POLITICAL SCIENCE IN ANCIENT GREEK THOUGHT (1992); ROBERT DAHL, DEMOCRACY AND ITS CRITICS 20–23 (1989).

[14] *See* ZEPHYR TEACHOUT, CORRUPTION IN AMERICA: FROM BENJAMIN FRANKLIN'S SNUFF BOX TO CITIZENS UNITED 358 (2014).

In early America, however, the republican argument against noncitizen suffrage was complicated by the fact that most states prior to the 1850s limited suffrage to property owners. This limitation was itself rooted in republican concerns about ensuring an independent electorate. To the extent noncitizens owned property, they might be counted on to be independent, and certainly more independent than the growing class of landless merchants, artisans, and urban dwellers who were then agitating for voting rights. As Jamin Raskin observes, "alien enfranchisement reflected the assumption that the propertied white male alien voter would be sufficiently similar to other electors so as not to threaten fundamental cultural and political norms."[15] Thus, enfranchisement of alien landowners was relatively uncontroversial.

Liberal ideology was similarly ambivalent on the question of alien suffrage. As Gerald Neuman describes, this ambivalence initially arose during the debates over the Alien and Sedition Acts, which subjected noncitizens to summary expulsion from the country on an executive order by the President. Defenders of the Act, citing the liberal theorist Emer de Vattel, argued that aliens had no constitutional rights because they were not members of the community and thus not subject to the social contract. The opposition, which included James Madison, also argued from liberal premises that the Constitution enshrined certain natural rights, and aliens had natural rights just as citizens did.[16] The debate was never really resolved, and the tension between the two approaches became evident once states extended the franchise to noncitizens. Proponents of alien suffrage argued, especially after the states had abolished the property qualification for voting, that all residents were within the community of the governed and thus entitled to vote. But opponents argued that extending voting rights to aliens diminished the distinction between members and non-members. Several states addressed this objection by finding – either through judicial decisions or enshrinement in state constitutions – that noncitizen residents were citizens of the *state*, even if they were not national citizens. Thus, even at this time there was an emerging trend to resolve ambiguities about the meaning of citizenship by using our nation's federal structure to divide citizenship in a scalar manner. Some states reached an interesting middle ground by enfranchising aliens who made a declaration of intent to seek citizenship. Such "declarant aliens" had many incidents of citizenship, such as the right to carry a passport and the duty to

---

[15] Raskin, *supra* note 8, at 1401.
[16] *See* GERALD L. NEUMAN, STRANGERS TO THE CONSTITUTION: IMMIGRANTS, BORDERS, AND FUNDAMENTAL LAW 52–63 (1996).

serve in the military if drafted. The declarant alien compromise recognized that citizenship was often a matter of degree rather than a binary distinction between citizens and noncitizens.[17]

Ultimately, the liberal and republican ambivalence about noncitizen suffrage was overwhelmed by ethno-nationalist opposition to the idea. The first stirrings of this opposition occurred after the War of 1812, which made many people suspicious of foreigners. It was during this same period that states began abolishing the property qualification for the franchise. According to Raskin, the newfound discomfort with foreigners, mixed with traditional concerns about nonproperty owners participating in government, raised serious questions about the prospect of propertyless immigrants voting. The idea that the franchise should be restricted to American citizens gained currency. Most states admitted to the union in the period after the war of 1812 limited the franchise to citizens.[18]

After the Civil War, the opposition to alien suffrage died down and many states, especially the sparsely settled western states, used the promise of suffrage to lure settlers.[19] However, alien suffrage became a matter of controversy again during the late nineteenth century, as three factors converged to create a resurgence of ethno-nationalist sentiment. First, where previous generations of immigrants had mostly been white people from central Europe, there was now a massive influx of immigrants into America's major cities from less desirable places like China and southern and eastern Europe. Second, American overseas expansion led to a need for a more explicitly racialized vision of citizenship so that territories like Guam, the Philippines, and Puerto Rico could be incorporated into the United States without needing to extend citizenship to their populations. Third and finally, the era was characterized by the emergence of quasi-scientific eugenic theories about the superiority of the white race.[20] As a result, the federal government began to enact strict immigration limits using expressly racial criteria, which met with the enthusiastic approval of courts. In *the Chinese Exclusion Case*, the Supreme Court upheld a federal law barring the admission of Chinese immigrants, noting the

---

[17] *See id.* at 63–71; *id.* at 64 ("The complex federal and territorial structure of the United States has fostered greater pluralism in the definition of political community and consequently a more flexible notion of popular sovereignty.").

[18] *See* Raskin, *supra* Note 8, at 1404.

[19] *See* Virginia Harper-Ho, *Noncitizen Voting Rights: The History, The Law, and Current Prospects for Change*, 18 L. & INEQUALITY 271, 277 (2000).

[20] *See generally* ROGERS M. SMITH, CIVIC IDEALS: CONFLICTING VISIONS OF CITIZENSHIP IN U.S. HISTORY 347–71 (discussing immigration); 429–48 (discussing overseas expansion and rise of "scientific" racial theories) (1997).

"differences of race," the refusal of the Chinese "to assimilate with our people," and the threat of "vast hordes" overrunning the nation.[21]

By the time the United States enacted its strict immigration laws, however, immigrants were already the predominant voting bloc in many cities, strong enough to elevate the storied Gilded Age political machines to power. Cities were overwhelmed by the huge population increases of the nineteenth century, and struggled to provide basic services. The vacuum was filled by political machines like New York City's infamous Tammany Hall, which delivered favors to their primarily immigrant constituents in return for unstinting loyalty and a blind eye toward the machines' penchant for graft. Horrified as much by the immigrant influence in municipal government as they were by the corruption scandals that characterized the machines, white upper- and middle-class reformers created the Progressive movement with the goal of limiting the influence of immigrants in politics and "reforming" city government. The progressives were enormously productive, enacting literacy tests, poll taxes, voter registration requirements, the secret ballot, and, ultimately, disfranchisement of noncitizens.[22] By 1926 every state in the union barred noncitizens from voting in state elections.[23]

5.1.2 *Dual Federalism and the Separation of Federal and Local Spheres of Citizenship*

It would be tempting to see the enactment of restrictive immigration laws and the disfranchisement of noncitizens as leading toward a predominantly ethno-nationalist conception of citizenship. In fact, these developments were part of a process by which citizenship was being bifurcated, with the federal level becoming the public sphere of ethno-nationalist citizenship and the local the private sphere of liberal citizenship. If one part of this emerging dichotomy was the exclusion of immigrants from the incidents of federal citizenship, another part was an evolving idea of local citizenship in which noncitizens might be included.

As described in Chapter 2, the ethno-nationalist underpinnings of our modern immigration law evident in *the Chinese Exclusion Case* led to a clear conceptual division of citizenship between the federal and local levels.

---

[21] Chae Chan Ping v. United States, 130 U.S. 581, 595, 606, 627 (1889).

[22] On the machines and reform, see ALEXANDER KEYSSAR, THE RIGHT TO VOTE: THE CONTESTED HISTORY OF DEMOCRACY IN THE UNITED STATES 119–46 (2001); RICHARD HOFSTADTER, THE AGE OF REFORM 175, 178–79 (1955); Samuel P. Hays, *The Politics of Reform in Municipal Government in the Progressive Era*, 55 PAC. NORTHWEST Q. 157 (1964).

[23] *See* KEYSSAR, *supra* Note 22, at 136–41, table A.12 (2001).

The perceived urgency to maintain a sense of national self-identity and the nation's existing racial composition in the face of mass immigration meant not only that the federal government required the power to shape the nation's demographic character through immigration control but also that this power must be *exclusive*. The federal law banning Chinese immigrants, which the Supreme Court upheld in *the Chinese Exclusion Case* in explicitly racial terms, came directly on the heels of the Court's decision in *Chy Lung v. Freeman*,[24] which held that states had no power to preclude Chinese immigrants, and is still often cited today for the principle that the federal government has the exclusive authority over immigration. According to Hiroshi Motomura, after *Chy Lung*, matters of "national self-definition" are exclusively federal. Thus, the idea of an exclusively federal immigration power is rooted directly in an ethno-nationalist conception of citizenship; conversely, ethno-nationalism is a distinctly *federal* idea of citizenship.[25]

As part of the new idea that the federal government alone had the power of national self-definition, in the early twentieth century the federal government withdrew from cities the power to naturalize citizens. As Rick Su notes, prior to that time local political machines were very active in naturalizing citizens. At its peak, Tammany Hall naturalized thousands of new citizens every year. The Progressive reformers put a stop to that, successfully urging the federal government to centralize the naturalization process in the newly created Bureau of Naturalization on the putative grounds that it would be more efficient and less prone to corruption.[26]

If the centralization of the naturalization process was part of a movement to make immigration exclusively federal, and thereby make the nation the locus of public, ethno-nationalist citizenship, it was also part of a movement to redefine local citizenship as purely private and liberal. The argument that naturalization processes should be centralized under expert control was one component of a comprehensive Progressive campaign to reform local government. As we saw in the previous chapter, municipal reformers wanted to make local government more efficient by reducing popular democratic control over various areas of local government and replacing them with expert commissions and appointed city managers. The reformers believed that local government was administrative or quasi-private rather than political in nature, and thus was entirely distinct

---

[24] 92 U.S. 275 (1875).

[25] *See* Hiroshi Motomura, *Whose Immigration Law? Citizens, Aliens and the Constitution*, 97 Colum. L. Rev. 1567, 1589–96 (1997). I discuss Motomura's article and the implications for citizenship at greater length in Chapter 2.

[26] *See* Rick Su, *Urban Politics and the Assimilation of Immigrant Voters*, 21 Wm. & Mary Bill Rts. J. 653, 667, 674–75 (2012).

from the public sphere of the state. In order to prevent state politicians from meddling with local bureaucratic control and facilitate municipal government's transformation into a nonpolitical entity, reformers argued that local governments should have a distinct sphere for autonomous activity, or "home rule." The original model of home rule, as described in the previous two chapters, thus made a strict division between "statewide" and "municipal" affairs.[27]

Therefore, at the same time the Supreme Court fashioned the federal government into the sphere of ethno-nationalist citizenship by conjuring the notion of an exclusively federal immigration authority, reformers were transforming local government into the sphere of liberal citizenship by creating the doctrine of home rule. These were hardly coincidental occurrences. As discussed in Chapter 3, both transformations were linked to a fashionable judicial ideology of the day called "dual federalism," in which courts considered national and state governments to have entirely distinct realms of authority. Under dual federalism, federal and state governments exist within "two mutually exclusive, reciprocally limiting fields of power."[28] For a long period, dual federalism animated the courts' interpretation of the Constitution's Interstate Commerce Clause, as courts attempted to draw the line between the "national" sphere of interstate commerce and the "local" sphere of intrastate commerce. Dual federalism's influence is clearly evident in both home rule and immigration law. Consistent with the commerce clause jurisprudence of the period, home rule divides the world of government activity into separate spheres for statewide and municipal affairs. Likewise, *Chy Lung's* apparent understanding of the immigration power as exclusively federal embodies the dual federalist idea that there are distinct realms of national and local power, each with a designated and exclusive set of functions.[29] Taken together, the

---

[27] *See* Keyssar, supra note 22, at 185–86, 232; David J. Barron, *Reclaiming Home Rule*, 116 Harv. L. Rev. 2257, 2292–2309 (2003). Barron describes three different, and in some ways competing, visions of home rule. Two of these three, the old conservative and administrative model, both conceptualized local government as distinct from politics, though the former saw local government as "private," whereas the latter saw it as "administrative."

[28] *See* Ernest A. Young, *Dual Federalism, Concurrent Jurisdiction, and the Foreign Affairs Exception*, 69 Geo. Wash. L. Rev. 139, 143–44 (2001) (quoting Alpheus Thomas Mason, *The Role of the Court*, in Federalism: Infinite Variety in Theory and Practice 8, 24–25 (Valerie Earle ed., 1968); *see also* Duncan Kennedy, *Toward an Historical Understanding of Legal Consciousness: The Case of Classical Legal Thought in America, 1850–1940*, 3 Res. Law & Soc. 3, 7 (1980).

[29] *See, e.g.*, Dale Krane et al., Home Rule in America: A Fifty-State Handbook 12 (2001) (noting that early home rule reforms were consistent with dual federalism); David S. Rubinstein & Pratheepan Gulasekaram, *Immigration Exceptionalism*, 111 N.W.U. L. Rev. 583, 605 (2017) (describing principle of federal government's exclusive control over immigration as "an exceptional relic of 'dual federalism'").

two doctrines helped to craft our current distinction between a public sphere of national citizenship that is understood as ethno-nationalist (with lingering hints of republicanism) and a private sphere of local citizenship that is understood as liberal.

5.1.3 *The Emergence of Local Citizenship for Foreign Nationals*

Ultimately, this distinction meant that certain classes of immigrants, while denied eligibility for citizenship at the federal level, could potentially become citizens at the local level. Though dual federalism circumscribed municipal power, it also freed municipalities to develop a more expansive view of citizenship precisely because the sphere of local authority was so restricted. As we have already seen, several municipalities used their home rule powers during this period to grant voting rights to women on the grounds that municipal government was a fully privatized sphere dedicated primarily to the home and child care, as distinct from the political affairs of the state. Alexander Keyssar reports that restrictions on the franchise slowed down beginning in the 1920s because the reform strategy shifted from disfranchisement to simply removing more matters from democratic control.[30]

The history of woman suffrage suggested that local governments also had the authority to expand voting rights to other groups not explicitly enfranchised in state constitutions, including immigrants. As discussed at the outset of this chapter, several cities have chosen in recent years to do just that, sometimes even citing woman suffrage as precedent.[31] Of far greater import, however, is that as the meaning of citizenship has expanded to encompass social rights like education, housing, and security, local governments have increasingly been providing immigrants with those rights. In doing so, as I argue later, they have recognized immigrants as local citizens.

The incorporation of immigrants as local citizens took some time to occur. Rick Su observes that by the 1920s the political machines had lost interest in politically mobilizing immigrants, and the municipal reforms in many cities had largely disempowered the political machine anyway, so there was little motivation for local governments to enfranchise immigrants.[32] The 1920s were also a period when anti-immigrant sentiment reached a crescendo, with

---

[30] *See* Keyssar, *supra* note 22, at 167–68; 185–87; 232.

[31] *See* John Saunders, *Non-Citizens' Politics*, in Acts of Citizenship 292, 293 (Engin F. Isin & Greg M. Nielsen eds. 2008) (quoting advocate for noncitizen voting rights in Cambridge, Massachusetts, citing precedent of women's enfranchisement in school board, tax, and bond elections in Cambridge).

[32] Su, *supra* note 26, at 677.

Congress passing a draconian immigration law that set strict quotas on immigration and essentially prohibited it from less desirable nations like Japan, China, and countries in southern and eastern Europe. This restrictive immigration regime remained in force until the 1960s.

Another reason why municipalities lost interest in incorporating immigrants as local citizens in the 1920s is that local government itself was undergoing a profound transformation at this time. During this period, city residents began moving in large numbers to suburban communities on the outskirts of major cities. The move to the suburbs was driven in part by a desire for lower taxes and high quality municipal services, but also to escape the throngs of immigrants congesting urban centers and transforming their politics. Suburbs used zoning regulations, endorsed by the US Commerce Department and declared constitutional by the Supreme Court in 1926, to limit the development of apartment buildings in which poorer immigrants could generally afford to live, zoning most land exclusively for single-family homes that were out of reach for immigrant families.[33]

Although partially motivated by anti-immigrant sentiment, the move to the suburbs actually hastened the bifurcation of citizenship that would eventually lead to the reincorporation of immigrants as local citizens. At the same time that Congress was closing the national borders and defining membership in terms of fixed racial identities, the streetcar, the automobile, and the suburbs were opening up local borders and making local membership a matter of mobility and individual choice. The era of suburbanization came to be defined by fairly extreme population movement.[34] This pattern intensified after World War II, as national citizenship remained fixed by the national origin system while interlocal mobility increased dramatically. The baby boom of the 1950s and the enactment of the Interstate Highway Act meant that more families were moving to the suburbs, and a variety of legal and political innovations caused the number of municipalities within metropolitan regions to skyrocket, giving families an abundance of choices of places to settle.[35] It was within this context of increasing interlocal mobility and choice that Charles Tiebout wrote his famous article, *A Pure Theory of Local*

---

[33] On zoning and suburbanization as strategies for escaping immigrants, *see* KENNETH T. JACKSON, CRABGRASS FRONTIER: THE SUBURBANIZATION OF THE UNITED STATES 150 (1985); Rick Su, *Local Fragmentation as Immigration Regulation*, 47 HOUS. L. REV. 367, 384–90 (2010).

[34] *See, e.g.,* ERIC H. MONKKONEN, AMERICA BECOMES URBAN: THE DEVELOPMENT OF U.S. CITIES & TOWNS 1780–1980, *at* 194–97 (1988) (describing persistence of population mobility in American life).

[35] *See* PETER HALL, CITIES OF TOMORROW 291–94 (1988).

Expenditures,[36] in which he conceptualized suburbanites as "consumer voters" who vote with their feet in choosing where to reside, and municipalities as essentially private firms that compete for residents by providing the most attractive package of municipal services.

In contrast to its rulings that the federal government had "plenary power" to control immigration across international borders, the Supreme Court frequently held during this period that states and local governments had no power to restrict movement across state and local lines. In cases like *Edwards v. California*[37] and *Shapiro v. Thompson*,[38] the Court struck down state laws restricting internal mobility, holding that the Constitution requires "that all citizens be free to travel throughout the length and breadth of our land uninhibited by statutes, rules or regulations which unreasonably burden or restrict this movement."[39] The Court thus placed its imprimatur on a dual conception of citizenship. Local citizenship was to be fluid and liberal, the product of mobility and private market choice, whereas national citizenship was to be ethno-nationalist, based on collective identity and closure.[40]

This conception of local citizenship as liberal and local citizens as mobile consumer-voters set the table for immigrants to be re-incorporated as local citizens. Given the highly mobile nature of local residence, immigrants' apparent rootlessness and uncertain loyalties were no longer all that different from any other local residents; to the contrary, their mobility made them paradigmatic local citizens.[41] The Supreme Court apparently affirmed as much when it held in *Graham v. Richardson*[42] that the equal protection clause prohibited states and local governments from discriminating in favor of American citizens and against legal immigrants in the distribution of public benefits. The Court reasoned that restricting welfare benefits to noncitizens would effectively limit where they could settle, thereby infringing on "the fundamental right of interstate movement,"[43] and also encroaching on the

---

[36] *See* Charles M. Tiebout, *A Pure Theory of Local Expenditures*, 64 J. Pol. Econ. 416, 418 (1956).

[37] 314 U.S. 160 (1941).

[38] 394 U.S. 618 (1969).

[39] *Id.* at 629.

[40] The Supreme Court resoundingly reaffirmed *Shapiro* and *Edwards* in *Saenz v. Roe*, 526 U.S. 489, 511 (1999). On the Supreme Court's increased attention to the "right to travel" in the postwar era, see Kunal M. Parker, Making Foreigners: Immigration and Citizenship Law in America, 1600–2000, at 192–96 (2015); Motomura, *supra* note 25, at 1588, 1596, 1598.

[41] *See* Monkkonen, *supra* note 34, at 194 (observing that many Americans falsely believed the immigrant experience of extreme mobility was distinct from the tradition among native-born Americans of rootedness; in fact, Americans were also extremely mobile).

[42] 403 U.S. 365 (1971).

[43] *Id.* at 375.

"exclusive federal power" to control the movement of immigrants. Interestingly, the Court cited *Shapiro* and *Edwards* for the principle that aliens have a right to travel, pointedly rejecting the state's argument that the right to travel belonged only to United States citizens. In doing so, the Court noted that treating noncitizens differently from citizens with regard to public benefits was irrational because aliens pay taxes, live and work in the state, and contribute to its economic growth.[44] In short, aliens were entitled to be treated the same as citizens because they were similarly situated in terms of residence and economic life. Of course, this logic only extended to state and local citizenship, not *federal* citizenship. A few years later, in *Mathews v. Diaz*,[45] the Court affirmed that while the equal protection clause prevented state and local governments from discriminating against noncitizens in the provision of public benefits, it did not prevent the federal government from doing so. In choosing whether to share its resources with "guests," Congress "may take into account the character of the relationship between the alien and the country ... "[46]

Graham ushered in a period in which noncitizens were extended many benefits of the welfare state, including rights to housing, education, security, and welfare. In an important essay, T. H. Marshall referred to these benefits as "social rights" of citizenship, and argued that as the state was taking more responsibility for securing the welfare of its citizens, these social rights had assumed great significance as markers of citizenship, eclipsing even political rights such as the right to vote.[47] If that is true, then immigrants were largely being granted rights of citizenship during this time. New civil rights statutes protected immigrants from discrimination in many areas and the Supreme Court expansively interpreted these statutes and constitutional provisions to guarantee social rights to noncitizens. The most significant of these decisions, *Plyler v. Doe*,[48] held that even undocumented immigrant children were entitled to a free public education, noting that education is "the very foundation of good citizenship." In the 1960s, Congress ended the racist national origins system and opened up a new era of large-scale immigration. The federal government had no official system for incorporating new immigrants into American life, and states had largely devolved responsibility for most

---

[44] *Id.* at 376.
[45] 426 U.S. 67 (1976).
[46] *Id.* at 80.
[47] *See* T. H. Marshall, *Citizenship and Social Class*, in CLASS, CITIZENSHIP, AND SOCIAL DEVELOPMENT 72 (1964).
[48] 457 U.S. 202, 205, 208–09 (1982).

social welfare programs to municipalities, so the new social rights that immigrants enjoyed were, as a de facto matter, rights of *local* citizenship.

5.1.4 The Social Rights of Local Citizenship

After *Graham*, *Mathews*, and *Plyler*, the question of noncitizens' rights as local citizens became immensely more complicated. First, the Court developed a "political function" exception to *Graham* that essentially allowed state and local governments to discriminate against noncitizens in matters considered "political," including voting, holding public office, and even working as teachers in public schools.[49] According to Linda Bosniak, the political function exception draws into question the distinction drawn in *Graham* and *Mathews* between federal and state alienage classifications (and by extension, federal and state conceptions of citizenship), because it suggests that state and local governments, like the national government, have the ability to determine the scope of their own political community on an ascriptive or nationalist basis. Second, during the anti-immigrant frenzy of the 1990s, the federal government enacted legislation allowing, and in some cases requiring, state and local governments to discriminate against noncitizens in the provision of many public benefits.[50]

Strikingly, however, many state and local governments have affirmatively *chosen* to extend social and political rights of citizenship to noncitizens even as the courts and the federal government have loosened these mandates. Although the 1990s welfare reform had actually been spurred by California's draconian Proposition 187, which sought to make undocumented immigrants ineligible for all sorts of public benefits in the state, conservatives reported with chagrin after the welfare reform legislation that many states and local governments had opted to restore several of the benefits welfare reform had taken away, including access to health care, in-state tuition discounts, and others.[51]

---

[49] *See* Cabell v. Chavez-Salido, 454 U.S. 432, 439 (1982); Foley v. Connelie, 435 U.S. 291 (1978); Ambach v. Norwick, 441 U.S. 68 (1979).

[50] *See* Jenny-Brooke Condon, *The Preempting of Equal Protection for Immigrants*, 73 Wash. & Lee L. Rev. 77 (2016); Congressional Research Service, Noncitizen Eligibility for Public Benefits: Legal Issues (Sep. 9, 2013), https://www.everycrsreport.com/files/20130909_R43221_6b375b0965db2c6cac9515d87d8d7b4b65ebbd10.pdf.

[51] *See, e.g.*, George Borjas, *Welfare Reform and Immigrant Participation in Welfare Programs*, 36 Int'l Mig. Rev. 1093, 1101–02, 1112 (2002); *see also* Peter Spiro, Beyond Citizenship: American Identity after Globalization 89–91 (2008); Edward J. W. Park & John S. W. Park, Probationary Americans: Contemporary Immigration Policies and the Shaping of Asian American Communities 74–75 (2005); S. Karthick Ramakrishnan & Allan Colbern, *The California Package: Immigrant Integration and the Evolving Nature of State Citizenship* 6 Pol. Matters 1, 5–6 (2015).

Abigail Fisher Williamson reports that the vast majority of cities receiving immigrants have taken a "welcoming" approach to immigrants, even if not always initially and often more in deed than in word. Interestingly, among the variety of steps municipalities have taken to incorporate noncitizens into their communities, Williamson finds that by far the most common has been *hiring immigrants as local government employees.*[52] If the courts are correct that communities are acting to define the boundaries of the political community when they choose whether to permit noncitizens to hold government positions, then it follows that most cities are choosing to define that community very expansively. The nascent movement to extend the franchise to noncitizens, although by no means inevitable, is a logical culmination of municipalities' efforts to confer local citizenship on noncitizen residents.

I contend that the reason municipalities have chosen to define community so expansively is because they have thoroughly internalized the logic of local citizenship as liberal, determined by interest and market choice rather than identity. As Williamson details, the mandatory duties imposed on local governments to provide services like housing, education, and security to all local residents, including immigrants, have caused local officials to see noncitizens as indistinguishable from other members of the community, as "clients" the city is bound to serve.[53] Perceived as clients, all residents have a broadly similar relationship with the city, and broadly similar interests in how they obtain and use municipal services, regardless of their immigration status. By contrast, as *Mathews* indicates, the "relationship between the alien and the country" may be very different from the relationship between the *citizen* and the country when it relates to matters of federal concern such as the character and boundaries of the national community. Jamin Raskin, who successfully advocated for noncitizen suffrage in the Maryland city of Takoma Park while serving in the state Senate, made the case for enfranchisement as follows:

> The idea of having foreign citizens vote in American national elections is . . . inherently more troubling than having them vote in local elections. At the local level, each resident's interests in good schools, public services, and transportation are very similar. If these interests diverge at all, it will be according to differences in neighborhood, income, or homeownership-not nationality or citizenship. At the national level, however, American, Mexican, and Canadian citizens arguably have numerous divergent interests as citizens of their respective states.[54]

---

[52] *See* ABIGAIL FISHER WILLIAMSON, WELCOMING NEW AMERICANS? LOCAL GOVERNMENTS AND IMMIGRANT INCORPORATION 67, 193 (2018).

[53] *See* WILLIAMSON, *supra* note 52, at 92–93; 127–29; 160–61.

[54] *See* Raskin, *supra* note 8, at 1468.

In addition, the liberal idea of local citizenship as a product of mobility and consumer choice has incentivized cities to incorporate immigrants as local citizens because the fluidity of local boundaries places cities in competition against each other for desirable residents, consumers, workers, and producers. Increasingly, immigrants are among those people cities are most eager to lure. Especially with the end of the Cold War and the massive cross-border migrations of the last few decades, immigrants are often coveted as consumers.[55] Moreover, highly skilled immigrants are particularly valued in a global economy that prizes innovation, creativity, and risk-taking, qualities disproportionately possessed by immigrants (who often require creativity and an appetite for risk in order to leave their home countries for a foreign land).[56] Places that wish to succeed in the new economy must compete for immigrants by adopting immigrant-friendly policies, much in the same way Tiebout envisioned municipalities competing for middle-class families in the 1950s. For all of these reasons, municipalities have often chosen to treat noncitizen residents as local citizens.

5.2 EDUCATION, SANCTUARY, AND LOCAL CITIZENSHIP FOR NONCITIZEN RESIDENTS

Noncitizen residents have been incorporated as local citizens in varous ways, but two rights of citizenship have stood out as particularly salient: the right to education enshrined in *Plyler* v. *Doe*,[57] and the right to security embodied in the "sanctuary city." The rights to education and security are among the most important of T. H. Marshall's social rights of citizenship, and they are both highly illustrative of the liberal nature of local citizenship, that is, how local citizenship is rooted in mobility and choice rather than nationality. They both also demonstrate, as we saw in the last chapter, the ambiguous promise of conceptualizing local citizenship in liberal terms. While local citizenship embraces noncitizen residents insofar as it is open to all on the basis of mobility and money, that accommodation is necessarily bounded because local citizenship is *only* available to those privileged enough to have mobility

---

[55] *See* WILLIAMSON, *supra* note 52, at 130–36; Ernesto Castañeda, *Urban Citizenship in New York, Paris, and Barcelona: Immigrant Organizations and the Right to Inhabit the City*, in REMAKING URBAN CITIZENSHIP: ORGANIZATIONS, INSTITUTIONS AND THE RIGHT TO THE CITY 57, 71–72 (Michael Peter Smith & Michael McQuarrie eds. 2012) (immigrants' acts as consumers constitute them as de facto urban citizens).

[56] *See* WILLIAMSON, *supra* note 52, at 130–36; Cristina M. Rodriguez, *The Significance of the Local in Immigration Regulation*, 106 MICH. L. REV. 567, 577 (2008).

[57] 457 U.S. 202 (1982).

and money – which many immigrants do not. Thus, liberal local citizenship has simultaneously an equalizing and a stratifying effect. In this way, the ambiguous character of liberal local citizenship reveals the roots of the modern discontent with citizenship as an organizing principle for membership in society.

5.2.1 Plyler *v.* Doe: *Education as a Right of Local Citizenship*

In *Plyler,* the Supreme Court confronted the question of whether the state of Texas violated the equal protection clause by barring undocumented immigrants from receiving a free public education in the state. The Court declined to recognize illegal immigrants as a suspect class and subject the Texas law to heightened scrutiny on that basis, but applied heightened scrutiny anyway and held that the state's rationale was insufficiently important to justify the law. The result was that all local resident children are entitled to a free public education, regardless of their immigration status.[58]

In recognizing that immigrant children had a right to education, the *Plyler* court was also essentially conferring on them a right to local citizenship. Indeed, T. H. Marshall considered education one of the foremost social rights of citizenship because education had always been perceived, since the days of the ancient Greek city-states, as fundamental training for citizenship. "[W]hen the state guarantees that all children shall be educated, it has the requirements and the nature of citizenship definitely in mind."[59] If an education is inadequate, the student will be unprepared for citizenship. Perhaps more importantly for Marshall, social rights like education had become more significant than political rights like voting because political rights were largely meaningless if inequalities within civil society created permanent class divisions. Inequalities in education, for example, could create permanent cleavages in life chances. Marshall observed a close correlation between education and future occupation. "The ticket obtained on leaving school or college is for a life journey. The man with a third-class ticket who later feels entitled to claim a seat in a first-class carriage will not be admitted, even if he is prepared to pay the difference."[60] Hence, Marshall asserted that guaranteeing a minimum level of educational attainment was necessary to ensure every citizen's equality of opportunity.

---

[58] 457 U.S. at 218–30.
[59] *See* T. H. Marshall, *Citizenship and Social Class*, in CLASS, CITIZENSHIP, AND SOCIAL DEVELOPMENT 100 (1964).
[60] *Id.* at 108.

Marshall's argument echoes throughout the Court's opinion in *Plyler*.
Noting that ineffective federal government enforcement of the immigration
laws and a high demand for immigrant labor had led to a "shadow population"
of undocumented immigrants, the Court warned of a new "caste" system of
people who are informally encouraged to stay in the United States "as a source
of cheap labor, but nevertheless denied the benefits that our society makes
available to citizens and lawful residents."[61] Reminiscent of Marshall, the
Court lamented that denying an education to undocumented immigrants
would lock them out of the opportunities available to other children. The
Court observed that "illiteracy is an enduring disability," that stigmatizes
uneducated children "for the rest of their lives" and denies them the most
fundamental opportunities for "individual achievement."[62] Therefore, the
Court found the law to be at odds with a central purpose of the equal
protection clause, "the abolition of governmental barriers presenting unrea-
sonable obstacles to advancement on the basis of individual merit."[63] But like
Marshall, the Court went even further, observing that in being denied an
education, undocumented children were being denied a fundamental right of
citizenship. After citing some of its previous precedents for the propositions
that the public school is "a most vital civic institution for the preservation of a
democratic system of government," the primary vehicle for transmitting "the
values on which our society rests," and "the very foundation of good citizenship," the Court found that the Texas law would deny to undocumented
immigrant children "the ability to live within the structure of our civic institutions, and foreclose any realistic possibility that they will contribute in even
the smallest way to the progress of our Nation."[64]

Read most broadly, *Plyler* is a resounding declaration of the rights of
undocumented immigrants. It not only reaffirms longstanding doctrine that
immigrants are entitled to the protections of the equal protection clause but
strongly suggests that, by mere virtue of their presence in the United States,
they are entitled to one of the most significant social benefits of *citizenship*,
namely, the right to an education. But insofar as *Plyler* confers a form of
citizenship, it is a peculiarly *local* form of citizenship. In the United States,
education is almost universally provided at the local level and has long been
associated with local self-government and the idea of local citizenship. In
Milliken v. *Bradley*, a case I return to shortly, the Court observed: "No single

---

[61] *Id.* at 218–19.
[62] *Id.* at 222; 223.
[63] *Id.* at 222.
[64] *Id.* at 205, 208–09.

tradition in public education is more deeply rooted than local control over the operation of schools; local autonomy has long been thought essential both to the maintenance of community concern and support for public schools and to quality of the educational process."[65] *Milliken* went on to note the relationship between citizenship and local control of education: "[L]ocal control over the educational process affords citizens an opportunity to participate in decision-making, permits the structuring of school programs to fit local needs, and encourages 'experimentation, innovation, and a healthy competition for educational excellence.'"[66]

5.2.2 *The Ambiguous Right to Education*

That education is a right of *local* citizenship makes it a far more equivocal right than *Plyler* acknowledges. Though *Plyler* contains the revolutionary implication that all children present in the United States are entitled to an education regardless of their immigration status, the limits of that implication became clear just one year later when, in *Martinez v. Bynum*,[67] the Court upheld a section of the Texas Educational Code limiting eligibility for free public schools to local *residents*. This is an enormously important qualification to *Plyler*. Local government authority in most metropolitan regions throughout the United States is highly fragmented, meaning that there are often dozens of municipalities within the region performing similar functions – land use, school control, and so forth. Wealth and the quality of local public schools vary greatly across district lines, even between neighboring districts, but tax-sharing among neighboring districts is generally limited. Most municipalities retain whatever tax revenue they generate locally. Attaining residence in high-performing school districts with strong tax bases is incredibly expensive and often cost-prohibitive for many lower-income families. This is hardly coincidental. Cities with quality schools are in demand, and demand pushes local home prices higher. Those cities respond to the demand by using zoning laws to restrict housing growth so that the schools do not get too congested, and those restrictions cause home prices to soar even higher. In essence, although public education is nominally "free," one must purchase eligibility for high quality public schools by buying or renting a home in the community at a price that reflects the quality of the school.[68]

---

[65] 418 U.S. 717, 741–42 (1974).
[66] *Id.* at 742 (*quoting* Rodriguez v. San Antonio School District Number 1, 411 U.S. 1, 50 (1973)).
[67] 461 U.S. 321 (1983).
[68] *See* Kenneth A. Stahl, *The Challenge of Inclusion*, 89 Temple L. Rev. 487, 496–99 (2017).

That the right of education is essentially a private right tied to purchasing a home is entirely consistent with the liberal idea of citizenship as rooted in interest, mobility, and market choice. Pursuant to the Tiebout model, which sees municipalities as competing firms and residents as mobile consumer-voters, metropolitan regions offer a buffet of municipalities with different price points and resources of varying quality so that consumers can "choose" where to reside based on the traditional market mechanism of their ability to pay. Anyone with the means to acquire residence in a community can thereby acquire citizenship, whereas anyone without such means cannot be a local citizen.

The limits of consumer choice are most significant, of course, because as T. H. Marshall and *Plyler* both point out, a quality public education is an essential characteristic of social citizenship. To the extent education is distributed unequally based on ability to pay, it means that the most essential aspects of citizenship are distributed unequally based on ability to pay. And the consequences of this inequality are severe. Studies increasingly show that a child's opportunities for social and economic advancement in life are almost entirely contingent on the zip code in which they were born or raised.[69] If *Plyler* worried that illiteracy was a stigma, it perhaps should have worried that *geography* was the real stigma.

Nevertheless, perhaps because the Court is wedded to a liberal view of local citizenship as determined by money and mobility, it has not worried excessively about the stigma of geography. To that point, *Plyler* and *Martinez* were both decided in the shadow of a third, epochal case about immigrants in Texas public schools, *Rodriguez v. San Antonio School District Number 1*.[70] *Rodriguez* presented two school districts within the city of San Antonio, Texas. The first, Edgewood Independent School District, was a poor district with a 90 percent Mexican American population, including a large number of immigrant children. The second, Alamo Heights, was a wealthy, mostly white school district with few immigrants. Under Texas's formula for funding public schools (widely shared across the country), school districts were required to finance a significant chunk of their school budgets out of their own local tax base. Because of the disparity in wealth between Edgewood and Alamo

---

[69] *See, e.g.*, Patrick Sharkey, Stuck in Place: Urban Neighborhoods and the End of Progress toward Racial Equality (2013); Robert J. Sampson, Great American City 121–48 (2012) (demonstrating that people residing in communities with high concentrations of poverty face fewer opportunities for economic and social mobility, lower quality schools, greater exposure to violence and crime, greater likelihood of incarceration, and a host of other negative consequences).

[70] 411 U.S. 1 (1973).

Heights, Alamo Heights had a much larger tax base, and was able to spend almost twice as much per student than Edgewood, while taxing its residents at a lower tax rate.[71] Parents in the Edgewood district asserted that Texas's school financing formula violated the Equal Protection clause by distributing educational benefits based on wealth and denied them the basic right to an education.

A dissenting opinion, echoing T. H. Marshall and anticipating *Plyler*, argued that Texas's system violated the equal protection clause because it denied "equality of educational opportunity" and deprived "children in their earliest years of the chance to reach their full potential as citizens."[72] The Court itself cited *Brown* v. *Board of Education* for the proposition that "education is the very foundation of good citizenship," and reaffirmed the Court's "abiding respect for the vital role of education in a free society."[73] Nevertheless, the Court found that the Texas scheme did not violate the equal protection clause. Unlike *Plyler*, which focused primarily on the right of citizens to be educated, *Rodriguez* focused on the right of citizens to control their local schools. According to the Court, local control of school financing entails "the freedom to devote more money to the education of one's children" and an opportunity "for participation in the decisionmaking process that determines how those local tax dollars will be spent."[74] A more state-centered financing system could "result in a comparable lessening of desired local autonomy."[75] Though *Rodriguez* itself did not explicitly draw a line between local control of education and citizenship, one year later in *Milliken* v. *Bradley* the Court cited *Rodriguez* for the proposition, cited earlier, that "local control over the educational process affords citizens an opportunity to participate in decision-making, permits the structuring of school programs to fit local needs, and encourages 'experimentation, innovation, and a healthy competition for educational excellence.'"[76]

The idea that local citizenship entails local control of education is consistent with the liberal conception of citizenship. Like the woman suffragists who saw local government as an enlarged household, *Rodriguez* envisions the municipality as simply an extension of the home and family. Local control of schools is the means through which parents ensure the quality

[71] *See id.* at 11–14 (describing a poorer district that spent approximately $356 per student, compared with $594 per student in an affluent district).
[72] *See id.* at 71 (Marshall, J., dissenting).
[73] *See id.* at 30.
[74] *See id.* at 49–50.
[75] *Id.* at 52.
[76] 418 U.S. 717, 742 (1974) (*quoting* Rodriguez, 411 U.S. at 50).

of their children's education. The broad aim of mandatory public education articulated in *Plyler* – to instill civic ideals, to bring children of diverse backgrounds together, to ensure a minimum level of opportunity for all children – is subordinated to the essentially private right to devote one's money to one's own children. That this right is unequally distributed among neighboring school districts based on the tax base is dismissed by the Court on the Tieboutian grounds that resources are footloose and wealth may shift between districts over time. As the Court stated, "Changes in the level of taxable wealth within any district may result from any number of events, some of which local residents can and do influence."[77] Subsequently, in *Martinez*, the Court found that restricting school eligibility based on residency was also consistent with the Tiebout model because "any person is free to move to a state and establish residence there."[78] Money, mobility, and choice in the care and raising of children are thus elevated as the hallmarks of local citizenship.

Of course, as Justice Marshall observed dissenting in *Rodriguez*, the Tieboutian picture is hardly so rosy because interlocal wealth inequalities are persistent and, in fact, reinforced by governmental policies such as zoning. "[G]overnmentally imposed land use controls have undoubtedly encouraged and rigidified natural trends in the allocation of particular areas for residential or commercial use, and thus determined each district's amount of taxable property wealth."[79] As I have already discussed, communities with high quality schools use their zoning regulations to restrict access to public schools by regulating the size and number of new homes, essentially transforming free, public schools into expensive, private schools. The bottom line is that in order to obtain residence in a community with quality schools, one must have the financial means to purchase it – and municipalities will often use zoning rules to make sure that anyone of modest means *cannot* purchase it. Local citizenship is a market transaction that one must pay to obtain. For immigrants, as well as everyone else, the consequences are quite clear. Market liberalism means that all those who can afford to live in an affluent municipality have the right to the social benefits of local citizenship regardless of nationality; but it also means that those who cannot afford to live in an affluent municipality have no entitlement to the social rights of local citizenship.

[77] 411 U.S. at 54.
[78] 461 U.S. at 328–29.
[79] Rodriguez, 411 U.S. at 123–24 (Marshall, J., dissenting).

5.2.3 *The Sanctuary City: Security as a Right of Local Citizenship*

Local citizenship's uncertain promise for immigrants is also evident in the controversial "sanctuary city." Though the term "sanctuary" is imprecise, it usually refers to cities that have in some way requested or directed local law enforcement officials to limit their cooperation with federal immigration authorities in the apprehension of undocumented immigrants.[80] The term may also refer to cities that have taken affirmative steps to integrate undocumented immigrants into the community, such as granting them municipal identification cards for the purpose of accessing banks and healthcare, authorizing and funding day laborer sites, and the like.[81] Dozens of cities (and some states) have adopted different types of sanctuary policies, and, as Abigail Williamson reports, many more have quietly engaged in similar practices, even if not formalized as policy.[82] Sanctuary policies stem from a variety of motivations, but whatever the intent, there is little doubt that the enactment of sanctuary policies, much like *Plyler*'s extending a right of public education to noncitizens, confers a de facto form of local citizenship on people who are not citizens at the national level. The effect of sanctuary policies is to incorporate immigrants, including undocumented immigrants, into the civic life of the municipality. In addition to giving undocumented immigrants many of the tangible benefits that other local citizens enjoy, such as access to housing and labor markets and financial institutions, sanctuary policies also reduce undocumented immigrants' sense of vulnerability so they can more freely participate in city life, and symbolically express the community's commitment to treating all its residents as equal members. In that light, Bill Ong Hing argues that sanctuary policies are analogous to *Plyler* insofar as both reject the idea of a permanent underclass relegated to live in the shadows.[83]

Like the promise of free public education, however, the protections of sanctuary are somewhat ephemeral and contingent on the liberal standards of money and mobility. Cities that have extended sanctuary protections to undocumented immigrants have rarely done so simply for humanitarian reasons. They have done so for several practical reasons. First, as explored in Chapter 2, cities have seen sanctuary policies as a critical component of

---

[80] *See, e.g.* Rose Cuison Villazor, *What Is a "Sanctuary"?* 61 SMU L. Rev. 133 (2008).
[81] *See* Cristina M. Rodriguez, *The Significance of the Local in Immigration Regulation*, 106 Mich. L. Rev. 567 (2008).
[82] *See* Williamson, *supra* note 52, at 60–63; 75–76; 160–61.
[83] *See* Bill Ong Hing, *Immigration Sanctuary Policies: Constitutional and Representative of Good Policing and Good Public Policy*, 2 U.C. Irvine L. Rev. 247, 307 (2012).

community policing strategies to make communities safer by encouraging immigrants to cooperate with local police without fear of immigration consequences.[84] Second, as I have already discussed, many cities have experienced substantial economic benefits from immigrants as workers and consumers. Cities are competing in Tieboutian fashion for immigrants, and sanctuary policies that signal friendliness toward immigrants make good economic sense as a strategy for luring immigrants.

The fact that cities have these practical reasons for enacting sanctuary protections necessarily makes those protections rather precarious. Because sanctuary policies are adopted for instrumental objectives having little to do with affection for immigrants, they may prove short-lived if sanctuary policies ever cease to serve those instrumental objectives. With regard to the community policing rationale, for example, Ingrid Eagly describes some recent studies finding that local law enforcement cooperation with immigration authorities does not diminish the willingness of immigrant communities to cooperate with police. Accordingly, she questions whether the community policing rationale for sanctuary cities has staying power.[85] With regard to the global competition for immigrant labor, not every city is "winning" this competition. In fragmented regions where cities are competing against each other, one city's gain may be another's loss. Many smaller, second-tier cities believe that they are losing out economically as a result of the increasing dependence on immigrant labor, leading to mostly debunked claims that immigrants are stealing jobs and prosperity from those communities. A number of states and localities during the past decade or so have attempted to pass laws that effectively bar undocumented immigrants from their communities or otherwise make life so difficult for such immigrants that they will choose to "self-deport."[86] Though the courts have found most of these efforts to be preempted by the federal immigration scheme, the point remains that cities' receptiveness to immigrants, and particularly undocumented immigrants, is often a function of those immigrants' perceived economic contributions.

5.2.4 Local Citizenship and Local Fragmentation

If I have portrayed the liberal nature of local citizenship as rather a mixed and contingent blessing for immigrants, I must also stress that liberal local

---

[84] See Ingrid V. Eagly, *Immigrant Protective Policies in Criminal Justice*, 95 Tex. L. Rev. 245, 281–87 (2016).

[85] *Id.* at 245, 281–87 (2016).

[86] *See, e.g.,* Stella Burch Elias, *The New Immigration Federalism*, 74 Ohio St. L.J. 703 (2013).

citizenship can indeed empower immigrants by offering them a form of emancipation from the stifling constraints of ethno-nationalism. In this section, I stake out some disagreement with Rick Su's important article *Local Fragmentation as Immigrant Regulation*.[87] Su argues that the fragmentation of municipal authority among numerous jurisdictions within metropolitan regions has functioned mostly to the detriment of immigrants. For example, he sees *Rodriguez*, which affirmed the ability of a local school district to hoard its taxable wealth from a neighboring district, as seriously limiting the promise of *Plyler*. According to Su:

> if an underlying message of *Plyler* was that the importance of education to our republic obligates us as a polity to collectively provide such a service as a public good, even to those who do not have formal membership in such a polity, *Rodriguez* affirms the practice of avoiding such obligations by defining oneself as being a part of a separate community, albeit on the local level.[88]

Likewise, Su is dismissive of the sanctuary city, which he sees as another instance of municipal fragmentation effectively segregating immigrants. The sanctuary city, according to Su, is a way of confining immigrants to particular places so that they cannot access the resources of other places.[89]

In Su's analysis, immigrants are hostages to local government policy. In my view, however, the relationship between immigrants and cities is not a one-way street. Particularly in an age of globalization, cities do not have absolute freedom to manipulate their borders to exclude or control immigrants because cities are increasingly dependent on immigrant labor. This dependency gives immigrants the ability to dictate terms – that is, to demand the incidents of citizenship. In fact, several cities that enacted anti-immigrant measures eventually reversed course after realizing the economic impact of discriminating against immigrants, including the city of Hazleton, Pennsylvania, which famously passed one of the first draconian local laws against unauthorized immigrants.[90] Moreover, municipal fragmentation may actually intensify immigrant leverage over cities because the more cities there are, the more competition there is for immigrant labor. As I have already noted, the sanctuary city is as much a response to the economic realities of globalizing

---

[87] 47 Hous. L. Rev. 367 (2010).

[88] *Id.* at 417–18.

[89] *Id.* at 394–96.

[90] See Williamson, *supra* note 52, at 50–52; 163–64; 176–77; Binyamin Applebaum, *In City Built by Immigrants, Immigration Is the Defining Issue*, N.Y. Times (Oct. 12, 2016), https://www.nytimes.com/2016/10/13/business/economy/hazleton-pennsylvania-donald-trump-immigrants.html?_r=0.

Tieboutian competition as it is an instantiation of human rights norms. Of course, it is precisely because sanctuary cities are a demonstration of immigrants' economic power that they have become such a flashpoint for controversy nationwide.

Furthermore, local citizenship is not wholly transactional. What begins as immigrants' economic integration into the community rarely ends there. Once people set down roots in the community and begin to interact with neighbors, it enables the formation of relationships, or what the sociologist Robert Putnam calls "bridging social capital."[91] Immigrants cease to be an abstraction and become a part of the community. As such, introducing immigrants into the community can lead to an increasing acceptance and embrace of diversity, and an awareness of the human cost of our national immigration policies.[92] In Jamin Raskin's view, "The move towards local noncitizen voting can be seen as part of the trend of communities accepting responsibility for participating in the enforcement of global human rights norms."[93] In undertaking to grant citizenship to foreign nationals, cities believe not only that they are improving their economic prospects but that they can stake out a cosmopolitan, inclusive identity that differentiates them from the ethnic nationalism at the federal level. As an advocate for noncitizen voting in San Francisco argued, "I think one of the most important things is to try to create an environment in this city that is different from what is happening in the state and certainly from what is happening in the nation."[94]

Of course, it is this very sentiment that has made sanctuary cities, and by extension the entire liberal idea of local citizenship, a matter of great controversy in our national politics. Once "global human rights norms" rather than domestic laws provide the basis for conferring rights, the ethno-nationalist foundation of citizenship is inevitably weakened. Further, to the extent immigrants can leverage their economic power to obtain political power, public life may be perceived as falling hostage to the corrupting influence of money. As one prominent opponent of noncitizen suffrage in San Francisco warned, municipal suffrage may be the "camel's nose under the tent" that upends the whole idea of citizenship.[95] Indeed, as we shall see in Chapter 7, globalization has placed pressure on nation-states to confer many incidents of *federal* citizenship on noncitizen residents, including undocumented immigrants.

---

[91] *See* ROBERT D. PUTNAM, BOWLING ALONE 143–45 (2000).
[92] *See* WILLIAMSON, *supra* note 52, at 255–58 (reporting that contact with immigrants increased local residents' positive perceptions).
[93] Raskin, *supra* note 8, at 1457.
[94] *Quoted in* HAYDUK, *supra* note 2, at 115.
[95] US Senator Dianne Feinstein *quoted in* HAYDUK, *supra* note 2, at 126.

What this discussion indicates is that the division between the local and federal spheres of citizenship is hardly as firm in practice as it is in the judicial imagination, and can easily collapse under the pressures of globalization. As that occurs, the meaning of citizenship is drawn into question and the status of immigrants becomes a highly charged political issue. Chapter 7 elaborates on these themes in greater detail, but first we must consider one final class of "noncitizen citizens" who often enjoy the benefits of local citizenship without the benefits of federal citizenship: landowners.

6

Local Citizenship for Nonresident Landowners

In addition to women and noncitizens, nonresident landowners have also sometimes been granted the incidents of local citizenship while being denied federal and state citizenship. The franchise again proves a useful point of comparison. Though it was once commonplace for states to condition the franchise on real property ownership, nearly every state had abolished the property qualification by the end of the 1850s.[1] Municipal suffrage followed a similar course, as states often insisted that local voting rules track state standards.[2] Today, though, nonresident landowners are occasionally enfranchised at the local level. More significantly, unlike our previous two cases, in which the municipal franchise has simply been expanded to include women and noncitizens, the municipal franchise is sometimes *contracted* to exclude everyone *except* landowners. Even where that is not the case, landownership is frequently a de facto prerequisite for voting in local elections, as municipalities use zoning rules to ensure that only those who can afford to purchase or (sometimes) rent a home in the community are permitted to reside there.

As in our previous cases, the distinctive treatment of landowners at the local level illustrates that local citizenship is constructed as private and liberal, meaning that it is based on mobility, interest, and individual market choice, whereas federal citizenship is constructed as republican, ethno-nationalist, and public, meaning that it is based on collective identity and a sense of organic solidarity. Furthermore, as in the previous cases, the status of landowners in local politics demonstrates the ambiguous character of local citizenship. On one hand, landowners' enjoyment of citizenship rights

[1] *See* Alexander Keyssar, The Right to Vote: The Contested History of Democracy in the United States 29 (2001).
[2] *See id.* at 30–33.

epitomizes a radically diluted conception of the citizen as an atomized "consumer-voter" whose interest in municipal life is primarily instrumental, and a similarly flaccid conception of the municipality as an essentially private firm with the limited purpose of serving its residents' consumption demands. On the other hand, the status of landowners as local citizens is also emblematic of a vision of citizenship that is more dynamic and cosmopolitan than the republican and ethno-nationalist conceptions, a vision in which the citizen is connected to the world and comfortable with innovation and diversity rather than isolated behind the walls of a community of identity.

This chapter begins by describing how liberal, republican, and ethno-nationalist conceptions of citizenship contributed to the abolition of the property qualification for state and federal elections. It then explains how, as part of the emergence of a distinctively local approach to citizenship, property ownership again became relevant in local elections. The salience of property ownership has manifested in the form of local governments both *expanding* the franchise to include nonresident landowners, and also *contracting* the franchise to exclude everyone but landowners. This latter development has been especially controversial in light of the Supreme Court's "one person, one vote" doctrine, and so this chapter spends some time elaborating how and why the Court has allowed certain local governments to circumvent the one person, one vote rule and limit the franchise to landowners. In short, it has done so because it perceives local citizenship as liberal and private, rooted in interest, money, and mobility rather than identity and nationality.

6.1 STATE AND FEDERAL CITIZENSHIP

At the time of the founding, every state limited the franchise to landowners or taxpayers. Noncitizens who owned land could often vote, but landless citizens could not. In the years after the revolution, however, states steadily abolished the property qualification for voting. Economic changes, particularly the move from an agricultural to a nascent industrial economy, played a key role in the movement to abolish the property requirement. More and more Americans were involved in commerce and did not own land. The result, according to Alexander Keyssar, was that there were "significant clusters of men who were full participants in economic and social life but who lacked political rights."[3] These economic changes coincided with the rise of a liberal

---

[3] KEYSSAR, *supra* note 1, at 34–35.

ideology that emphasized the natural equality of all white men.[4] Not surprisingly, it was often the very artisans and merchants who were disfranchised by the property qualification who most forcefully pushed this liberal argument. In addition to liberalism, the abolition of the property requirement was also driven in part, as Robert Steinfeld notes, by a change in republican ideology. The old republican idea that independence could only be secured through ownership of real property was displaced by a newer idea, consistent with the emerging commercial economy, that wage workers could also be independent because, although they did not own property, they had "self-ownership." Property ownership, in consequence, became an irrelevant characteristic in the public realm and was reconceived as something purely private. According to Steinfeld, "Governance was to occupy one realm, the public realm; property ownership was to be consigned to another, the realm of purely private relationships between juridical equals."[5] Property came to be perceived, paradoxically, as just another liberal interest, rather than as something that assured freedom from self-interest.[6]

Finally, ethno-nationalism was also linked with the abolition of the property qualification. By elevating wealth over national identity within the political sphere, the property qualification undermined the idea that all Americans shared some unique ascriptive character. Accordingly, the demise of the property qualification gave rise to a more openly ethno-nationalist conception of citizenship. As Rogers Smith explains, efforts by nativists to restrict the franchise on the grounds of race or nationality emerged after, and in reaction to, the widespread abolition of the property qualification.[7] While property qualifications sometimes re-emerged in forms such as the poll tax, often as a pretext to deny racial or national-origin minorities the right to vote, today neither states nor the federal government can permissibly impose a requirement that citizens pay taxes or own property as a prerequisite to vote.[8] Further, property owners and taxpayers cannot vote in federal elections if they are not

---

[4] *See* Robert J. Steinfeld, *Property and Suffrage in the Early American Republic*, 41 STAN. L. REV. 335, 352 (1989).

[5] *Id.* at 367; *see also* GORDON S. WOOD, THE RADICALISM OF THE AMERICAN REVOLUTION 268–70 (1991) (describing transformation in thinking about the nature of property in the early republic).

[6] KEYSSAR, *supra* note 1, at 47–50.

[7] ROGERS M. SMITH, CIVIC IDEALS: CONFLICTING VISIONS OF CITIZENSHIP IN U.S. HISTORY 212–16 (1997).

[8] The federal government is prohibited from enacting a poll tax by the 24th Amendment, ratified in 1964. States are prohibited from enacting a poll tax under the equal protection clause as interpreted by Harper v. Virginia State Bd. Of Elections, 383 U.S. 663 (1966), as well as the federal Voting Rights Act.

United States citizens, nor can they vote in state elections if they are not residents of the state.

6.2 LOCAL CITIZENSHIP

In some local elections, however, nonresident landowners do have the right to vote, and sometimes they actually have the *exclusive* right to vote. The reason this occurs is because local citizenship is typically perceived as qualitatively distinct from state and national citizenship. It is liberal, based on a privatized idea of the municipality as a nonpolitical site of commerce and administration, rather than an organic community of shared fate and identity. To reiterate a point I have stressed, local citizenship is not *always* perceived this way, especially by local residents themselves, and I consider some alternative views of local citizenship in the next part. Nevertheless, this liberal view of local citizenship has been predominant in our legal and political culture, what I have called a "structure of consciousness."

6.2.1 *The Historical Context*

From the medieval period until the early American republic, cities were corporate entities that typically granted voting rights, often exclusively, to landowners, taxpayers, and others who participated in commerce in the city. It was a fairly uncontroversial proposition that local politics was primarily about economic interest and so those who were interested should be the ones to govern. This view was stated succinctly by the novelist James Fenimore Cooper, who wrote: "towns and villages regulating property chiefly, there is a peculiar propriety in excluding those from the suffrage who have no immediate local interests in them."[9] Once the states moved to abolish the property qualification, however, they often insisted that cities do so as well.[10]

The thinking shifted back in the opposite direction during the Progressive period. Scandalized by the political machines and what they saw as profligate municipal spending, the Progressive reformers sought to return cities to the privatized mold of their medieval forbears and treat them as corporate rather than political entities. According to one writer, Andrew White, the idea that the city was a political body was an "evil theory." As he wrote:

[9]　*Quoted in* KEYSSAR, *supra* note 1, at 31.
[10]　*Id.* at 30–32.

The questions in a city are not political questions. They have reference to the laying out of streets; to the erection of buildings; to sanitary arrangements, sewerage, water supply, gas supply, electrical supply; to the control of franchises and the like; and to provisions for the public health and comfort in parks, boulevards, libraries, and museums.[11]

Consistent with this view, as the previous chapter explained, the Progressives instituted a series of reforms designed to make cities operate more like businesses and less like political entities: nonpartisan elections, devolution of power to expert commissions and professional city managers, the institution of inflexible home rule charters, and so on. But it also followed from this way of perceiving municipal government that only property owners should have a voice in municipal government. According to White: "The work of a city being the creation and control of the city property, it should logically be managed as a piece of property by those who have created it, who have a title to it, or a real substantial part in it, and can therefore feel strongly their duty to it."[12] During this period, many states enacted or came close to enacting property qualifications for voting in municipal elections. These efforts were justified on the grounds "that municipal affairs are business affairs, to be managed on business principles."[13] As Chapter 4 discussed, several cities enfranchised women during the Progressive era on similar grounds that local elections were distinct from national elections in that they involved matters of "housekeeping" rather than the civic affairs of state. The analogy was not lost on the courts, which typically upheld the property qualification for municipal elections, and sometimes cited municipal enfranchisement of women as precedent for the notion that municipalities could have distinctive suffrage rules.[14]

A general property requirement for municipal suffrage never emerged, however, perhaps because it proved unnecessary. Beginning in the early twentieth century, as the last chapter explained, it became easy for property owners to simply leave central cities for suburban communities where they could control the character of the population and protect their property from redistribution. During this time, as Kenneth Jackson's definitive history of suburbanization explains, changes in the law made the incorporation of new cities easier, at the same time that the improved quality of suburban services such as schools and sewers made exit from central cities feasible. Zoning,

[11] Andrew White, *The Government of American Cities*, 10 THE FORUM 357, 368 (Dec. 1890).
[12] *Id.*
[13] *Quoted in* KEYSSAR, *supra* note 1, at 132.
[14] KEYSSAR, *supra* note 1, at 133–34 and n. 27.

introduced from Germany, became exceptionally popular in these newly incorporated communities because it allowed cities to restrict undesirable uses such as apartment buildings, thereby ensuring that homeowners would have most of the political power.[15] According to one advocate for suburban separation from the city: "Under local government we can absolutely control every objectionable thing that may try to enter our limits … "[16] As I mentioned in the previous chapter, the suburbanization movement put the brakes on efforts to disfranchise noncitizens, since affluent city residents now had the option of redefining the municipal electorate by fleeing to the suburbs. Likewise, property qualifications became less relevant because, once communities could control their own zoning, they could effectively restrict the franchise to landowners anyway by using municipal borders and zoning laws to ensure that most of the voters were the community's homeowners. In effect, as the economist Robert Nelson writes, zoning creates a "de facto property qualification" for residency.[17] Nelson argues, accordingly, that suburbs are properly considered private entities, more akin to homeowners' associations than governments.[18]

The phenomenon of suburbanization made abundantly clear, if it had not been sufficiently clear already, that local citizenship was about interest rather than nationality. While many Progressive urban policies such as free public education, housing reform, temperance, and investment in public parks had been designed to "Americanize" immigrants, the movement to the suburbs was driven not by a desire to create a nationalist community of shared identity and meaning but a desire to obtain quality public services without urban problems.[19] This was well understood by the courts that facilitated suburbanization by interpreting state laws to liberally allow municipal incorporations. According to Richard Briffault's classic discussion, although many state laws insisted that only areas constituting "urban communities" could incorporate as municipalities, "courts defined 'urbanness' and 'community' to fit the economic and social characteristics of the emerging suburbs."[20] One court, for

[15] *See* KENNETH T. JACKSON, CRABGRASS FRONTIER: THE SUBURBANIZATION OF THE UNITED STATES 148–56 (1985); SEYMOUR I. TOLL, ZONED AMERICAN 188–210 (1969).

[16] *Quoted in* JACKSON, *supra* note 15, at 151.

[17] ROBERT NELSON, PRIVATE NEIGHBORHOODS AND THE TRANSFORMATION OF LOCAL GOVERNMENT 420–21 (2005).

[18] *Id.* at 4–6.

[19] *See* JACKSON, *supra* note 15, at 150–53; Gerald E. Frug, *City Services*, 73 N.Y.U. L. Rev. 23, 39–41 (1998) (describing the nineteenth-century vision of city services as designed to assimilate immigrants, and contrasting it with the current consumer-oriented model of city services).

[20] Richard Briffault, *Our Localism: Part II: Localism and Legal Theory*, 90 COLUM. L. REV. 346, 359 (1990).

example, found that residents of a suburban area constituted a "community" because they had "similar business interests, professions and occupations."[21] Another found the element of community satisfied by residents' common desire for police and fire services and "protection for their property or persons."[22] Thus, the very term "community" was being redefined from an organic unit marked by a general public interest into an aggregation of private self-interests, what sociologist Morris Janowitz would later call a "community of limited liability."[23]

Having acknowledged that the very purpose of community was the "protection" of private property, courts gave municipalities a wide berth to take actions that preserved and enhanced residents' property rights. In the early 1920s, for example, the Supreme Court established the constitutionality of zoning, which is perhaps the most significant and far-reaching power most municipalities possess.[24] Zoning enables communities to establish permitted and prohibited uses, determine the location, density, and timing of new land uses, set minimum lot sizes and square footage, and so forth. In so doing, zoning can affect the local and regional supply of housing and thus profoundly affect property values. Further, as described earlier, zoning can have the additional purpose of shaping the community's population to ensure that demands for additional housing or redistribution of local wealth are defeated. Courts have repeatedly cited the protection of property values as one of zoning's central purposes and have found that purpose sufficiently weighty to immunize zoning against all manner of legal challenges. Similarly, courts have frequently held that the protection of neighboring landowners' reliance interests in a preexisting regulatory scheme is a legitimate reason for municipalities to decline to change their zoning regulations. Modern courts have also upheld sweeping aesthetic and historic preservation laws, often by citing the connection between aesthetic or historic significance and neighborhood property values.[25]

6.2.2 *Expanding the Franchise*

Once courts accepted that the protection of private property was a legitimate function of local government, it followed that there was nothing improper

---

[21] State ex. Rel. Pickrell v. Downey, 430 P.2d 122, 128 (1967).

[22] In re Village of Chenequa, 221 N.W. 856, 859 (Wisc. 1928).

[23] Morris Janowitz, The Community Press in an Urban Setting 207–13, 218, 222–25 (1952).

[24] See Vill. of Euclid v. Ambler Realty Co., 272 U.S. 365 (1926).

[25] See Kenneth A. Stahl, *Reliance in Land Use*, 2013 BYU L. Rev. 949, 983–85 (collecting cases).

about enfranchising property owners in local elections. Accordingly, courts have on occasion upheld efforts by municipalities to enfranchise nonresident landowners on the grounds that they, much like noncitizen residents, have an interest in the affairs of local government. In the case of *May* v. *Mountain Village*, the 10th Circuit Court of Appeals held that a Colorado resort town had the home rule authority to extend the franchise in municipal elections to nonresident landowners, and that doing so did not violate the equal protection clause, because in light of the effects of municipal government on property, landowners have a "sufficient interest in town affairs" to justify granting them voting rights.[26] As we have seen in the last few chapters, this logic is entirely consistent with a liberal model of local citizenship in which participation is based on interest rather than identity. Women were enfranchised in local elections where they had "a legitimate interest in common with men."[27] Noncitizens won the right to vote in Takoma Park by arguing that "I have as much interest in the community as anyone."[28]

Another way in which the enfranchisement of landowners in municipal elections reflects the liberal idea of local citizenship is that it is premised on a view of citizens as mobile consumer-voters who choose where to live or invest based on the amenities the community offers, and a view of municipalities as competing firms that tailor their municipal services and regulatory policies to lure footloose residents and mobile capital. As we have seen, during the nineteenth century frontier states extended the franchise to women and noncitizens as a way of luring new residents to sparsely settled territories. Likewise, enfranchising nonresident landowners may be a shrewd mechanism for luring and maintaining a robust tax base by ensuring that those who pay taxes will have a voice in how much they are taxed and how that tax revenue is spent. In *May*, for example, Mountain Village enfranchised nonresident landowners through a charter amendment that was approved by the overwhelming majority of the town's existing residents.

[26] 132 F.3d 576, 578–83 (10th Cir. 1997). *See also* Glisson v. Mayor & Councilmen of Town of Savannah Beach, 346 F.2d 135, 137 (5th Cir. 1965) (upholding enfranchisement of nonresident landowners because each landowner "obviously has an interest in the operation of city government"); *but see* Brown v. Chattanooga Board of Commissioners, 722 F. Supp. 380 (E.D. Tenn. 1989) (invalidating local charter provision allowing nonresident landowners to vote on grounds that it placed no limits on how many people can vote on a single piece of real property, while leaving in place state law permitting nonresident "property qualification" as a basis for voting in municipal elections).

[27] Spatgen v. O'Neil, 169 N.W. 491, 493 (ND 1918).

[28] *See* Jamin B. Raskin, *Legal Aliens, Local Citizens: The Historical, Constitutional, and Theoretical Meanings of Alien Suffrage*, 141 U. PA. L. REV. 391, 1464 (1993) (quoting Beth Kaiman, *Takoma Park Weighs Noncitizen Vote*, WASH. POST, Oct. 31, 1991, at M2).

The reason why these residents voted to dilute their own voting power is fairly evident. Mountain Village is a resort town with a substantial number of vacation-home owners and, as the court noted, nonresidents paid over eight times more in property taxes than residents.[29] Losing those vacation-home owners to neighboring resort communities could have had a devastating impact on Mountain View's economy. Enfranchising nonresident landowners was thus an inducement to continue investing in the community. As before, it is money and mobility that determine membership at the local level, not primordial national identifications.

6.2.3 Contracting the Franchise

The logic of *May* opens up a more fraught question, which is whether cities may not only *expand* the franchise to include landowners, but also *contract* the franchise to exclude everyone but landowners. After all, if the idea is that all those who are interested should vote, it may follow that *only* those who are interested should vote. And as I have described, many cities already have a "de facto property qualification" insofar as zoning rules raise the cost of housing and thus require prospective residents to purchase their right to live and vote in the community at whatever price the community sets. If we see local citizenship as liberal, that is, as a product of market choice and interest, then the idea that the franchise is something that consumers must acquire in the manner of a market purchase has a certain logic.

Logical or not, contracting the franchise is far more controversial than expanding it because it affronts one of the main foundations of our democracy, the principle of "one person, one vote." The idea that we would allow wealth to be a prerequisite for political participation recalls the radically unequal relations of a feudal society.[30] Notwithstanding the one person, one vote rule, however, courts have sometimes arrived at the conclusion that the franchise in *local* elections can be expressly limited to landowners. We are once again confronted with the ambiguity of liberal local citizenship – it is open to all of those who can purchase it, without regard to identity or ethnicity, but it is also closed to those who cannot. This section describes how and why courts have carved out an exception to the one person, one vote

---

[29] See 132 F.3d at 579, 582.

[30] See ALEXANDER BICKEL, THE SUPREME COURT AND THE IDEA OF PROGRESS 157 (1970) (discussing one person/one vote, writes: "The structuring of government in terms of clearly defined interests ... raises the specter of the corporate state, or of the medieval state, which classified people by status, and held them to the status in which they were classified.")

rule and allowed landowners to control municipal governments in certain circumstances.

The One Person/One Vote Rule and Its Exceptions

As described earlier, restricting the franchise to landowners became a moot point in many places once middle class residents had the option of escaping cities instead of trying to reform them. The composition of the electorate could be controlled by lighting out to the suburbs rather than changing the voting rules. This option was not universally available, however. After World War II, much of the nation's growth occurred in the sunbelt, but this growth did not happen in the same way it had happened in the east. Sunbelt cities did not experience eastern-style suburbanization because these cities, with support from state law, aggressively annexed their suburbs. The need to coordinate expensive water supplies in the arid west made it necessary to have larger cities to spread out the costs of municipal infrastructure. As a result, affluent residents could not as easily exit the city as they could in the east. Perhaps for that reason, sunbelt cities adopted progressive municipal reforms much more readily than older rust belt cities did. As Amy Bridges' excellent history MORNING GLORIES recounts, sunbelt cities like Albuquerque, Phoenix, Austin, San Jose, and others instituted a raft of Progressive-era reforms designed to ensure that political participation was limited to a white land-owning elite, such as strict voter registration laws, poll taxes, literacy tests, the delegation of authority to professional city managers, and local elections that were off-cycle, non-partisan, and at-large.[31] In at least some circumstances, such as bond elections and special assessments to finance municipal infra-structure, the franchise has also been expressly limited to landowners.[32]

The validity of confining the franchise in this way was thrown into considerable doubt by a series of important Supreme Court decisions on voting rights in the 1960s that, among other things, invalidated the poll tax and held that states were required to apportion votes to elective office in accordance with the "one person, one vote" principle. For a short time, there was some question whether the one person, one vote rule would apply to *local* elections, given the ways in which local governments had always been perceived as distinct from the state. In *Avery* v. *Midland County*,[33]

---

[31] *See* AMY BRIDGES, MORNING GLORIES: MUNICIPAL REFORM IN THE SOUTHWEST (1997).

[32] On the sunbelt style of development, see ROBERT E. LANG & JENNIFER B. LEFURGY, BOOMBURBS: THE RISE OF AMERICA'S ACCIDENTAL CITIES (2007); CARL ABBOTT, THE METROPOLITAN FRONTIER: CITIES IN THE MODERN AMERICAN WEST (1993); CARL ABBOTT, THE NEW URBAN AMERICA: GROWTH AND POLITICS IN SUNBELT CITIES (rev. ed. 1987).

[33] 390 U.S. 474(1968).

however, the Supreme Court held that local governments exercising general municipal functions were required to abide by the one person, one vote rule. In sweeping language, the Court stated that "[t]he actions of local government *are* the actions of the State,"[34] and thus determined that local governments are bound by the terms of the equal protection clause to the same extent as the State itself. Several subsequent cases affirmed the broad reach of the one person, one vote principle to local governments.[35] In one such case, *City of Phoenix* v. *Kolodziejski*,[36] the Court struck down an effort by the city of Phoenix to limit voting rights to taxpayers on a referendum to issue bonds financed by property tax revenue.

Much like *Plyler* v. *Doe*, *Avery* and *Phoenix* are subject to at least two different readings on the meaning of local citizenship, reflecting the ambiguous nature of liberalism. On one hand, they could be read as a broad affirmation of the rights of all local residents to equal citizenship. Just as immigrants are entitled to a free public education in order to prevent the formation of a permanent underclass, all residents of a municipal government are entitled to be treated equally in the weighting of their votes, regardless of geography, landownership, or other particularistic considerations. On the other hand, *Avery* closed with an important caveat – the one person, one vote rule might not apply to "a special-purpose unit of government assigned the performance of functions affecting definable groups of constituents more than other constituents."[37] In other words, local citizenship can legitimately be limited to those who are disproportionately interested *if the municipality can demonstrate such a disproportionate interest*. Like *Plyler*, then, the right to equality that *Avery* affirms is contingent upon one's financial means. It is a right to be measured by money rather than identity.

Avery's implication became explicit in two later cases, in which the Court relied upon *Avery*'s caveat to find that municipal governments whose activities disproportionately affected landowners could in fact constitutionally limit the franchise to landowners. The second and more significant of these cases, *Ball* v. *James*,[38] involved the Salt River District in Arizona. The Salt River

---

[34] *Id.* at 480.
[35] Kramer v. Union Free School District No. 15, 395 U.S. 621, 622 (1969); Hadley v. Junior College District of Metro. Kansas City, Mo., 397 U.S. 50, 51–52 (1970); City of Phoenix v. Kolodziejski, 399 U.S. 204, 205–07 (1970); Hill v. Stone, 421 U.S. 289, 307–08 (1975); *Cipriano* v. *Houma*, 395 U.S. 701, 702, 705 (1969).
[36] 399 U.S. 204, 205–07 (1970).
[37] *Id.* at 483–84.
[38] 451 U.S. 355, 371 (1981). The earlier case was Salyer Land Co. v. Tulare Lake Basin Water Storage District, 410 U.S. 719, 728 (1973).

District, originally a private water management district that subsequently became a public entity, financed its operations partially through mandatory assessments imposed on landowners who received water from the district. The size of the assessment was based on the benefit each parcel of land was deemed to receive, and voting rights for the directors of the districts were allocated based on the acreage of land owned. The Court held that the district was exempt from *Avery*'s one person, one vote rule because the district served only the limited purpose of providing water and disproportionately impacted the landowners who paid the assessments and whose land received the benefit of water provision. The Court reached this conclusion notwithstanding the fact that the water district in *Ball* included almost half the population of the state of Arizona, including the entire Phoenix metropolitan region, and that it generated and sold electric power in addition to its water management functions, thus making the district a significant factor in the overall development of an arid region. The Court found that the district did not administer "such normal functions of government as the maintenance of streets, the operations of schools, or sanitation, health, or welfare services."[39] Furthermore, the district's weighted voting structure was legitimate because the landowners empowered to vote were the principal beneficiaries of the district and bore the principal burden of financing the district's operations through the mandatory assessments.[40]

Ball illustrates the liberal conception of local citizenship, in which membership correlates precisely with one's financial interest. According to Richard Briffault, *Ball* represents a "proprietary" model of local government, which "validates governance only by those within the community who can be seen as investors."[41] But the full implications of *Ball* for local citizenship were not immediately evident. The Court emphasized the exceptional nature of the Salt River District, and the fact that it did not carry out the sort of governmental functions typically associated with local government.

Kessler v. Grand Central District Management Association

In subsequent lower court cases, however, *Ball*'s exception has been expanded in ways that show how fully the liberal idea of citizenship has taken hold at the local level. This is well demonstrated by one especially important decision from the Second Circuit Court of Appeals, *Kessler v. Grand Central District*

---

[39] 451 U.S. at 366.
[40] *Id.* at 371.
[41] *See, e.g.*, Richard Briffault, *Who Rules at Home?: One Person/One Vote and Local Governments*, 60 U. Chi. L. Rev. 339, 370 (1993).

Management Association.[42] *Kessler* addressed the constitutionality of a voting scheme for the board of directors of a "business improvement district" (BID) that governed the area surrounding the historic Grand Central terminal in New York City. Beginning in the late 1980s, as declining revenues and disinvestment made it difficult for many cities to finance municipal services through the traditional mechanisms of property taxation and intergovernmental transfers, cities turned to BIDs as an alternative financing technique. BIDs typically function, as in the case of the Grand Central District Management Association (GCDMA), by assessing a mandatory charge upon real property within a territorially bounded district, and then using those assessments to furnish services such as sanitation, security, maintenance, and street-signage within that area for the benefit of the assessed property. A board of directors is elected to manage the assessed funds. The GCDMA, like most other BIDs, allocated voting power for the board of directors in a way that ensured that the property owners who paid the assessments had the ability to elect the majority of the board.[43] Hence, the BID was not consistent with the "one person, one vote" principle. Nevertheless, the *Kessler* court found that one person/one vote did not apply to the GCDMA because the district had the limited purpose of promoting business within the area, performed a narrow set of functions, lacked regulatory authority, and was subject to substantial governmental oversight.[44] Furthermore, the GCDMA's operation had a disproportionately greater effect on the assessed property owners than others, both insofar as property owners alone would bear the economic burden of paying the assessments, and property owners would reap the principal economic benefits from the assessments in the form of increased property values.[45] Thus, according to *Kessler*, limiting the franchise to landowners was legitimate because the BID's fundamental purpose is to maximize the value of real property for the benefit of landowners.

Kessler reflects the liberal nature of local citizenship in several ways. First, to the extent it ties the franchise to economic interest – the benefits landowners will receive in the form of property values – *Kessler* evokes the reasoning we have seen used to justify *expanding* the municipal franchise beyond the core electorate of adult citizen residents. In the case of both nonresident landowners and noncitizen residents, courts and advocates for expanding suffrage have repeatedly emphasized that those who reside in the community or who

---

[42] 158 F.3d 92 (2d Cir. 1998).
[43] See id. at 97.
[44] See id. at 104–07.
[45] Id. at 107–08.

have a financial interest there have a sufficient interest to warrant a vote. Second, *Kessler* relies upon the same rhetoric of mobility that has frequently undergirded the extension of local citizenship beyond the core electorate. Cities that have conferred social and political rights on landowners or non-citizen residents have often done so on the rationale that landowners and immigrants are desirable but mobile, and could easily be lost to competing cities if they were not given the rights of citizens. BIDs, likewise, are rationalized with a public choice logic that presumes urban landowners are mobile and indifferent to particular urban spaces, and will therefore exit to the suburbs at relatively low cost unless the exchange value of their land can be maximized. As Richard Briffault writes, the BID is a critical piece of a narrative of urban decline and subsequent revitalization, in which affluent individuals fled the city in search of the more favorable environments in the suburbs, and then flocked back to the downtown areas once the BID was able to provide landowners with a dedicated revenue stream.[46] The *Kessler* decision internalizes this narrative. The very purpose of the BID, *Kessler* asserts, is to "attract and keep businesses by assisting property owners to achieve the remunerative use of" commercial space.[47] Implicitly, landowners have a choice of jurisdictions in which to invest and will only be "attracted" to urban spaces if their property can be made sufficiently "remunerative."

Of course, though *Kessler* employs the same logic often used to expand municipal suffrage, it uses that logic to reach exactly the opposite conclusion – that the franchise should be *limited* to landowners only. The idea that cities are in a relentless zero-sum competition for footloose revenue, a competition that some cities will inevitably win and others will lose, means that cities must do whatever it takes to win that competition. If the only way to secure investment in formerly disinvested places is to guarantee landowners that they can have sole control over a revenue stream for their own benefit, then democracy becomes a luxury that those places cannot afford. According to Don Mitchell, the rhetoric of capital mobility "allows local officials, along with local business and property owners, to argue that they have no choice but to prostrate themselves before the god capital."[48] *Kessler* thus represents the full realization of the problematic implications of liberal local citizenship – once we say that

---

[46] See Richard Briffault, *A Government for Our Time: Business Improvement Districts and Urban Governance*, 99 COLUM. L. REV. 365, 420–29 (1999).

[47] 158 F.3d at 104; *see also* 2nd Roc-Jersey Assocs. v. Town of Morristown, 731 A.2d 1, 13 (N.J. 1999) (accepting that "special improvement district" (SID) was necessary to enable declining city to compete with nearby suburbs for mobile businesses).

[48] DON MITCHELL, THE RIGHT TO THE CITY: SOCIAL JUSTICE AND THE FIGHT FOR PUBLIC SPACE 166 (2003) (deploring "suburbanization of downtown").

citizenship is determined by interest rather than nationality, it rapidly leads to the conclusion that *only* those with a sufficient interest should have the privilege of being called citizens.

"Interest" in this context means money. Those who own property have political power, whereas those who do not have none. This is more troubling in *Kessler* than in *Ball* because, while the Salt River District provided services like water and electricity that fall outside the ordinary domain of a general purpose municipality, BIDs like GCDMA are fundamentally land-use authorities, managing public space for the benefit of landowners. They act aggressively against street vendors, food trucks, adult businesses, or any other use of space deemed inconsistent with the BID's central goal to increase property values. BIDs have vigorously lobbied city governments for favorable zoning changes and the enforcement of existing zoning laws. According to Robert Ellickson, one of the BID's "central functions" is "the control of disorderly street people" like the homeless and aggressive panhandlers.[49] Yet, although the BID's control of land use affects many people aside from landowners, including tenants, visitors, street vendors, the homeless, and others, those people's voices are discounted in the governing process because their "interest" is not commodifiable in the same way that landowners' interests are, and they do not have the same ability that landowners do to threaten to withdraw capital from the city. Again, *Kessler* makes local citizenship contingent upon money and mobility.

Finally, *Kessler* reflects the liberal character of local citizenship in another way as well. Just as it depicts the citizen as primarily a self-interested consumer, it also depicts the municipality as a truncated, privatized sphere of administration. As we have seen previously, the expansion of suffrage to encompass women and noncitizens was often coupled with a portrayal of municipal government as quotidian, preoccupied with matters such as the home and the care of children, street sweeping, security, and garbage collection, rather than the civic affairs of state. This portrayal served to contrast the privatized, consensual, and interest-based nature of municipal citizenship from the civic-minded and ethno-nationalist sphere of federal citizenship. *Kessler* does this as well, emphasizing the narrow purpose of the BID, its lack of regulatory authority, and the limited nature of the services it provides. Although as a de facto matter, as I have just described, BIDs exercise fairly wide-ranging land use powers, the court depicts the GCDMA as doing nothing more than some aesthetic improvements "to make the district more

---

[49] Robert C. Ellickson, *Controlling Chronic Misconduct in City Spaces: Of Panhandlers, Skid Rows, and Public-Space Zoning*, 105 YALE L.J. 1165, 1199 (1996).

attractive to tourists and other consumers."[50] In doing so, the Court conceptually transforms the BID from a public entity exercising public powers into a private entity protecting private property rights; that is, the BID exists within the realm of the marketplace rather than the realm of politics, and therefore can base the franchise on financial interest and mobility. As the court states, "the purpose of the Grand Central BID is the promotion of business."[51] Thus, while *Kessler* attempts to portray the BID as exceptional, it is in fact emblematic of the modern approach to local citizenship. Courts have often been at pains to present local citizenship as a privatized realm of consumption and self-interest in contrast to the public realm of the state.

On the other hand, and as I elaborate further in Chapter 10, mechanisms like the BID may foster a kind of openness to difference and tolerance for diversity that we often treasure in urban life. As we saw in Chapters 4 and 5, the loosening of traditional moral and ethnic communities and their displacement by money, mobility, and interest is correlated with a more cosmopolitan view of citizenship. In this case, the BID arguably solves an important problem posed by the influential Tiebout model, discussed earlier. Under this model, people migrate to whichever community has the most attractive bundle of municipal services. The model thus predicts that cities will become increasingly homogeneous as individuals with similar tastes gravitate toward the same cities, and those with divergent tastes choose different cities.[52] Consistent with this prediction, for at least a generation affluent residents and investors eschewed diverse cities for exclusive and homogeneous suburbs where they could obtain their preferred level of public goods and services without having to worry about congestion or compromise with groups that have different demands.[53] One way to reverse this pattern of suburban migration and maintain a diverse city, however, is to unbundle residence from public goods and services so that individuals can choose their preferred package of municipal amenities while remaining within the city.[54] This is precisely what the BID is intended to accomplish – to keep investors, tourists, and middle-class residents

---

[50] *Id.* at 105–06.
[51] *Id.* at 104.
[52] *See* Kenneth A. Stahl, *Mobility and Community: An Essay on* Great American City *by Robert J. Sampson,* 46 Urb. L.J. 625, 634–40 (2014) (discussing various implications of the Tiebout model).
[53] *See generally* Gary J. Miller, Cities by Contract: The Politics of Municipal Incorporation (1981) (describing fiscal motivations that led small suburban communities in Los Angeles County to resist consolidation with larger, more diverse cities).
[54] *See* Nicole Stelle Garnett, *Affordable Private Education and the Middle Class City,* 77 U. Chi. L. Rev. 201, 210–17 (2010) (explaining how private schools help urban residents "unbundle" educational decisions from residential ones).

within the city.[55] As Richard Ford argues, there is a limit to how much exposure to diversity city dwellers can take before they recoil from it.[56] BIDs may provide a necessary buffer against unlimited exposure that enables people to confront diversity more confidently. Indeed, social science research demonstrates that people are initially hostile to diversity, but develop "ego strength" to tolerate and embrace it over time.[57] As in the case of sanctuary cities, what begins as a purely economic calculation may become a normative ideal of citizenship.

From the ethno-nationalist perspective, however, the embrace of strangers and the use of money as a criterion for citizenship may also lead to a dilution of the cultural distinctions between people, and a nondescript corporate homogeneity in place of authentic civic traditions. If the private sphere of money is not kept rigidly segregated from the public sphere of the state, the ethno-nationalist conception of citizenship may be threatened. That is the subject of the next chapter.

---

[55] To be clear, there is considerable debate about the role the BID has played in reversing urban decline and bringing the middle class back downtown. Though the BID is often credited for this trend, there is also evidence that the changing fortune of many cities was a result of long-term macroeconomic and demographic changes with which the advent of the BID merely coincided. *See* Richard C. Schragger, *Rethinking the Theory and Practice of Local Economic Development*, 77 U. CHI. L. REV. 311–13, 326–31 (2010) (doubting claims that BID has driven urban resurgence, and casting doubt on the validity of the Tiebout model more generally).

[56] *See* Richard Thompson Ford, *Bourgeois Communities: A Review of Gerald Frug's City Making*, 56 STAN. L. REV. 231, 243–46 (2003).

[57] Robert D. Putnam, E Pluribus Unum: *Diversity and Community in the Twenty-First Century*, 30 SCANDINAVIAN POL. STUD. 137, 138–44 (2007).

7

Globalization and the Collapsing Distinction between Local and Federal Citizenship

The argument of this book so far is that the distinction between federal and local citizenship has been designed to achieve an accommodation between three different models of citizenship, the liberal, republican, and ethno-nationalist models. Liberal citizenship emphasizes individual consumption and the pursuit of self-interest, republican citizenship stresses collective civic activity, and ethno-nationalist citizenship rests on a foundation of shared identity and linked fate. Where republicanism and ethno-nationalism have been relatively easily reconciled, especially as republicanism has faded in importance, the collectivist premises of republican and ethno-nationalist citizenship have been more difficult to square with the individualist premises of liberal citizenship. The case studies in the three previous chapters – women, noncitizens, and landowners – all attempted to demonstrate how the courts and policymakers have reached an accommodation among these different models by dividing citizenship jurisdictionally between the federal and the local levels. In short, they have constructed local citizenship as liberal, rooted in money, mobility, and choice, and federal citizenship as ethno-nationalist and republican, rooted in identity and linked fate. The dichotomy between federal and local citizenship mirrors a distinction, long prevalent in western thought and central to the very idea of citizenship, between the private sphere of individual self-seeking and the public sphere of collective civic activity. Hence, as we saw in each of our three cases, advocates for a distinctive municipal suffrage emphasized that local citizenship was purely private, in contrast to the public sphere of national citizenship. Where nation-state citizenship is predicated on primordial identifications and deep loyalties, local citizenship is tailored to mobile consumer-voters who seek to obtain quality municipal services for themselves and their families with relative indifference to the cultures of particular places. For that reason, local citizenship could easily be extended to those, such as women, noncitizens, or landowners, who share the characteristics of mobile consumer voters, even if they are at the same time deemed incapable, undeserving, or ill-suited for federal citizenship. For many years, the distinction between the public sphere of federal citizenship and the private sphere of local citizenship has enabled the ethno-nationalist, republican, and liberal approaches to citizenship to coexist by confining them to separate spheres where they will not come into conflict.

Today, however, as I show in this chapter, globalization is destabilizing the public/private distinction, and, as it does so, the distinction between local and federal citizenship is breaking down. The result is that the liberal conception of citizenship that prevails at the local level has bled into the federal level, conceptually unsettling the ethno-nationalist and republican conceptions thought to be safely enshrined there. Increasingly, federal citizenship is being extended beyond its traditional boundaries of identity and territory and conferred, just as local citizenship has long been, on the basis of money, mobility, and consumption.

The shift from an ethno-nationalist toward a more liberal idea of federal citizenship has had significant, and ambiguous, implications for our politics and society. As I stressed in the last few chapters, the liberal nature of local citizenship has been a double-edged sword for cities and their residents. On the one hand, defining local citizenship in liberal terms as the provision of quality municipal services has allowed local citizenship to be far more expansive and, in a sense, cosmopolitan than federal citizenship. On the other hand, however, the liberality of local citizenship is tied up with its subjection to the forces of money and mobility, and the stratification of wealth inequality. Women, noncitizens, and landowners became valued as local citizens to the extent of their economic contributions to the local economy and tax base, but no further. Municipalities with resources treat citizenship like membership in a private club, using zoning laws to ensure that only those with sufficient financial means to purchase residence can become local citizens. In short, where the ethno-nationalist model divides people by ethnicity and identity, the liberal model divides them based on wealth and mobility.

As the local conception of citizenship invades the federal, all the ambivalences and contradictions within liberal local citizenship now burst onto the national political stage, threatening to undermine the ethno-nationalist character of federal citizenship by making federal citizenship contingent on consumption and mobility rather than identity. As globalization has loosened national borders, those who have the ability to traverse those borders freely can leverage that mobility to attain the benefits once reserved for citizens. Mobility replaces identity as the key dividing line in our society. As Zygmunt Bauman writes: "The freedom to move, perpetually a scarce and unequally distributed commodity, fast becomes the main stratifying factor" in our global age.[1] The shift from identity to mobility has unleashed a huge wave of resentment, especially among those who feel they have been on the losing end of that shift as a result of outsourcing, mechanization, brain drain, and changing demographics. That resentment has taken the form of a renewed ethno-nationalist sentiment, designed to turn back the liberal tide and reinstate a more primordial conception of citizenship rooted in identity. Donald Trump's election to the US Presidency on an anti-urban, anti-immigrant, and anti-globalization platform represents the apotheosis of ethno-nationalism's resurgence.

This chapter returns to each of the three case studies discussed in this part: women, noncitizens, and landowners. In each case, what began as a distinctly municipal form of citizenship eventually burst out of its sphere and challenged the nature of federal citizenship. As it did so, it caused a crisis in the meaning of citizenship and a backlash of nationalist sentiment. That backlash has often taken the form of resentment against cities and their liberal approach to citizenship, exemplified above all by the controversy over sanctuary cities. For that same reason, many on the left have seen cities as the cure for our current spasm of ethno-nationalism. The last section of this chapter, therefore, considers possible futures for local citizenship.

7.1 KARL MARX ON GLOBALIZATION AND THE COLLAPSING PUBLIC/PRIVATE DISTINCTION

At the outset, let me provide some context on globalization, cities, and citizenship. I use the term globalization here generally to mean the liberalization of international barriers to trade, immigration, and capital mobility that has taken place since the end of the Cold War. Long before the end of the Cold War, however, Karl Marx saw clearly that capitalism would collapse the neat boundary that liberal nation-states attempted to draw between public and private, threatening the idea of citizenship.[2] The flow of money could not be contained within borders, and so efforts to contain capitalism within a

---

[1] ZYGMUNT BAUMAN, GLOBALIZATION 2 (1998).

[2] *See* Karl Marx, *On the Jewish Question,* in THE MARX-ENGELS READER 26, 31, 33–34 (Robert C. Tucker ed., 2nd ed. 1978); KARL MARX & FRIEDRICH ENGELS, THE GERMAN IDEOLOGY 47 (Prometheus Books 1998) (1845).

"private" sphere would inevitably prove fruitless.[3] Marx accordingly mocked as an "unreal universality" the idea that citizens can be divorced from their private interests.[4] Taking note of the contemporaneous abolition of the property qualification for voting in America, Marx argued that citizens are emancipated "politically" from their private affiliations insofar as wealth is abolished as a criterion for political participation, but citizens fail to achieve genuine "human" emancipation because distinctions based on wealth and the like are allowed to persist in civil society outside the realm of the state.[5] Although liberalism may free women or the working classes to participate in politics, it does not truly free them from class distinctions. As such, where citizenship in the ancient republic was based on "real slavery," modern citizenship in the liberal democratic state is based on "emancipated slavery."[6] And though the modern state attempts to suppress this contradiction by dividing the public and private spheres, when global capitalism explodes the boundaries between those spheres the inherently unsustainable character of emancipated slavery is exposed.

Though Marx thought little about the city, viewing it as an epiphenomenon of the rise of capitalism, his analysis is readily applicable to the changing relationship between local and federal citizenship. One of the things that have made local citizenship so distinctive, as I have stressed throughout, is the need of cities to attract mobile labor and capital. Many places extended the franchise to women, noncitizens, and landowners in order to lure desirable residents or revenue to their communities. Cities have nearly always depended on trade, which has caused them to both cooperate with and compete against other places for resources. They could never rely on borders to protect

---

[3] See GEORGE RITZER, GLOBALIZATION: A BASIC TEXT 6 (2010) (describing how, according to Marx, "many of the solid, material realities that preceded capitalism (e.g.[,] the structures of feudalism) were 'melted' by it and transformed into liquids"); Michael Walzer, *Liberalism and the Art of Separation*, 12 POL. THEORY 315, 317 (1984) (noting that Marxists have been skeptical of the liberal "art of separation" because they "have generally stressed both the radical interdependence of the different social spheres and the direct and indirect causal links that radiate outward from the economy"); see also PETER SAUNDERS, SOCIAL THEORY AND THE URBAN QUESTION 16–17 (2nd. ed. 1986) (for Marx, "any explanation of the part can only be accomplished through an analysis of the whole").

[4] See Marx, *supra* note 2, at 32–34. For a discussion of Marx's essay that stresses its connections to local government law in the United States, specifically the applicability of the "one person, one vote" rule to local governments, see Kenneth A. Stahl, *Local Government, "One Person, One Vote," and the Jewish Question*, 49 HARV. C.R.-C.L. L. REV. 1 (2014).

[5] See Marx, *supra* note 2, at 30–34.

[6] See KARL MARX & FRIEDRICH ENGELS, THE HOLY FAMILY 164 (1956) [1844]; Michael Walzer, *Citizenship*, in POLITICAL INNOVATION AND CONCEPTUAL CHANGE 211 (Terence Ball et al. eds., 1989).

themselves against competition. This reality practically forced cities to adopt a liberal, cosmopolitan understanding of citizenship based on market choice and private self-interest as a way of securing a competitive advantage. Nation-states, by contrast, are creatures of their boundaries, and they have used those boundaries to craft a notion of citizenship that is not beholden to the market-place. As Marx predicted, however, the pressures of global capitalism have melted the solidity of national borders, enabling the private market to invade the sphere of the state, and citizenship to become contingent on interest. Globalization is making states subject to the same liberal forces of mobility and money that have long shaped local citizenship. Both labor and capital can now "vote with their feet" in choosing nation-states in which to locate, placing pressures on states that wish to succeed in a global economy to cater to their demands. Nation-states have been forced to conform national citizenship to the liberal standards of money, mobility, and residence, rather than shared nationality and civic virtue.

Each of our three case studies illustrates this trend. What began as a distinctly municipal form of citizenship – liberal, cosmopolitan, and private – eventually erupted out of its sphere and threatened to undermine federal citizenship. As that has happened, concerns over the diminishing significance of citizenship have begotten calls to strengthen borders and more sharply delineate the line between citizens and noncitizens in ethno-nationalist terms.

7.2 WOMAN SUFFRAGE AND CITIZENSHIP

The case of woman suffrage provides an important historical example of how, during an earlier era of globalization, liberal ideas about citizenship crept out of the local sphere and into the national sphere, challenging the foundation of federal citizenship. The example is not entirely historical, however, for the question of women's citizenship has become salient again during our current political crisis.

As discussed in Chapter 4, prior to the enactment of the Nineteenth Amendment the main anti-suffrage argument was that women were unqualified for citizenship because they were creatures of the private sphere of the home, unsuited for the public realm of the state. Nevertheless, women attained suffrage rights in many municipalities by stressing that local governments were principally concerned with matters of private "housekeeping" as to which women were especially adept, and were careful to contrast the quotidian nature of municipal government from the civic affairs of state. As we now know, however, woman suffrage did not stay confined to the municipal sphere, but was extended via the Nineteenth Amendment to state and federal elections as well. Rather than entailing a re-evaluation of women's role in society, though, the expansion of woman suffrage entailed a transformation in the conception of federal citizenship to dovetail with women's privatized status. During a time period, much like our own, when economies were globalizing and developed nations were shifting from mass production to mass consumption, the nation itself now came to be seen as an enlarged private household in which, according to Hannah Arendt, "private interests assume public significance."[7] Arendt observed that in the modern nation-state, "housekeeping and all matters pertaining formerly to the private sphere of the family have become a 'collective' concern."[8] Consumption, previously considered a private activity taking place within the sphere of the family and the market, now became the principal public duty of the citizen. According to one pamphlet from the time period, "The first responsibility of an American to his country is no longer that of a citizen, but of a consumer."[9] The public sphere of politics now fused with the private sphere of the home and market.[10]

Reconceptualizing the citizen as a consumer meant that women, rather than enjoying an exceptional status, were paradigmatic American citizens. Sociologist Christine Frederick dubbed the married woman "Mrs. Consumer," and assigned her the critical role of boosting domestic consumption.[11] The commentator Walter Lippman predicted that woman suffrage would herald a new consumer society because "the mass of women do not look at the world as workers, but as consumers."[12] While citizenship therefore expanded to include women, the meaning of citizenship itself was narrowed to coincide with women's privatized status. Where republican ideology once demanded the strict exclusion of private interests from the public sphere of government, the realization of private interests now became the central end of the state. Arendt writes: "The fact that the modern age emancipated the working classes and the women at nearly the same historical moment must

---

[7] HANNAH ARENDT, THE HUMAN CONDITION 35 (1958).
[8] *Id.* at 33.
[9] DOLORES HAYDEN, THE GRAND DOMESTIC REVOLUTION: A HISTORY OF FEMINIST DESIGNS FOR AMERICAN HOMES, NEIGHBORHOODS, AND CITIES 276 (1981).
[10] On the fusion between citizen and consumer during this period and the role of women within it, see LIZABETH COHEN, A CONSUMERS' REPUBLIC: THE POLITICS OF MASS CONSUMPTION IN POSTWAR AMERICA 31–41; 75–83 (2003).
[11] On Frederick and the concept of "Mrs. Consumer," see *id.* at 283–89; *see also* DOLORES HAYDEN, REDESIGNING THE AMERICAN DREAM: GENDER, HOUSING AND AMERICAN LIFE 33–34 (2002).
[12] WALTER LIPPMAN, DRIFT AND MASTERY 54–55 (1914); *see also* MICHAEL SANDEL, DEMOCRACY'S DISCONTENT: AMERICA IN SEARCH OF A PUBLIC PHILOSOPHY 221–27 (1996) (on the new consumer society of the twentieth century).

certainly be counted among the characteristics of an age which no longer believes that bodily functions and material concerns should be hidden."[13] Consumption and self-interest – those liberal standards that had long defined municipal citizenship – now became the hallmarks of national citizenship.

If woman suffrage in one sense truncated the meaning of citizenship, it also enabled women to expand it by challenging the traditional boundary between public and private. As described in Chapter 4, the extension of municipal suffrage to include women codified the woman's role within the home, but also broadened the domain of the home into the political sphere. As a result, matters once considered private, and therefore not political, could be rearticulated as political matters of the most significant order. Since the enactment of the Nineteenth Amendment, efforts to reconceive citizenship on feminist terms have thus tended to proceed in some form from the slogan that "the personal is political." Feminist theorists like Ruth Lister have emphasized that women's rights to bodily integrity, including reproductive freedom and protections against domestic violence, must be taken out of the realm of the private and made matters of political concern because they are "preconditions of women's full and free access in the public sphere."[14] Without these issues on the table, women's "agency, and hence their citizenship, is profoundly compromised."[15] As advocates for women's citizenship introduced matters formerly relegated to the sphere of the home into the public sphere, blurring the boundary between public and private, gays and lesbians also claimed a right to "sexual citizenship," a right to be incorporated as members of the polity without being forced to hide their sexual identities within a "private" sphere.[16]

This reconfiguration of citizenship, however, can easily be perceived as threatening to republican and ethno-nationalist ideas about citizenship. As Leti Volpp explains, women's reproductive capacities are central to those ideas; women reproduce citizens. They are thus "the symbolic center and boundary marker of the nation."[17] The emphasis that the republican and ethno-nationalist conceptions place on birth and lineage as signifiers of citizenship demonstrates the importance of women's reproductive function

---

[13] ARENDT, *supra* note 7, at 73.

[14] RUTH LISTER, CITIZENSHIP: FEMINIST PERSPECTIVES 125 (2003); *see also* BEYOND CITIZENSHIP: FEMINISM AND THE TRANSFORMATION OF BELONGING (Sasha Roseneil ed. 2013).

[15] *See* LISTER, *supra* note 14, at 126.

[16] *See* SHANE PHELAN, SEXUAL STRANGERS: GAYS, LESBIANS, AND DILEMMAS OF CITIZENSHIP (2001); *see also* Leti Volpp, *Feminist, Sexual and Queer Citizenship*, in THE OXFORD HANDBOOK OF CITIZENSHIP 153, 167–71 (Shachar et al. eds. 2017).

[17] *See* Volpp, *supra* note 16, at 160.

to citizenship. Women "represent the nation's purity and honor" and as such, their bodies are "sites of conflict about national cultural identity."[18] As Volpp observes, the fear of "anchor babies," or pregnant women entering the United States in order to give birth to American citizens, is a fear that women's reproductive capacity can be used to undermine national borders and national identity.[19] For that reason, women's bodies and especially their reproductive functions are subject to tight control, as our ceaseless political controversies over abortion attest. The insistence among feminists that reproductive rights are essential to women's citizenship thus poses a conflict with this more primordial idea of citizenship.

That primordial idea of citizenship has reached a crescendo under Donald Trump. As globalization and mechanization have hollowed out once well-paying manufacturing jobs, many men in declining rust belt areas lost their status as breadwinners, causing anxieties about their own masculinity and resentment toward society's demographic and cultural changes, including changing ideas about women's role in society. Men accustomed to predominance in the social and cultural sphere outside the home were scandalized by occurrences such as an all-female reboot of *Ghostbusters* and the election of several young minority women to Congress. These men were obviously drawn to Donald Trump, who in addition to targeting globalization, racial minorities, and immigrants, was the ultimate symbol of male chauvinism, a thrice-married philanderer who boasted of his sexual assaults while promising to punish women who sought abortions.

In short, once the liberal idea of citizenship that long predominated at the local level seeped into the national sphere, it undermined the republican and ethno-nationalist foundations of federal citizenship, triggering an immense political backlash and an effort to reinstate those foundations in a most vulgar fashion. This same trend is evident as well in our other case studies.

7.3 NONCITIZEN RESIDENTS AND CITIZENSHIP

In our current political environment, there are few issues more polarizing throughout the world than immigration and the status of noncitizens within the state. As was the case with the incorporation of women as national citizens, the controversy over immigration has been spurred at least in part by the way that globalization has caused the liberal model of local citizenship to invade the national level, as noncitizen residents have increasingly

---

[18] *Id.* at 160–61.
[19] *See id.* at 161.

attained many of the rights of federal citizens on liberal grounds. The idea of a "noncitizen citizen," while a tolerable oxymoron at the local level, has threatened to undermine the very idea of federal citizenship.

Chapter 5 explained that while noncitizens were considered unsuited for national citizenship because of their questionable loyalties, they have often been granted the incidents of local citizenship because local citizenship is about interest and mobility, not loyalty, and all local residents share similar interests in the enjoyment of municipal services regardless of their immigration status. As a practical matter, because immigrant labor is mobile and cities are in constant competition with each other for the economic benefits of that labor, cities have been eager to extend the benefits of local citizenship to noncitizens as a way of luring immigrants to settle there. As local citizenship has expanded to encompass noncitizens, however, advocates have been careful to emphasize the distinction between local and federal citizenship in order to ensure that federal citizenship's foundation in cultural identity and civic allegiance is not diminished. For example, advocates of local noncitizen suffrage often stress that local elections do not implicate questions of ultimate allegiance because they are primarily about the common interests among consumers of municipal services. According to one such advocate: "While my Canadian or Brazilian neighbors and I may have different interests or approaches on international issues like acid rain or regional trade, we presumably have identical interests in efficient garbage collection, good public schools, speedy road repair, and so on."[20]

Today, echoing the trajectory of woman suffrage, the boundary between local and federal citizenship as it pertains to noncitizens is collapsing. Globalization is placing pressure on nation-states to grant the benefits of federal citizenship, as local governments long have, on the basis of residence rather than identity. As goods and people move freely across borders, nation-states now face the same competition for mobile labor and capital that cities have confronted for centuries. Desirable, highly skilled immigrants carry multiple passports and can "vote with their feet" in choosing a nation-state in which to locate. As Aihwa Ong writes, "Although citizenship is conventionally thought of as based on political rights and participation within a

---

[20] Jamin B. Raskin, *Legal Aliens, Local Citizens: The Historical, Constitutional, and Theoretical Meanings of Alien Suffrage*, 141 U. Pa. L. Rev. 391, 1452 (1993). Raskin, a resident of Takoma Park and Congressman from Maryland, previously represented a district including Takoma Park in the Maryland state legislature and was one of the advocates for extending voting rights to noncitizens there.

sovereign state, globalization has made economic calculation a major element in diasporan subjects' choice of citizenship, as well as the ways nation-states redefine immigration laws."[21] States now find, as cities did ages ago, that they can "win" the competition for global labor by offering up the prospect of citizenship, or at least the tangible benefits that typically accompany it, to desirable immigrants. Ayelet Shachar explains that many states have responded to the global market for skilled immigrant labor and immigrant money by essentially putting citizenship up for sale.[22] The United States and several other countries offer an expedited pathway to citizenship for those who make substantial investments in that nation's economy or participate in the high-skilled labor market. According to Ong, citizenship has become "flexible," adapted by nation-states as necessary to lure desirable immigrants and understood by migrants themselves as purely transactional. Shachar observes that the rise of "citizenship for sale" marks a harrowing transformation in the nature of citizenship "from 'sacred' bond to marketable 'commodity.'"[23] Of course, *local* citizenship has long been seen as a commodity one could purchase by acquiring residence, so the trend Shachar identifies represents one way in which federal citizenship is transforming to resemble local citizenship.

For immigrants without desired skills or money, of course, border migration hardly works as smoothly. Though there is an enormous demand in the United States for low-wage workers, the politics of expressly permitting large numbers of poor people of color to cross the Mexican border into the United States has meant that these immigrants must be kept in a permanent in-between status, formally excluded but informally encouraged to come and work.[24] Nevertheless, liberal ideas about natural equality have placed pressure on nation-states to grant benefits of citizenship to all residents, even undocumented immigrants. Where cases like *Plyler* v. *Doe*[25] recognized that residence within the community entitled noncitizens to social rights of local citizenship such as education, international law and norms of governance

---

[21] Aihwa Ong, Flexible Citizenship: The Cultural Logics of Transnationality 112 (1999).

[22] Ayelet Shachar, *Citizenship for Sale*, in The Oxford Handbook of Citizenship, *supra* note 16, at 789.

[23] *Id.* at 792.

[24] On our ambivalent attitudes towards "illegal" immigrants, see Mae M. Ngai, Impossible Subjects: Illegal Aliens and the Making of Modern America 2, 266 (2004) (noting Americans' "schizophrenic attitude towards undocumented immigrants"); Bonnie Honig, Democracy and the Foreigner (2001) (exploring ambivalent attitudes of Americans toward immigrants).

[25] 457 U.S. 202 (1982).

now impose obligations on nation-states to accord certain basic rights to all residents within their territory, irrespective of nationality.[26] In most places, immigrants have the same rights to access the courts, housing and labor markets, and others, often regardless of immigration status. According to David Jacobson, "citizenship today is less about national self-determination and more a vehicle for protecting individual human rights."[27] Yasemin Soysal argues that the incorporation of human rights norms into national law means that we are moving toward a "postnational" citizenship based on the individual rights of the person rather than nationality, and distributed by nation-states to all who are present within their territory.[28] Essentially, the liberal idea that all residents are entitled to the incidents of citizenship has been scaled up from the local to the federal level.[29]

The pressure to extend the benefits of citizenship to all residents also comes from within. As immigrants have come into the United States, immigrant communities have grown and become more politically powerful. They have increasingly flexed their muscles, demanding more humane immigration policies as well as distinctive cultural rights.[30] At the same time, Americans have become increasingly uncomfortable with the idea of a permanent underclass. It is partly for this reason, of course, that so many cities and states have chosen to confer many of the benefits of citizenship on noncitizens. But what began at the sub-federal level did not stay there, as immigration advocates pushed laws like the DREAM Act that would give certain unauthorized immigrants a path to citizenship. Though the DREAM Act was defeated by a Republican filibuster, the Obama administration's Deferred Action for Childhood Arrivals (DACA) and Deferred Action for Parents of Americans (DAPA) programs were efforts to confer a citizen-like status on unauthorized residents by removing their vulnerability to immigration enforcement actions. Even the Trump Administration has run into both legal and political problems trying to repeal these programs. In sum, federal citizenship is evolving to reflect both market liberalism and liberal humanitarian ideals about equality.

---

[26] *See* Yasemin Nuhoğlu Soysal, Limits of Citizenship 189–91 (1994).

[27] David Jacobson, Rights across Borders: Immigration and the Decline of Citizenship 70 (1996).

[28] *See* Soysal, *supra* note 26, at 136–62.

[29] *See generally* Peter Spiro, Beyond Citizenship: American Identity after Globalization 81–108 (2008) (describing ways in which residence has become more important than citizenship for acquiring rights).

[30] *See, e.g., id.* at 93–94 (describing numerous ways that noncitizens can exercise political influence).

As the distinction between citizens and noncitizens has blurred, nation-states have attempted to shore up the distinction by setting aside some rights exclusively for citizens, particularly the right to participate in politics. For a variety of reasons, as explained earlier, suffrage has increasingly come to be seen as synonymous with citizenship. Accordingly, while nation-states have conferred a wide variety of economic and social benefits on noncitizen residents, many continue to limit the franchise and other aspects of public life to citizens. In the United States, noncitizens are prohibited from voting in every state as well as in federal elections.

The use of political participation as a strict dividing line between citizens and noncitizens will become more challenging, however, as immigrants continue to be integrated into our economic and social life. Jamin Raskin argues that "[t]he possibilities for exploiting displaced persons are too great if we make capital and labor mobile but political rights immobile. We cannot treat the world as a global economic village but define it as a collection of remote islands for the purposes of political participation."[31] In a Marxian vein, Raskin implies that it is inevitable for the "private" sphere of the economy to invade the "public" sphere of the state, and for the liberal conception of citizenship to overturn the ethno-nationalist conception. Indeed, as Yasemin Soysal notes, there is a growing movement to recognize that noncitizen residents are entitled to the franchise because "voting rights are human rights" – the motto of a voting rights campaign in Austria.[32]

Raskin's argument is especially interesting because, in the very same article, he distinguishes municipal suffrage from national suffrage on the familiar grounds that municipalities are primarily concerned with quotidian things like "good schools, public services and transportation," and he acknowledges that the arguments for citizen suffrage at the federal level are different and more complex. But he also anticipates, and celebrates, that what begins at the municipal level will ultimately undermine federal citizenship altogether, writing of his hope that "the spread of local alien suffrage would sufficiently relax the global ideological hold of nationalism as to make people all over the world comfortable with the idea of making voting rights mobile between nation-states."[33] In short, Raskin sees liberal local citizenship as an opening move toward destroying ethno-nationalism in a global age of population mobility. His argument thus confirms the fears of those who believe that granting local voting rights for noncitizens is the "camel's nose under the

---

[31] Raskin, *supra* note 20, at 1460.
[32] See SOYSAL, *supra* note 26, at 154.
[33] Raskin, *supra* note 20, at 1468, 1469.

tent" that will eventually upend national citizenship.[34] Once we permit economic and political life to become enmeshed, they will be difficult to disentangle. That is, indeed, exactly what Raskin appears to intend in advocating for noncitizen voting at the local level, for the local is the gateway through which we allow economic life to invade political life. This disruption of the public/private distinction, as globalization forces economic issues into the public sphere, is precisely what Marx presaged in warning that liberal citizenship posited an "unreal" separation between the public sphere of the state and the private sphere of material concerns.

Needless to say, the invasion of the private sphere of the market into the public sphere of the state is profoundly destabilizing to our ideas about citizenship, and in different ways troubling to people on all sides of the political spectrum. For one thing, according to Shachar, the idea of "citizenship for sale" offends our republican and nationalist notions that citizenship is supposed to be about *political* rather than market relations, that citizenship "is expected to both reflect and generate notions of participation, co-governance, risk-sharing, and some measure of solidarity among those constituting the body politic."[35] For another, while the increasing commodification of citizenship liberates people from being stratified by the accidents of birth and identity, it substitutes wealth and mobility in their place as the principal lines of stratification. As we have seen in the case of local citizenship, where borders are relatively porous mobility becomes a proxy for wealth, as those with resources can move with ease across borders, settling wherever they find most attractive. In this era of globalization, people with mobility are generally moving away from declining rural and manufacturing areas and toward the urban areas that are the hubs of the new global knowledge-based economy, leaving people with obsolete job skills and little education stuck in deteriorating places.[36]

The resurgence of ethno-nationalism on the national political scene in the last few years can well be called the revolt of the immobile against the mobile. Those who have been left behind by the new global economy resent that

---

[34] *See* Ron Hayduk, Democracy for All 126 (2006) (quoting US Senator Dianne Feinstein).
[35] Shachar, *supra* note 16, at 805.
[36] *See* Alana Semuels, *The Graying of Rural America*, CityLab (Jun. 2, 2016), http://www.citylab.com/housing/2016/06/the-graying-of-rural-america/485288/ [https://perma.cc/9MAQ-TFN8] (on rural population loss); Laura Meckler & Dante Chinni, *City vs. Country: How Where We Live Deepens the Nation's Political Divide*, Wall St. J. (Mar. 21, 2014, 7:45 AM), http://www.wsj.com/articles/SB10001424052702303636404579395532755485004 [https://perma.cc/9AEQ-556E] (describing how loss of manufacturing jobs in rural areas has led to population exodus and insulation from cultural change).

citizenship has been redefined to advantage those with mobility, and they lash out against those who are the most visible symbols of a mobile society, immigrants.[37] Their reaction is to retrench a definition of citizenship deeply rooted in place and a fixed sense of identity. Donald Trump's victory in the US Presidential election was powered largely by white people in rural and smaller metropolitan areas who believe themselves to be "losers" under globalization, and Trump fed into that resentment by targeting immigrants, racial minorities, trade, and everything to do with cities.[38] One signature attribute of the Trump administration has been a drive to firm up the distinction between citizens and noncitizens. As discussed in Chapter 2, the Trump administration's cruel and arbitrary treatment of different groups of immigrants and would-be immigrants, including a confusing quasi-repeal of the DACA and DAPA executive orders, efforts to change standards for legal immigration, separation of immigrant families at the border, targeting of sanctuary cities, the Muslim ban, and so forth, should be seen as part of a grand performative effort to shore up the salience of citizenship by demonstrating the precarious status of noncitizens.[39] No one today would argue, as the great scholar and Holocaust refugee Alexander Bickel once did, that citizenship is an irrelevant status.[40] And that seems to be the point.

7.4 LANDOWNERS, MOBILE CAPITAL, AND CITIZENSHIP

As globalization has enhanced labor mobility, placing pressure on nation-states to give many of the trappings of citizenship to immigrants, it has similarly enhanced *capital* mobility. Nation-states have accordingly felt

---

[37] *See generally* KATHERINE J. CRAMER, THE POLITICS OF RESENTMENT (2016) (describing "rural consciousness" in Wisconsin that drives political participation, characterized by resentment of perceived urban values, antipathy toward government, and racist attitudes); HONIG, *supra* note 24, at 80–98 (discussing how immigrants are perceived, and resented, as symbols of a mobile consumer culture).

[38] *See* Ashley Jardina, WHITE IDENTITY POLITICS 207–11 (2019) (observing that globalization enhanced the sense among Trump's white supporters that the white race was losing status); James Surowiecki, *Losers!*, NEW YORKER (June 6 & 13, 2016), http://www.newyorker.com/magazine/2016/06/06/losers-for-trump [https://perma.cc/VS6F-4QMR] (noting that Trump's campaign was driven by a sense of loss among his supporters).

[39] *See* Adam Serwer, *The Cruelty is the Point*, THE ATLANTIC (Oct. 3, 2018), https://www.theatlantic.com/ideas/archive/2018/10/the-cruelty-is-the-point/572104/ (arguing that Trump's policies of inflicting suffering on innocent groups of people are designed to send a message to his white male supporters that they are the only ones entitled to rights).

[40] *See* ALEXANDER BICKEL, THE MORALITY OF CONSENT 33, 36 (1975); *see also* SPIRO, *supra* note 29, at 159 (arguing that citizenship had lost significance and that "[t]he real prize is legal residency, not citizenship").

pressure to confer many of the benefits of citizenship on bearers of mobile capital, most controversially including artificial "persons" like corporations. The recognition of corporations as citizens, described in this section, represents another invasion of liberal ideas about citizenship, long prevalent at the local level, into the ethno-nationalist sphere of federal citizenship. As we saw in Chapter 6, landowners' ease of mobility within metropolitan regions and the intense competition among neighboring municipalities for scarce revenue has forced many cities to confer a citizenship status upon landowners in order to lure or keep them within the jurisdiction. The extension of such citizenship rights has often been justified on the familiar grounds that local citizenship is more about interest and mobility than nationality. The new phenomenon of corporate citizenship demonstrates a similar movement underway at the national level. Corporations have no loyalty to any nation or civic ideal; their sole purpose is to increase wealth for shareholders. Indeed, when consumer advocate Ralph Nader asked the CEOs of America's largest corporations if they would show some appreciation for the government that showers them with subsidies by calling for the Pledge of Allegiance to be recited at their annual shareholders' meeting, most rejected the request out of hand, many of them likening the request to a "loyalty oath."[41] So, when the Supreme Court held in *Citizens United* v. *Federal Election Commission*[42] that corporations could spend unlimited sums of money influencing elections, the sacrosanct process that is often equated with citizenship, Americans on all sides of the political spectrum were left wondering what it means to be a citizen.

The expansion of citizenship rights to corporations culminating in *Citizens United* did not happen overnight but evolved over a long period of time, punctuated by the pressures of globalization. By the 1830s, corporations were becoming powerful and, where once they had mostly operated within their states of incorporation, now sought to do business across state lines. These corporations often found that they were subjected to discriminatory treatment by state legislatures who favored in-state interests over out-of-state concerns. When one such corporation, the Bank of Augusta, complained to the Supreme Court that this sort of discrimination amounted to a denial of the "privileges and immunities" of citizenship, it found a very hostile audience. The courts of the Jacksonian age were highly suspicious of increasing corporate power, which they denounced as the result "privilege" and "monopoly."

---

[41] *See* SAMUEL HUNTINGTON, WHO ARE WE? THE CHALLENGE TO AMERICA'S NATIONAL IDENTITY 7 (2004).
[42] 558 U.S. 310 (2010).

In *Bank of Augusta* v. *Earle*,[43] the Supreme Court held that corporations were not citizens and therefore not entitled to the protections of the privileges and immunities clause.[44]

Less than fifty years later, the Court began reversing course, recognizing that corporations did indeed have many of the rights of citizens. Technological advancements in society and, most importantly, the emergence of the railroads as the most significant businesses in America meant that the United States was rapidly becoming an integrated economic market. It was widely believed that the railroads had measurably improved the quality of life for Americans, and the restrictions the Jacksonian courts had placed on corporations doing business outside their state seemed anachronistic.[45] In addition, the Fourteenth Amendment now extended many constitutional protections beyond "citizens" to "persons." In the famous *Santa Clara*[46] case in 1886, the Supreme Court declared that corporations were legal persons under the Constitution. During this same era, the Court significantly scaled back the impact of the *Bank of Augusta* decision, finding that the Fourteenth Amendment's equal protection clause as well as the dormant commerce clause prohibited states from discriminating against out-of-state corporations. In effect, corporations now enjoyed the same rights under these clauses to be free of discrimination that citizens enjoyed under the privileges and immunities clause.[47] As we recall, *Graham* v. *Richardson*[48] conferred upon immigrants a similar right of interstate mobility under the equal protection clause in the guise of the "right to travel," pointedly denying that the right to travel pertained only to citizens under the privileges and immunities clauses. In short, the expansion of constitutional rights to "persons" allowed two very different classes of noncitizens – immigrants and corporations – to enjoy rights once reserved exclusively for citizens.

But the Court remained hesitant to extend the full benefits of citizenship to corporations. While extending some Constitutional protections to corporations, such as protections against unlawful searches and seizures under the Fourth Amendment, the Court withheld others, like the right against self-incrimination under the 5th Amendment. According to Morton Horwitz, the decision highlighted "the Court's continuing reluctance to entirely personify

---

[43]   38 U.S. 519 (1839).
[44]   On the early treatment of corporations, see ADAM WINKLER: WE THE CORPORATIONS: HOW AMERICAN BUSINESSES WON THEIR CIVIL RIGHTS 90–103 (2018).
[45]   *See id.* at 103–10; 140–43.
[46]   Santa Clara County v. Southern Pac. R.R, 118 U.S. 394 (1886).
[47]   *See* WINKLER, *supra* note 44, at 145–46.
[48]   403 U.S. 365 (1971).

the corporation . . . "[49] Most significantly, when Congress prohibited corporations from making financial contributions to elections, the courts found this to be a permissible restriction on corporate freedom because participation in the political process was reserved to citizens. According to one federal court, corporations "are not citizens of the United States, and, so far as the franchise is concerned, must at all times be held subservient to the government and the citizenship of which it is composed." The court found that spending money on elections was one of the principal "means of participation in the government,"[50] and so, like the right of suffrage, was limited to citizens. As in the case of immigrants, courts were able to preserve the basic ethno-nationalist conception of political community in the face of the liberalizing pressures of the marketplace by placing some of the essential attributes of citizenship off limits to noncitizens.

As Marx predicted, however, capital is not easily contained within the private sphere of the market. In Chapter 6 we saw how mobile capital elides the public/private distinction and introduces liberal ideas about citizenship into the ethno-nationalist sphere of the state. Though the Supreme Court's "one person/one vote" doctrine is careful to distinguish the public sphere of politics from the private sphere of the market, that distinction is persistently undermined by a variety of judicially crafted exceptions that allow local citizenship to be based on financial self-interest. With the approval of the courts, cities have made landownership a de facto prerequisite for local citizenship, using their zoning authority to ensure that only those with adequate means can purchase residence, and therefore citizenship, in the community. As Marx explained, the separation of the public and private spheres is "unreal" because the economic concerns of the private sphere constantly threaten to enter the public. In short, the purportedly "public" sphere of citizenship is itself a disguised extension of the private sphere.

In the same way that mobile capital eroded the distinction between public and private in local citizenship, today it is similarly eroding that distinction when it comes to federal citizenship. The state's efforts to give corporations only select trappings of citizenship, and thus to contain capital within the private sphere, have proven utterly fruitless. As that has happened, money bleeds into the sphere of the state, and liberalism overtakes ethno-nationalist and republican ideas of citizenship. Nowhere is this more evident than in the

---

[49] Morton J. Horwitz, Santa Clara *Revisited: The Development of Corporate Theory*, 88 W. Va. L. Rev. 173, 182 (1986).

[50] *See* United States v. United States Brewers Ass'n, 239 F. 163 (W.D. Pa. 1916); Winkler, *supra* note 44, at 224–26.

infamous *Citizens United* case, which broke with Progressive-era precedent and held that corporations have a First Amendment right to spend unlimited sums of money influencing political campaigns. Much like the Court's application of the one person, one vote rule to local elections, *Citizens United* is predicated on a distinction between the public and private spheres that collapses almost as quickly as it is articulated. Relying on the precedent of *Buckley* v. *Valeo*,[51] *Citizens United* distinguishes campaign *contributions* from campaign *expenditures*. According to the Court, contributions are efforts to influence government decisions, and can therefore be limited to prevent the occurrence or appearance of *quid pro quo* corruption. But expenditures, if they are uncoordinated with a candidate's campaign, are simply expressions of opinion protected by the First Amendment.[52] In essence, the Court drew a distinction between the private sphere of money and the public sphere of politics. Expenditures on political speech fall entirely within the private sphere of money and do not risk corrupting the political sphere as long as the money is not directed toward, or coordinated with, a candidate's campaign. Money is free to call the tune within the private sphere because that sphere is walled off from the public sphere of politics.

However, the distinction between expenditures and contributions has failed to prevent money from invading the public sphere of politics. Just a few years before *Citizens United*, in *McConnell* v. *Federal Election Commission*,[53] the Supreme Court upheld portions of the very same law invalidated in *Citizens United*, the McCain-Feingold Bipartisan Campaign Reform Act. *McConnell* extensively detailed the way that supposedly uncoordinated expenditures had influenced politicians in the performance of their public duties. The Court chronicled, for instance, how the major political parties sold access to public officials with "menus of opportunities," in which the degree of access escalated as the contribution to the party increased.[54] Nevertheless, in *Citizens United*, the Court reaffirmed its commitment to the expenditure/contribution divide, stating clearly that expenditures, regardless of their size, can never corrupt politicians.[55]

As Zephyr Teachout argues, *Citizens United* turns on a radical transformation of "corruption" from a republican conception into a liberal one. Where republican ideology had understood corruption broadly to mean private

---

[51] 424 U.S. 1 (1976).
[52] 558 U.S. 310, 345–47, 356–61.
[53] 540 U.S. 93 (2003).
[54] *Id.* at 151.
[55] 558 U.S. at 360 ("[I]ndependent expenditures do not lead to, or create the appearance of, *quid pro quo* corruption.").

interest invading the public sphere, *Citizens United* adopts a shrunken liberal meaning of the term, which assumes that private interest runs rampant within the public sphere and holds public officials to only the very minimal standard of avoiding an explicit exchange of government services for something of value.[56] According to Teachout, *Citizens United* is animated above all by the "belief that the corrupting influence of money is moot because everyone in politics is already on the take."[57] And thus, with the collapse of the private sphere of money into the public sphere of politics, the invasion of a liberal idea of citizenship into the sphere of republican and ethno-nationalist citizenship, corporations were granted one of the key rights of American citizens, the right to influence elections.[58]

While *Citizens United* conferred this incident of citizenship on corporations, globalization's enhancement of capital mobility has given corporations leverage to make additional demands on the state, such as lower taxes and lighter regulation.[59] This represents another way in which increasing corporate power in an age of market liberalization appears to be diminishing the significance of nation-state citizenship. As Darren Rosenblum notes, corporations use "inversion" – merger with an overseas firm – to become "traveling corporations" that can avoid taxes by magically changing their home country. According to Rosenblum, inversions demonstrate the weakened power of nation-state borders and the limited ability of nation-states to protect their citizens against labor and capital mobility.[60]

As we have seen in the previous section, many Americans have not taken kindly to the idea of corporate citizenship because it means that money and

---

[56] Zephyr Teachout, Corruption in America: From Benjamin Franklin's Snuff Box to Citizens United 8–9; 229–64 (2014).

[57] *Id.* at 9.

[58] Notably, federal law permits legal permanent residents and minors to spend money influencing elections, even to make contributions directly to candidates. Thus, spending money on elections is perceived as distinct from voting. See 52 U.S.C. § 30121; 11 CFR 110.20

[59] See, e.g., Debora L. Spar & David B. Yoffie, *A Race to the Bottom or Governance from the Top*, in Coping with Globalization 31 (Aseem Prakish & Jeffrey A. Hart eds., 2000) (arguing that increased capital mobility leads nation-states into a "race to the bottom" as they compete for capital). There is some disagreement about whether capital mobility leads to a "race to the bottom" or conversely a "race to the top," but even the "race to the top" theories recognize that mobile capital is dictating terms. For example, incumbent businesses in a regulated industry may favor maintaining regulatory standards that give them a competitive advantage. See David Vogel & Robert A. Kagan, *Introduction*, in Dynamics of Regulatory Change: How Globalization Affects National Regulatory Policies 1 (David Vogel & Robert A. Kagan eds. 2004).

[60] See Darren Rosenblum, *The Futility of Walls: How Traveling Corporations Threaten State Sovereignty*, 93 Tulane L. Rev. 645 (2019).

mobility become the most sacred values. Trade, long the lifeblood of commercial cities along with immigrant labor, is now seen as antithetical to prosperity, and trade barriers become the complement to the physical barriers preventing immigrants from entering the country.[61] The Trump administration has imposed an escalating series of tariffs on Chinese imports, which appear to be popular with Trump's voters despite the fact that those voters are the ones most economically harmed by the tariffs. Meanwhile, cases like *Citizens United* induced a widespread cynicism about the role of corporate money in politics that allowed demagogues like Donald Trump to rise above the pack of bought-off politicians by cultivating the appearance of authenticity through the clearly unmediated use of social media and unhinged populist rallies.

Multinational corporations have often been the targets of this populist rage (even as the "populist" politicians continue to favor them with tax breaks) because they are increasingly perceived as being at the vanguard of our mobile liberal urban culture that is weakening the meaning of citizenship. As I mentioned earlier, corporations are increasingly eschewing any loyalty to their home countries. Moreover, as corporations increasingly locate their headquarters in cosmopolitan urban centers, they have become harbingers of liberal urban values. As Tom Lin describes, in recent years corporations have greatly stepped up their social activism, particularly around socially liberal political causes. For example, companies like Google, Apple, and Lyft pressured North Carolina into a partial repeal of its anti-transgender "bathroom bill," banks such as Citigroup and Bank of America ceased doing business with clients that manufacture military-style firearms or sell high-capacity magazines, and companies like Starbucks, Nike, Facebook, and Amazon have openly opposed several Trump immigration initiatives like the Muslim ban and the repeal of the DACA and DAPA protections. As these global corporations have fought Trump's efforts to more narrowly define citizenship along ethno-nationalist terms, Trump supporters reacted furiously by smashing their Keurig coffee machines and cutting up their Nike socks, demonstrating contempt for the urban corporate culture.[62] Among political liberals as well, the question lingers why one's rights as a citizen must apparently depend on the willingness of multinational corporations to go to bat for them.

---

[61] On the politics of trade, see KIMBERLY CLAUSING, OPEN: THE PROGRESSIVE CASE FOR FREE TRADE, IMMIGRATION AND GLOBAL CAPITAL 92–114 (2019).

[62] *See* Tom C. W. Lin, *Incorporating Social Activism*, 98 B. U. L. REV. 1535, 1547–58 (2018).

7.5 CONCLUSION: LOCAL CITIZENSHIP'S FUTURE?

In each case discussed in this chapter, a crisis in the meaning of citizenship occurred because what was once a distinctively local approach to citizenship invaded the sphere of federal citizenship. For that reason, the nationalist backlash against the changing nature of citizenship has often manifested in the form of vilifying localities, cities in particular. Local governments' willingness to confer citizenship on the basis of interest and mobility embodies the threat that globalization poses to federal citizenship. Indeed, the city has played a key role in each of the three cases discussed in this chapter. Woman suffrage and the rise of the citizen-consumer were spurred by an urbanizing society that fundamentally changed women's role in society and catalyzed a new era of mass consumption. Cities are critical nodes in the global knowledge-based economy that requires open borders; immigrants and corporations have both found friendly environments in cities that benefit from their presence. The re-awakening of a nostalgic vision of citizenship based on blood and belonging thus leads to the demonization of cities, with the sanctuary city becoming the pivotal flashpoint in a reckoning over the meaning of citizenship. Donald Trump ran a Presidential campaign that, despite his status as a lifelong New Yorker, was anti-urban to its core, and he has since persistently attacked cities like Chicago and San Francisco and fomented outrage against sanctuary cities.[63]

That cities have taken a central role in the debate over citizenship is not surprising because, as Rogers Smith states, cities have always been "political symbols," for better or for worse, of what our political community could be.[64] Many nationalist movements have demonized cities as the Trojan horses within that corrode the nation's authentic spirit by introducing the forces of

---

[63] *See* David Dudley, *The GOP Is Afraid of My City*, CITYLAB (July 22, 2016), http://www.citylab .com/crime/2016/07/the-gop-is-afraid-of-baltimore-chicago-detroit-st-louis/492671 [https://perma .cc/PWG3-QDUQ] (arguing that Trump's anti-urban platform is aimed at scaring rural voters who are terrified of cities); Vann R. Newkirk II, *Mayors vs. Trump*, CITYLAB (July 27, 2016), http://www.citylab.com/politics/2016/07/cities-mayors-trump/493211 [https://perma.cc/DQ9F-43V6] (observing that Trump's message on crime, immigration, and other issues is essentially anti-urban); Josh Stephens, *Trump to Cities: You're Dead to Me*, PLANETIZEN (July 26, 2016, 8:00 AM), http://www.planetizen.com/node/87620/trump-cities-you're-dead-me [https://perma .cc/ANF8-NR57] (comparing Trump's "law and order" message to its Nixonian forerunner in the 1970s and noting the anti-urban roots of the message). Rumore, *When Trump Talks about Chicago, We Track It*, CHI. TRIBUNE (Mar. 28, 2019 8:10 AM), https://www.chicagotribune .com/news/local/breaking/ct-trump-tweets-quotes-chicago-htmlstory.html.

[64] Rogers M. Smith, *American Cities and American Citizenship*, in URBAN CITIZENSHIP AND AMERICAN DEMOCRACY 211, 214 (Amy Bridges & Michael Javen Fortner eds. 2016).

modernity, capitalism, and homogenization. On the other hand, and for that same reason, many on the political left see cities as the great hope to save democracy against the horrors of ethnic nationalism.[65] According to Benjamin Barber, cities are inherently cooperative and cosmopolitan because they are dependent on friendly trade relations with other cities. "[C]ooperation and linguistic facility as well as cosmopolitanism and mobility are virtues that benefit cities as cultural, economic, and trading enterprises."[66] Cities' interdependence immunizes them against ethnic nationalism, which "affords integral unity only by diminishing or nullifying the 'other' or the 'stranger' just the other side of the common border."[67]

There is some irony in this celebration of cities because for years left-leaning urbanists have bemoaned local governments' subjection to the very liberal forces now championed as an antidote to nationalism – a citizenship defined by money, interest, and mobility. For example, Jerry Frug and David Barron lament that cities, forced into a zero-sum competition for revenue by the fragmentation of metropolitan regions and a political and legal structure that leaves cities constantly desperate for money, have ignored the demands of residents as they chase dollars from tourists and global financiers.[68] The philosopher Michael Sandel bemoans the ways cities have degraded themselves with "privatization," citing examples such as soda companies sponsoring educational programs in exchange for exclusive marketing agreements and police vehicles decked out in advertisements like NASCAR race cars. Sandel analogizes these practices to immigration policies like those described by Shachar, in which citizenship is placed "up for sale." In all of these cases, Sandel argues, substituting a market for a nonmarket interaction corrupts the relationship because it expresses an attitude that what is being exchanged is no longer a civic engagement but a commodity transaction. Ultimately, he asks: "Do we have a market economy, or a market society?"[69]

---

[65] *See* Nilanjana Roy, *Cities Offer Sanctuary against the Insularity of Nationalism*, Fin. Times (Apr. 4, 2017), https://www.ft.com/content/b54093f0-191f-11e7-9c35-0dd2cb31823a; Robert Muggah & Misha Glenny, *Populism is Poison. Plural Cities are the Antidote*, World Econ. Forum (Jan. 4, 2017), https://www.weforum.org/agenda/2017/01/populism-is-poison-plural-cities-are-the-antidote/; Benjamin Barber, *In the Age of Donald Trump, the Resistance Will be Localized*, The Nation (Jan. 18, 2017), https://www.thenation.com/article/in-the-age-of-donald-trump-the-resistance-will-be-localized/.

[66] *See* Benjamin R. Barber, If Mayors Ruled the World: Dysfunctional Nations, Rising Cities 116 (2013).

[67] *Id.* at 115.

[68] *See* Gerald E. Frug & David J. Barron, City Bound 141–84 (2008).

[69] *See* Michael Sandel, What Money Can't Buy 9, 35, 139–40 (2013).

The most troubling aspect of liberal local citizenship, as I discuss further in the next part is surely its treatment of America's racial minorities. One defining feature of our metropolitan regions is a persistent pattern of interlocal inequality and racial segregation. The liberal rhetoric of mobility and choice has always belied the ugly reality that mobility for some has been premised on suppressing mobility for others. Zoning regulations, as described in Chapters 5 and 6, are often justified in neutral terms as allowing anyone to settle in the community if they can afford to acquire residence there, but in practice and often in intent these laws have entrenched patterns of racial and class segregation. That liberalism's promise of equality is undermined by its own segregatory practices is, however, often shrouded by judicial decisions that describe segregation in liberal terms as a product of individual consumer choice.[70]

We should thus take pause before celebrating the liberal nature of local citizenship as an antidote to ethno-nationalism. If liberalism promises the emancipating potential of universal human rights, it also offers the debasement of economic self-seeking and the shame of racial segregation. This paradox is well illustrated by a city like San Francisco. On one hand, the city touts its openness to all by declaring itself a "sanctuary city" and even extending voting rights to noncitizens, while on the other hand its zoning laws are so incredibly restrictive, and it produces so little new housing, that only the extremely affluent can afford to live there and most of its black population has been displaced by escalating rents.[71]

If local citizenship is to be the hope of our globally networked future, therefore, we must determine whether it is possible to place it on a foundation that avoids the perils of both liberalism and ethno-nationalism. As it turns out, and as I explore in the next part, cities have not always meekly accepted their fate as sites of liberal citizenship. In a variety of ways, they have tried (often unsuccessfully) to manage the flow of labor and capital, to create and preserve a sense of authentic community in the face of globalization, to cultivate and recognize alternative forms of identity, and to protect low-income and minority communities against exploitation. In all of these efforts, cities have attempted to create meaningful alternatives to the ethno-nationalist and liberal conceptions embodied in our predominant mode of citizenship. That mode, as I have described, is a "structure of consciousness," or a way in which elites

---

[70] *See* Jessica Trounstine, Segregation by Design: Local Politics and Inequality in American Cities 33–36, 188–89 (2018) (noting how suburban homeowners shifted from explicitly racist arguments to "colorblind" arguments of neighborhood character, property values, taxes, and the like as racial arguments became less politically palatable).

[71] *See, e.g.,* Thomas Fuller, *The Loneliness of Being Black in San Francisco*, N.Y. Times (July 20, 2016), https://www.nytimes.com/2016/07/21/us/black-exodus-from-san-francisco.html.

have organized their thinking about citizenship in order to advance the goals of the nation-state. But as I have also stressed, because this structure of consciousness is a product of elite reasoning and not a reflection of the way people actually live, it is always subject to popular contestation.

One of the key sites of contestation has been the very nature of the public/private distinction that underlies the modern idea of citizenship. As described in Chapter 1, "public" and "private" are fluid terms subject to a variety of interpretations. Our current way of thinking about citizenship uses the public/private distinction to contrast that which pertains to the state versus that which pertains to the individual, or that which concerns the whole as opposed to what concerns the particular. The public, as understood by theorists such as Jean-Jacques Rousseau, means an organic association pointed toward a single aim, the realization of a society's collective and indivisible will. The private refers to an aggregation of individuals collectively pursuing their self-interest. This division roughly corresponds to the distinction I have described between ethno-nationalist and liberal citizenship, which our legal and political tradition has implemented through a distinction between federal and local citizenship. But the public/private distinction may mean something else entirely. It can be used, for example, to contrast "[w]hat is hidden or withdrawn versus what is open, revealed, or accessible."[72] This contrast is perhaps best captured in the distinction we draw between public and private space, the former referring to places that are generally open "to the public" and the latter to places that are reserved for "private" use and off limits to the public. Indeed, according to the philosopher Phillipe Aries, the term "public" literally means "a *place* where people who do not know each other can meet and enjoy each other's company."[73] On this view, the public is not an organic national unity but its opposite, a place of spontaneous meeting of strangers – that is, a city. The city's openness, while not nationalist, is not liberal either because it arises from the very nature of urban space to throw people together rather than captivity to market logic – in fact, when spaces fall prey to market logic, they become closed. The idea of the city as a public space thus may allow us to navigate between liberalism and ethno-nationalism. I explore that possibility in the next part.

---

[72] *See* Jeff Weintraub, *The Theory and Politics of the Public/Private Distinction,* in PUBLIC AND PRIVATE IN THOUGHT AND PRACTICE 1, 5 (Jeff Weintraub & Krishan Kumar eds., 1997).

[73] *See* PHILLIPE ARIES, 3 A HISTORY OF PRIVATE LIFE 9 (1989) (emphasis added); *see also* Weintraub, *supra* note 72, at 17–20.

PART III

Race, Space, Place, and Urban Citizenship

8

A Return to Urban Citizenship?

In 1968, after a series of devastating urban riots exposed the corrosive effects of a society segregated by race and class, a commission convened by President Lyndon Johnson popularly known as the "Kerner commission" concluded that the riots were the direct product of white racism. Years of segregatory practices like discriminatory mortgage lending, bulldozing of minority neighborhoods, racially restrictive deed restrictions, and exclusionary zoning, designed to benefit white communities, had trapped black Americans in deteriorating urban ghettos. "White institutions created [the ghetto,] white institutions maintain it, and white society condones it."[1]

Embarrassed policymakers ignored the report, and just a few years later the Supreme Court came to an entirely different conclusion about the causes of segregation. In *Milliken* v. *Bradley*,[2] the Court held that a district court exceeded its equitable powers in crafting a remedy for racial segregation in the Detroit public school system by requiring Detroit's predominantly white suburbs to participate in a desegregation plan for the metropolitan area as a whole. The Court found that the suburbs bore no responsibility for the predominantly black population of the Detroit public school system, which was instead the product of "unknown and perhaps unknowable factors such as in-migration, birth rates, economic changes, or cumulative acts of private racial fears."[3] The following year, in the case of *Warth* v. *Seldin*,[4] a group of plaintiffs identifying themselves as residents or taxpayers of the city of Rochester, New York, challenged the zoning practices of a neighboring

---

[1] REPORT OF THE NATIONAL ADVISORY COMMISSION ON CIVIL DISORDERS 1 (1968) (Kerner Commission Report).

[2] 418 U.S. 717 (1974).

[3] *Id.* at 756 n.2.

[4] 422 U.S. 490 (1975).

suburban community called Penfield, which like many suburbs was zoned almost exclusively for expensive, low-density single-family housing. The plaintiffs claimed that Penfield's zoning practices directly affected them insofar as Rochester was forced to absorb the need for affordable housing that Penfield refused to accommodate, at considerable cost to Rochester's own taxpayers. The Court found, however, that the causal link between high taxes in Rochester and Penfield's zoning practices was too speculative. "Whatever may occur in Penfield, the injury complained of – increases in taxation – results only from decisions made by the appropriate Rochester authorities, who are not parties to this case."[5]

According to Richard Ford, cases like *Milliken* and *Warth* reflect the Supreme Court's belief that racial segregation is the product of private choice, rather than government action. On this view, "spatial communities are seen as marketplace commodities into which anyone with enough cash can buy entry, and the political process is understood to occur in a neutral political space and to consist of individuals who form groups for purely strategic purposes."[6] Residents "are mobile and rootless; they are rational profit maximizers and technocratic modern citizens."[7] I have previously described this view of local citizenship as "liberal," part of a tradition in which citizenship is a function of market choice, self-interest, and mobility. The liberal idea of local citizenship is epitomized by Charles Tiebout's model of local government, which perceives residents as consumer-voters who choose a place to live the same way they would buy a pair of socks at the store. But the freedom of choice and mobility offered by the liberal consumer society has never been fully available to racial minorities, especially blacks. As Regina Austin explains, blacks have often been excluded from places of white leisure like parks, theaters, beaches, and shopping centers.[8] And affluent suburbs, which epitomize our individualistic, mobile consumer society, have always been characterized by the relentless exclusion of blacks, through a combination of government policies and private prejudice. As Ford observes, the liberal/Tiebout model of citizenship "ignores the fact that the marketplace is spatially located and spatially

---

[5] *Id.* at 509.

[6] Richard Thompson Ford, *The Boundaries of Race: Political Geography in Legal Analysis*, 107 HARV. L. REV. 1841, 1888–89 (1994).

[7] *See id.; see also* Richard T. Ford, *Law's Territory (A History of Jurisdiction)*, 97 MICH. L. REV. 843, 861 (1999); Richard Thompson Ford, *Geography and Sovereignty: Jurisdictional Formation and Racial Segregation*, 49 STAN. L. REV. 1365, 1368 (1997).

[8] Regina Austin, *"Not Just for the Fun of It:" Governmental Restraints on Black Leisure, Social Inequality and the Privatization of Public Space*, 71 S. CAL. L. REV. 667, 681–84, 697 (1998). I discuss Austin's work in more depth in Chapter 10.

segregated. Racially identified spaces make movement across boundaries much more costly than this model acknowledges. With boundaries racially less permeable, racial groups have fewer choices in the community marketplace."[9]

Accordingly, Ford notes that there is another view of local spaces, which emphasizes that local borders are hard and "opaque," rather than permeable and "transparent" in the manner the Tiebout model presents them. This "opaque" view "constructs political subjects who understand themselves as – and in this sense in fact are – intimately connected in groups that are defended by territorial autonomy. This discourse encourages individuals and groups to present themselves as organically connected to other people and to territory in a way that requires jurisdictional autonomy."[10] In contrast to the Tieboutian ideal of the citizen as a footloose and capricious consumer, Ford's idea conceptualizes the citizen as someone with deep ties to the community, and citizenship as a mechanism for protecting the community against the intrusion of outside forces, whether those forces be the commodification of liberalism or the noxious structural racism of exclusionary zoning.

This Part will show that, despite the predominance of the liberal idea of local citizenship in our legal discourse, local governments have frequently sought to construct citizenship in the manner Ford describes. In recent years, for example, cities have attempted to regulate the financial institutions that caused the global recession of 2008, banned big box stores that threaten local businesses, enacted local hiring mandates, joined with other cities to enact climate change legislation, created community economic development programs to ensure capital investment in neighborhoods often overlooked by global capital, enacted rent control or condominium conversion legislation to protect traditionally disinvested neighborhoods against a flood of investment that may disrupt those communities and displace residents, and more.[11] In enacting these sorts of policies, cities are advancing an idea of citizens not as mobile consumers but as people deeply embedded in particular places and shielded by their membership within those places against the vagaries of global economic markets and institutional racism. And these cities embrace a vision of citizenship in which citizens enjoy economic and cultural rights as a community, not just the individual political or social rights that liberalism confers.

---

[9]   *See* Ford, *supra* note 6, at 1889.
[10] *See* Ford, *supra* note 7, at 899.
[11] I described many of these local efforts to address the effects of globalization in Kenneth A. Stahl, *Local Home Rule in the Time of Globalization*, 2016 BYU L. Rev. 177.

This chapter describes that vision in further detail, situating it within a body of geographical literature that emphasizes the importance of "place" in cultivating a citizenship that is not beholden to liberalism. The following three chapters then introduce three models of local citizenship that all embrace, in different ways, some version of local citizenship rooted in place and immunized against liberalism: the republican, postmodern, and differentiated citizenship models. As each chapter explores, however, cities' efforts to overthrow the liberal idea of local citizenship and implement a conception of citizenship rooted in place have frequently been rebuffed by the courts, who insist on seeing local citizenship as purely liberal in character.

8.1 A RETURN TO URBAN CITIZENSHIP?

When cities reject the liberal, Tieboutian idea of local citizenship as unmoored from the urban terrain and celebrate an idea of citizenship rooted in particular places, they are evoking, intentionally or not, a view of citizenship inspired by the French urban theorist Henri LeFebvre.[12] According to LeFebvre, the idea that cities are permeable spaces that consumers pass through with relative indifference was a product of capitalism and the modern state, which saw the republican citizenship of the ancient city-state as a threat to their centralizing ambitions and sought to destroy the vibrant civic spaces in which republican citizenship flourished. Followers of LeFebvre have accordingly argued that when urban dwellers, and particularly historically marginalized groups like women, minorities, and gays, appropriate the public spaces of the city for political struggle, social organization, or even leisure, they are in fact exercising an oppositional form of "urban citizenship," a rejection of the liberal idea of citizenship that treats urban space as a fungible commodity. According to Mark Purcell, urban citizenship is produced by "the collective daily life routines of urban dwellers," and urban space, instead of being "valued as a commodity for exchange," is "an oeuvre that is created and

---

[12] I discussed the work of LeFebvre and some of his followers in the book's introduction. For some of the key works on "urban citizenship" inspired by LeFebvre, see REMAKING URBAN CITIZENSHIP: ORGANIZATIONS, INSTITUTIONS AND THE RIGHT TO THE CITY (Michael Peter Smith & Michael McQuarrie eds. 2012); DON MITCHELL, THE RIGHT TO THE CITY: SOCIAL JUSTICE AND THE FIGHT FOR PUBLIC SPACE 140 (2003); DEMOCRACY, CITIZENSHIP AND THE GLOBAL CITY (Engin Isin ed., 2000); CITIES AND CITIZENSHIP (James Holston ed. 1999); Richard T. Ford, *City-States and Citizenship*, in CITIZENSHIP TODAY: GLOBAL PERSPECTIVES AND PRACTICES 209, 210 (T. Alexander Aleinikoff & Douglas Klusmeyer eds., 2001); Mark Purcell, *Citizenship and the Right to the Global City*, 27.3 INT'L. J. URB. & REGIONAL RESEARCH 564 (2003).

recreated every day by the quotidian practices of urban inhabitants."[13] For Don Mitchell, urban citizenship occurs when people *take* a private space and *make* it public.[14]

As described in Chapter 7, the champions of urban citizenship view the term "public" in a very different light than the policymakers and courts who constructed our prevailing conception of citizenship. Where the elites see the "public" as something deliberately created by the federal government in order to construct and police the boundaries of the nation, the urban citizenship advocates see the public as something that arises spontaneously as people socialize in urban places. The public is not the sphere of identity and closure, but a sphere of openness and sociability, the "being together of strangers," in Iris Young's evocative phrase.[15] This notion of the public "entails some common problems and common interests" but does "not create a community of shared final ends, of mutual identification and reciprocity."[16] Viewing the public sphere this way has two important implications. The first is that it promises to avoid the pitfalls of both liberal and ethno-nationalist citizenship. By embracing diversity and eschewing closure, it rejects the organic solidarity of ethno-nationalism; by conceptualizing the public as a place where people come together to socialize rather than to consume, it rejects the market orientation of liberalism. The second implication is that the idea of the public as a sphere of sociability is necessarily *urban* in nature. Only a city where people are thrown together in all their diversity can be a "public" in this sense – indeed, Young uses the term "being together of strangers" to describe the city itself. For that reason, where I have used the term "local citizenship" in describing our prevalent way of thinking about citizenship at the local level, this oppositional model is more accurately named "urban citizenship." While suburbs are in some ways the archetypes of "local citizenship" insofar as they represent the Tieboutian ideal of the mobile consumer-voters, suburbs largely lack the places for meaningful social interaction that make urban citizenship possible.

It is evident that urban citizenship is deeply tied up with the idea of *place.* Unlike the liberal Tieboutian conception of citizenship, which perceives citizens as floating through an undifferentiated realm of fungible spaces, the urban citizenship model views citizens as rooted in concrete and historically contingent places. As it happens, this distinction reflects an important

---

[13] *See* Purcell, *supra* note 12, at 578.
[14] *See* MITCHELL, *supra* note 12, at 35, 105.
[15] IRIS MARION YOUNG, JUSTICE AND THE POLITICS OF DIFFERENCE 227(1990).
[16] *Id.* at 237–39.

dichotomy described by geographers between "space" and "place." Recalling the public/private distinction, the space/place distinction proves to be a key dividing line in the debate about how urban citizenship can transcend liberalism and ethno-nationalism. Accordingly, the next section describes the space/place distinction in somewhat more detail. The following section will then relate that distinction back to urban citizenship.

8.2 SPACE AND PLACE

A place is a meaningful location, a location filled with culture, tradition, and memory. Space is a location that has been stripped of meaning, homogenized, and abstracted from all historical particularity. Space is the tax collector's map, the general plan, the administrative capital; place is the village, the home, the neighborhood. The geographer Yi-Fu Tuan says that space is where we walk or run, place is where we sit. Space is associated with reason, rational choice, and capitalism; place is perceived as pre-capitalist, primordial, sentimental. Space is individualized – it can be chopped into bits, exchanged between buyers and sellers in the market. Place is collective – it is bound up with the community's sense of identity, and cannot be divided or alienated.[17]

According to many students of geography, a signature attribute of the modern age has been for place to yield to space. On this view, according to John Agnew, space "represents the transcending of the past by overcoming the rootedness of social relations and landscape in place through mobility and the increased similarity of everyday life from place to place."[18] Three interlinked phenomena caused this transformation to occur: the rise of capitalism, the emergence of the nation-state, and globalization. First, capitalism and a money economy have turned land into a commodity. To facilitate the exchange of land for money, land needed to become "abstract, objective, homogenous, and universal."[19] Second, as the nation-state has sought to assert its authority over a vast terrain of diverse peoples, it emptied places of their sentimental meaning and imbued them with the abstraction of impersonal authority, creating "territory." According to Saskia Sassen, territorial sovereignty means that an entity has "exclusive authority over a given territory and

---

[17] *See* TIM CRESWELL, PLACE: A SHORT INTRODUCTION (2004); John A. Agnew, *Space and Place*, in THE SAGE HANDBOOK OF GEOGRAPHICAL KNOWLEDGE 316–30 (John A. Agnew & David N. Livingstone eds. 2011); YI-FU TUAN, SPACE AND PLACE (1977); DOREEN MASSEY, RACE, PLACE AND GENDER (1994).

[18] *See* Agnew, *supra* note 17, at 319.

[19] David Harvey, *Money, Time, Space and the City, in* CONSCIOUSNESS AND THE URBAN EXPERIENCE 1, 13 (1989).

at the same time this territory is constructed as coterminous with that author-ity."[20] Territory substituted impersonal relationship between the sovereign and the land for the in-kind, personal relationships that undergirded feudalism. Third and finally, the hypermobility and mass cultural homogenization of globalization have also caused space to overtake place. According to Edward Relph, extreme population mobility creates "a weakening of the identity of places to the point where they not only look alike and feel alike, but offer the same bland possibilities for experience." Globalization thus leads to "a grow-ing uniformity of landscape and a lessening diversity of places by encouraging and transmitting general and standardized tastes and fashions."[21]

At the same time, however, modernity also intensifies attachments to place because people long for the comfort of places imbued with meaning and authenticity as they lose their moorings in the world. According to David Harvey, a sense of place "gives a certain kind of 'permanence' in the midst of the fluxes and flows of urban life." Place becomes a "locus of collective memory," a site of resistance to global capitalism and the centralizing demands of the nation-state.[22] When communities attempt to assert control of their food sources, jealously guard local languages against homogenization, or prevent real estate investors from transforming neighborhood character, they are all elevating "place" over "space" in this way.

As place has become a potent source of resistance to space, the nation-state and capital investors have in turn attempted to appropriate place for their own ends. The nation-state leverages the attachment to places in order to create an idea of the nation's particularity and cultivate loyalty to itself. According to Tuan, "the sentiment that once tied people to their village, city or region had to be transferred to the larger political unit."[23] Hence, as Richard Ford writes, the state uses decentralization of power in a paradoxical fashion as a "strategy for consolidating and maintaining centralized power."[24] In addition, as cap-ital becomes more mobile, forcing different locations to compete for it, so capital becomes more sensitive to the particular qualities of specific places.

---

[20] SASKIA SASSEN, TERRITORY, AUTHORITY, RIGHTS 6 (2006).

[21] *See* EDWARD RELPH, PLACE AND PLACELESSNESS 90, 92 (1974).

[22] DAVID HARVEY, JUSTICE, NATURE, AND THE GEOGRAPHY OF DIFFERENCE 296, 306 (1996); *see also id.* at 293 ("When place becomes threatened, it becomes more meaningful to us."); Creswell, *supra* note 17, at 56.

[23] *See* Tuan, *supra* note 17, at 176–77.

[24] Ford, *supra* note 12, at 845; *see also* ROBERT SACK, PLACE, MODERNITY AND THE CONSUMER'S WORLD 92 (1992) (a nation needs a specific connection to real places, because places help define the uniqueness of the nation); JOHN AGNEW, PLACE AND POLITICS 38–39 (decentralization is a tool of centralization).

The phenomenon of the "global city" described by Sassen, in which a handful of prestigious cities can command capital's presence due to their concentration of both highly skilled and low-wage workers, is one key example of how capital's mobility actually enhances the relative importance of particular places.[25]

When the nation-state and capital institutions embraced place, however, they transformed it into something more like space, creating oxymoronic "placeless places" or "non-place urban realms."[26] Capital investors, realizing the attractions of place in an age of global mobility, have created "places of consumption," locations that evoke the authenticity of places but whose sense of place has been manufactured in order to induce consumption, such as shopping malls, faux historic districts, and soulless suburbs. Interactions with these places are inauthentic, shallow, superficial. And while each place is presented as a unique product of its local culture, they are all essentially interchangeable.[27]

Similarly, the places of the nation-state, though drawing inspiration from and grafted on authentic places, are actually artifacts created by the state to serve its centralizing ambitions. As Richard Ford describes the French modernization project, France displaced the welter of organic local dialects by grouping them into regional languages, creating "regional literary traditions when for centuries there had been only the spoken patois of rural life, different from village to village." Those who opposed the French centralization project by attempting to revive "place" thus unwittingly abetted that project by defending a French regional tradition that the modern state had invented. "The provinces were led to defend, not organic local life but an image of the organic that was itself an artifact of the centralization effort they opposed."[28]

8.3 PLACE, SPACE, AND URBAN CITIZENSHIP

Within our predominant model of citizenship, as we have seen in Parts I and II, the state is constructed as the fixed sphere of identity and solidarity, and the local is the sphere of mobility and choice. Where cities are unbounded "nodes" within a network of capital and labor flows, the nation-state is a "container" with rigid boundaries that enforces its authority over all within

---

[25] *See* Saskia Sassen, The Global City (1989).

[26] *See* Michael Sorkin, *Introduction*, in Variations on a Theme Park xi, xii (Michael Sorkin ed. 1992).

[27] *See* Sack, *supra* note 24, at 3, 134; Relph, *supra* note 21, at 83–105.

[28] Ford, *supra* note 12, at 878–80.

those boundaries.[29] Another way of putting it is that the nation-state represents "place" whereas the localities within it represent "space." Consider again the quote from Michael Walzer with which I opened this book:

> Neighborhoods can be open only if countries are at least potentially closed. Only if the state makes a selection among would-be members and guarantees the loyalty, security and welfare of the individuals it selects, can local communities take shape as "indifferent" associations, determined solely by personal preference and market capacity.[30]

The idea is that localities must be understood as spaces so that the nation-state can be the only relevant place. Local citizenship must be seen as freely chosen, so national citizenship can be our primary identity.

In light of the discussion in this chapter, however, we can now see that this formulation is far too flippant. Cities have never been "indifferent" associations, as their long history of racial segregation makes evident, nor has the "closure" of the nation-state protected localities against the pressures of globalization sufficiently to ensure individual "loyalty, security and welfare." The idea of "urban citizenship" elaborated by LeFebvre, Ford, and Young, and implemented by countless urban dwellers worldwide, is a direct response to the failures of nation-state citizenship embodied in Walzer's formulation. Rather than accepting that local citizenship is liberal, privatized, and unbounded in space, they have attempted to resuscitate an idea of urban citizenship that is public and rooted in place, in which, indeed, the public *is* a place.

The next three chapters explore three distinct models of place-based local citizenship that all attempt, in different ways, to resist the liberal idea of local citizenship unmoored from place. These are the republican, postmodern, and differentiated citizenship models. As we will see, however, these models have all run into the same two problems. The first problem is that the nation-state has not taken kindly to those who would challenge its monopoly on place. Courts and policymakers have been ruthlessly insistent that local citizenship must be liberal and unbounded in space. At the same time, because the state recognizes people's attachment to local places, it has often sought not to eradicate those places but to recapitulate them in liberal terms as "places of consumption." Courts and policymakers have, for example, shown a marked favoritism toward the suburb over the city. Urban citizenship has usually existed as something purely oppositional and aspirational, a citizenship of

---

[29] *See* Yishai Blank, *Spheres of Citizenship*, 8 THEORETICAL INQUIRIES L. 411, 414 (2007).
[30] MICHAEL WALZER, SPHERES OF JUSTICE 38–39 (1983).

resistance to the dominant paradigm. The second problem is that because place is so bound up with emotional attachments to territory, building citizenship on the idea of place may lead cities down the path to ethno-nationalism, exclusion, and xenophobia. Attempting to inoculate themselves against liberalism with a place-based citizenship may, therefore, actually push cities to embrace a more destructive form of belonging. Nevertheless, these three models provide much needed insight into how local citizenship can be reconstructed for our global age.

9

Republican Citizenship

Part I described how the American political tradition has attempted to reconcile liberal, republican, and ethno-nationalist conceptions of citizenship by creating a public sphere where citizenship is expressed in nationalist terms as a matter of collective identity, and a private sphere where citizenship is expressed in liberal terms as a matter of individual consumer choice. One effect of this reconciliation was to largely suppress republicanism's traditional concern with civic virtue and public participation in favor of structural protections against corruption. Beginning in the 1980s, however, a group of scholars became disenchanted with what they saw as the absence of virtue in the liberal nation-state, specifically the aggressively acquisitive, deregulatory culture of the "greed is good" Reagan years. These scholars led an effort to revive a public-minded, communitarian ideal of civic life that would stand in contrast to the individualistic, privatized liberal order. They discovered this ideal by reaching back to the republican tradition of the Greek city-state, which they recalled as anti-capitalist, collectivist, and dedicated to engaging citizens in a spirit of civic activity.[1]

The contrast these scholars drew between liberalism and republicanism in many ways mirrors the contrast geographers have drawn between space and place, described in the previous chapter. Just as the geographers see modernity eradicating meaningful "places" where people gather in a spirit of solidarity in

---

[1] The revival of the Republican tradition is recounted well in LAURA KALMAN, THE STRANGE CAREER OF LEGAL LIBERALISM 132–63 (1996). Some of the significant works related to the Republican revival include MICHAEL SANDEL, LIBERALISM AND THE LIMITS OF JUSTICE (2nd ed. 1998); J. G. A. POCOCK, THE MACHIAVELLIAN MOMENT: FLORENTINE POLITICAL THOUGHT AND THE ATLANTIC REPUBLICAN TRADITION (1975); Frank Michelman, *Law's Republic* 97 Yale. L.J. 1493 (1988); Suzanna Sherry, *Civic Virtue and the Feminine Voice in Constitutional Adjudication*, 72 VA. L. REV. 543 (1986); Cass R. Sunstein, *Interest Groups in American Law*, 38 STAN. L. REV. 29 (1985).

favor of abstract, homogenous "spaces" traversed by footloose consuming individuals, republican theorists worry that capitalism and the liberal state are giving precedence to the individual over the community, the consumer over the citizen, and mobility over solidarity. And just like the geographers chronicled a renewed commitment to place as space became more dominant in society, republicans have sought to revive the ancient spirit of republicanism at the precise moment liberalism appeared triumphant. In doing so, republicans have often drawn on the idea of place, and in particular they have championed the *local* as the sphere in which a republican conception of place could successfully germinate. At the same time, they have articulated a republican and place-based vision of local citizenship that stands in contrast to our predominantly liberal and nationalist conceptions of citizenship. This chapter describes that republican conception of local citizenship, details its (unfavorable) treatment in our political and legal traditions, and weighs its strengths and failings.

9.1 THE CHAIN STORE BATTLE AND ITS AFTERMATH

The clearest call for a republican and place-based local citizenship has come from Michael Sandel, one of the intellectual leaders of the republican revival. Sandel derives a republican ideal of citizenship, as well as its liberal antithesis, from a historical conflict between space and place: the chain store battles of the 1920s.[2] As global brands with headquarters in distant cities began spreading into small towns, threatening independent local retailers, the local retailers and their advocates fought back by articulating a republican vision of citizenship rooted in place. According to these advocates, citizenship could only be exercised within local communities that enjoyed collective economic independence from global forces. Louis D. Brandeis, one of the most famous enemies of the chain system, argued that "you cannot have true American citizenship" unless local communities had economic independence from the chains.[3] The chain system, by robbing localities of their independence, sapped the community spirit that instilled the virtues of citizenship. According to Sandel, local economic independence was deemed necessary "to form in citizens the qualities of character necessary to self-government," specifically

---

[2]   *See* MICHAEL SANDEL, DEMOCRACY'S DISCONTENT: AMERICA IN SEARCH OF A PUBLIC
      PHILOSOPHY 201–49 (1996). Richard Schragger provides excellent commentary on Sandel's
      book, and additional context on the chain store battles, in Richard C. Schragger, *The Anti-*
      Chain Store Movement in Localist Ideology, and the Remnants of the Progressive Constitution,
      1920–1940, 90 IOWA L. REV. 1011 (2005).

[3]   Brandeis quoted in SANDEL, *supra* note 2, at 237.

the "sense of community and civic engagement" that gives rise to democratic activity.[4] As we saw in Chapter 1, it was a staple of republican ideology that people need freedom from economic necessity in order to meaningfully participate in politics. In republican thinking, those who are economically dependent are unable to see beyond their narrow self-interest, and thus incapable of participating in politics in a spirit of civic mindedness.[5]

For the Progressive reformers and anti-chain store activists, citizenship was synonymous with local self-government because local self-government was what ensured economic independence. Echoing Brandeis, Woodrow Wilson lamented that "If America discourages the locality, the community, the self-contained town, she will kill the nation."[6] Reformers like Frederic Howe believed in an activist, participatory local government, and Howe was among the advocates pushing for local home rule. These reformers, however, rejected the liberal meaning of home rule as a constraint on cities' economic freedom, seeing it conversely as "expanding the ability of municipalities to pursue social ends, freed from dependence on private businessmen and private capital," in Rich Schragger's words.[7]

This vision of citizenship rooted in the local quickly gave way, however, to our modern, liberal view of the citizen as an atomized consumer indifferent to place. The chain stores prevailed in their struggle against local retailers – in the courts, in the legislatures, and ultimately in the battle for public opinion – by successfully elevating the consumer over the community. As Sandel explains, Brandeis's vision of local citizenship was defeated by a competing strand of Progressivism that sought to create a model of citizenship located not at the local but at the national scale, a model of citizenship that would "transcend differences of occupation, ethnicity, and class."[8] On this view, consumption provided the glue that united people of all backgrounds – the basis of our liberal-nationalist citizenship. According to journalist Walter Weyl, "In America today the unifying economic force ... is the common interest of the citizen as a consumer."[9] The idea of the citizen as an individual

---

[4] *See id.* at 224; 6.
[5] *See* HANNAH ARENDT, THE HUMAN CONDITION 27 (1958) (slaves and women were defined as being outside the political community because of their material dependence; J. G. A. Pocock, *The Ideal of Citizenship since Classical Times,* in THE CITIZENSHIP DEBATES 32, 34 (Gershon Shafir ed., 1998) (slaves and women could never leave the material world of the household); Robert Steinfeld, *Property and Suffrage in the Early Republic,* 41 STAN. L. REV. 335, 337–50 (1989) (describing the republican ideology of dependence during the early American republic).
[6] Wilson *quoted in* SANDEL, *supra* note 2, at 216.
[7] Schragger, *supra* note 2, at 1046.
[8] Sandel, *supra* note 2, at 221.
[9] *Id.* at 223–24.

consumer-voter, untethered to local communities and freely moving through space, thus triumphed over the republican conception of the citizen as bound to place, embedded in the community.[10]

For Sandel, what's been lost in the process is significant. Our liberal state, while allowing individuals to choose their own moral and political commitments, "soon generates its own disenchantment" because it offers citizens a robust freedom of choice during a time when globalization is rapidly depriving us of meaningful choices, sapping our economic independence, and subjecting us to global forces far beyond our control.[11] Liberalism thus "creates a moral void that opens the way for narrow, intolerant moralisms," presumably including our now prevalent ethnic nationalism.[12] Not surprisingly, Sandel argues that we should revive the place-based view of citizenship, "shore up the public spaces that gather people together in common experiences and form the habits of citizenship."[13] In Sandel's view, common spaces like parks, libraries, and schools are "sites for the promotion of civic identity, neighborliness, and community."[14] Like Sandel, Zadie Smith praises the library, "the only thing left on the high street that doesn't want either your soul or your wallet." For Smith, the library is the kind of social reality, "which by its very existence teaches a system of values beyond the fiscal."[15]

In true republican fashion, Sandel sees citizenship as an activity rather than a status, a coming together of the public in a spirit of civic engagement. Importantly, for Sandel, as for the ancient Athenians, this activity necessarily occurs in the city's places, as people freed from economic dependency interact with each other and share "common experiences." But the city's places can only serve this role if they are purified of the corrupt influence of global economic forces, so that people can have the economic independence on which self-government depends. For instance, Sandel rails against the introduction of commercial advertising in public schools, lamenting that "[A]dvertising teaches us to want things; schools teach us to reflect critically on our desires."[16] Ben Barber, also writing in the republican tradition, observes that it is only places like churches,

---

[10] *See generally* Lizabeth Cohen, A Consumers' Republic: The Politics of Mass Consumption in Postwar America 8 (2003) (describing emergence of a culture of consumption in which consumer and citizen "often overlapped, reflecting "permeability of political and econ spheres").

[11] *Id.* at 22–24.

[12] *Id.; see also id.* at 201–02.

[13] *Id.* at 333.

[14] *Id.* at 332.

[15] Zadie Smith, *Northwest London Blues*, in Feel Free 12 (2018).

[16] Michael Sandel, What Money Can't Buy 200 (2013).

schools, and libraries that "elicit active and engaged public behavior and ask us to define ourselves as autonomous members of civic communities marked by culture or religion or other public values."[17]

9.2 COMMUNITY ECONOMIC DEVELOPMENT

According to Sandel, the way to ensure that places (and their citizens) thrive is to create institutions that enable local economic independence. For example, Sandel briefly discusses community development corporations (CDCs), which are nonprofit corporations that invest in low-income communities and attempt to give residents of those communities the opportunity to exercise control over their own economic fortunes. CDCs are a key component of the community economic development (CED) movement, which seeks to attract investment to lower-income communities for the benefit of existing residents.[18]

Like the chain store movement before it, CED can easily be seen as a republican reaction against the liberal effort to turn urban places into commodifiable spaces. CED grew out of the era of "urban renewal," a period roughly from the 1940s through the 1960s during which cities and real estate interests, aided by federal money, decimated poor neighborhoods so they could reclaim those areas for more profitable uses. These neighborhoods were systematically deprived of investment, divided and isolated by freeways, and bulldozed to make way for stadiums and performing arts centers.[19] The concerns of community residents were ignored. Eventually, as discontent with urban renewal increased, neighborhood organizing movements emerged across the country to create collective resistance to urban renewal schemes and to give neighborhood residents positive control over community life.[20]

---

[17] BENJAMIN BARBER, JIHAD V. MCWORLD 97–98 (1995). Barber goes on to state that the market empowers consumers to choose, "but the choice is always about which items to buy and consume, never about *whether* to buy and consume anything at all … " *Id.* at 98.

[18] *See* SANDEL, *supra* note 2, at 333–38. On community economic development, see, for example, EDWARD G. GOETZ, THE ONE-WAY STREET OF INTEGRATION: FAIR HOUSING AND THE PURSUIT OF RACIAL JUSTICE IN AMERICAN CITIES (2018); SUSAN BENNETT, ET AL., COMMUNITY ECONOMIC DEVELOPMENT LAW (2012); WILLIAM H. SIMON, THE COMMUNITY ECONOMIC DEVELOPMENT (2001); Scott L. Cummings, *Community Economic Development as Progressive Politics: Toward a Grassroots Movement for Economic Justice*, 54 STAN. L. REV. 399 (2001); Audrey G. McFarlane, *Race, Space and Place: The Geography of Economic Development*, 36 SAN DIEGO L. REV. 295 (1999).

[19] *See* McFarlane, *supra* note 18, at 318; Wendell E. Pritchett, The *"Public Menace" of Blight: Urban Renewal and the Private Uses of Eminent Domain*, 21 YALE L. & POL. REV. 1 (2003).

[20] See, e.g., JEFFREY M. BERRY ET AL., THE REBIRTH OF URBAN DEMOCRACY (1993); MILTON KOTLER, NEIGHBORHOOD GOVERNMENT (1969); Audrey G. McFarlane, *When Inclusion Leads to Exclusion: The Uncharted Terrain of Community Participation in Economic Development*, 66 BROOK. L. REV. 861 (2001).

The legacy of urban renewal and neighborhood organizing echoes in modern debates about globalization and gentrification. As cities have emerged from a long period of urban decline and experienced a revitalization sparked by demographic shifts and the comparative advantage cities enjoy in the global knowledge-based economy, a lingering problem is how to protect existing poor and minority residents from being priced out of their communities by an influx of global capital and affluent newcomers with disposable income.[21] Worried that "[i]ntegration into broad-based markets subjects the community to forces beyond the reach of self-government," CED advocates like William Simon favor strategies such as rent control, community banking, and condominium-conversion legislation that attempt to give communities a degree of self-sufficiency and the ability to resist global economic forces. According to Simon's treatment of the community economic development movement, CED is "republican" because at its core is "a preference for economic self-sufficiency and a concern about non-resident, 'absentee' ownership."[22]

While Sandel and Simon praise community economic development for giving lower-income urban communities the ability to obtain some economic independence, they do not care much for what Simon calls the "dark side" of CED, exclusionary suburbs.[23] As we have seen, affluent suburban communities throughout the country use strict zoning regulations to limit the supply and raise the cost of housing, with the effect (and arguably the purpose) of making it harder and more expensive for others to move there. In the process, many residents of the metropolitan region, especially poor and minority residents, are locked out of places with good jobs, good schools, low crime, and rising property values.[24] Several scholars have observed similarities between suburban zoning and CED strategies like rent control, which are similarly designed to maintain the character of the preexisting community by limiting and controlling the entry of new residents and development.[25]

---

[21] On gentrification, see generally JOHN JOE SCHLICHTMAN ET AL., GENTRIFIER (2017); THE GENTRIFICATION READER (Loretta Lees et al. eds. 2010); THE GENTRIFICATION DEBATES (Japonica Brown-Saracino ed. 2010).

[22] *See* SIMON, *supra* note 18, at 62–67, 93–95, 113–41.

[23] *Id.* at 73.

[24] *See generally* JESSICA TROUNSTINE, SEGREGATION BY DESIGN: LOCAL POLITICS AND INEQUALITY IN AMERICAN CITIES (2018).

[25] *See* Jerry Frug, *Decentering Decentralization*, 60 U. CHI. L. REV. 253, 287 (1993) (condominium conversion legislation, like zoning, is designed "to preserve an existing community by excluding outsiders"); Margaret Jane Radin, *Residential Rent Control*, PHIL. & PUB. AFF. 350, 379 (1986) (rent control, like exclusionary zoning, has "the effect of keeping out would-be entrants"); *see also* SIMON, *supra* note 18, at 73–75 (comparing CED to suburban zoning).

From the perspective of Sandel, Simon, and many other republican-minded theorists, however, these two things are not alike at all. Where CED seeks to expel the influence of commerce so citizens can gather together in public space in a spirit of civic engagement, exclusionary suburbs eradicate public space to instill an ethos of isolated consumption. Where CED tries to knit the community together through common institutions and build trust through personal relationships, exclusionary suburbs reject the public streets, sidewalks and porches in which people congregate, favoring enlarged domestic spaces in which goods can be privately stored and consumed, wide thoroughfares for speedy automobile traffic, and shopping malls marooned in vast parking lots and dedicated to mass consumption. The spatial separation wrought by the suburbs – enforced by zoning laws that mandate single-use zones – deadens civic participation and the breeding of connections among neighbors. Furthermore, suburban exclusion is a tool of commodification and consumption because its goal is to enrich individual homeowners by enhancing their property values. Rent control and limits on condo conversions, on the other hand, preserve the fabric of the community without commodifying it and *prevent* the enrichment of private landowners who would profit from changing the community. Thus, where CED stands athwart the global capital forces bearing down on urban neighborhoods, suburbs are inseparable from those very global forces. In short, exclusionary suburbs are not real places, in the sense of authentic communities with a deep sense of connection to the territory, but inauthentic "places of consumption."[26]

9.3 CITIZENSHIP, THE STATE, AND SPACE

Unfortunately for the republican theorists, however, courts have been far more favorably inclined toward suburban exclusionary zoning than community economic development. This inversion of the republican preference makes perfect sense because, as we have seen throughout this book, our political and legal tradition persistently characterizes local citizenship as liberal, based on mobility and consumer choice rather than deep connections to territory. In the geographic lingo, this means that citizens must be apprehended as moving through space, rather than embedded in opaque and impenetrable places.

[26] There is a voluminous literature on how suburbia has ushered in a culture of isolated consumption and suppressed civic engagement. *See, e.g.,* COHEN, *supra* note 10, at 254–56; ROBERT PUTNAM, BOWLING ALONE, 204–15 (2000); ROBERT SACK, PLACE, MODERNITY AND THE CONSUMER'S WORLD 134–73 (1992); VARIATIONS ON A THEME PARK: THE NEW AMERICAN CITY AND THE END OF PUBLIC SPACE (Michael Sorkin ed. 1992).

Courts have insisted that local citizens have a "right to travel," and therefore that states and municipalities cannot use their powers to impede population mobility.[27] States and municipalities are prohibited from enacting immigration laws or placing length-of-residency requirements on eligibility to vote or access to public benefits.[28] Furthermore, the idea of local citizens as mobile consumers means that state and local governments must also be prohibited from hindering the workings of an integrated national economic market for the sake of insulating themselves against market forces. Many courts have accordingly found that local hiring preferences, rent control, predatory lending ordinances, and other efforts to regulate the economy at the local level are invalid.[29] Courts have also barred states from favoring in-state over out-of-state economic interests, or even placing an excessive burden on interstate commerce.[30] In summary, as Simon laments, "[t]he Supreme Court considers that the federal structure of the constitution implies rights of interstate mobility that are inconsistent with encompassing notions of local citizenship."[31]

On the other hand, courts have seen suburban exclusionary zoning as furthering the mobility and consumer choice that underlie liberal local citizenship. Although the courts have been clear that state and local governments are prohibited from infringing on the right to travel, they have consistently held that zoning regulations do not interfere with this right because they "merely make it more difficult for the outsider to establish his residence in the place of his choosing."[32] Further, unlike CED, exclusionary suburbs are fully consistent with the consumerist premise of liberal local citizenship – precisely because they are the perceived as the sort of "places of consumption" that Simon and

---

[27] *See* Saenz v. Roe, 526 U.S. 489, 511 (1999); Shapiro v. Thompson, 394 U.S. 618 (1969); Edwards v. California, 314 U.S. 160 (1941); Hiroshi Motomura, *Whose Immigration Law? Citizens, Aliens and the Constitution*, 97 COLUM. L. REV. 1567, 1597–98 (1997). The right to travel as an incident of local citizenship is discussed further in Chapters 2 and 5.

[28] See the discussion in Chapter 2.

[29] *See, e.g.*, American Financial Services Ass'n v. City of Oakland 104 P.3d 813 (Cal. 2005) (invalidating local ordinance addressing predatory lending); United Bldg. & Construction Trades Council of Camden Cty. v. Camden, 465 U.S. 208 (1984) (casting doubt on the validity of local hiring requirements); Marshal House, Inc. v. Rent Review & Grievance Bd. Of Brookline, 260 N.E.2d 200 (Ma. 1970) (holding the municipality lacked home rule authority to enact rent control ordinance); Ngai Pindell, *Home Sweet Home? The Efficacy of Rental Restrictions to Promote Neighborhood Stability*, 29 ST. LOUIS U. PUB. L. REV. 41 (2009) (discussing court decisions addressing validity of alienability restrictions).

[30] *See* Richard C. Schragger, *Cities, Economic Development, and the Free Trade Constitution*, 94 VA. L. REV. 1091, 1110–12; 1117–18 (2008).

[31] SIMON, *supra* note 18, at 88.

[32] *See* Assoc. Homebuilders v. City of Livermore, 557 P.2d 473, 484 (1976); Vill. of Belle Terre v. Boraas, 416 U.S. 1, 7 (1973).

Sandel condemn. Policymakers have long seen suburban homeownership as the very foundation of good citizenship because it facilitates consumption. Since the 1920s, it has been widely understood that "a more spacious, mass produced form of housing was essential to enable workers and their families to consume."[33] According to Lizabeth Cohen, policymakers often connected the consumerism exemplified by suburbia with citizenship, tying "free choice as consumers with political freedom."[34] On that premise, the federal government has subsidized and incentivized suburban homeownership in various ways, including issuing mortgage guarantees, offering tax deductions, subsidizing roads and automobiles, and encouraging the use of zoning. Courts have repeatedly upheld zoning ordinances against a variety of legal challenges on the grounds that zoning protects homeowners' property values.[35]

Even where it has been evident that suburban zoning laws were motivated by something *other* than property values, courts have nevertheless perceived them that way. For instance, in *Village of Arlington Heights* v. *Metropolitan Housing Dev. Corp.*,[36] perhaps its most significant modern decision on zoning, the Supreme Court upheld a Chicago suburb's refusal to rezone property to permit low-income housing, despite the fact that the city was zoned almost uniformly to exclude low-income housing and only 27 of its 64,000 residents were black. The Court found that the zoning decision was designed to protect homeowners' property values and not racially motivated, despite the fact that several homeowners specifically objected to the proposed rezoning on racial grounds.[37] The Court also said nothing about the long-standing historical connection between white homeowners' fears of property value decline and fears of racial change.[38] Under the Court's view, as Richard Ford has explained, "spatial communities are seen as marketplace commodities into which anyone with enough cash can buy entry, and the political process is understood to occur in a neutral political space and to consist of individuals who form groups for purely strategic purposes."[39]

---

[33] DOLORES HAYDEN, REDESIGNING THE AMERICAN DREAM: GENDER, HOUSING AND AMERICAN LIFE 33 (2002); *see also* COHEN, *supra* note 10, at 194–95 (suburbanization was a key element of the "commitment to rebuild the American economy after World War II around the mass consumer market").

[34] *See* COHEN, *supra* note 10, at 126.

[35] Kenneth A. Stahl, *Reliance in Land Use*, 2013 BYU L. REV. 949, 983–85 (collecting cases).

[36] 429 U.S. 252 (1977).

[37] *See id.* at 257–58 (noting community objections to racially integrated housing); *id.* at 270 (finding that village acted without discriminatory purpose).

[38] *See* TROUNSTINE, *supra* note 24, at 29–32.

[39] Richard Thompson Ford, *The Boundaries of Race: Political Geography in Legal Analysis*, 107 HARV. L. REV. 1841, 1888–89 (1994).

9.4 CRITIQUE OF REPUBLICAN CITIZENSHIP

Sandel and the other republican theorists have good reason to lament the way that local citizenship in our political and legal tradition has been constructed as liberal. There is little doubt that the decline of genuine public places has led to a loss of civic engagement and diminished the ability of communities to provide a sense of self-sufficiency and moral purpose. The longstanding policy preference for exclusionary suburbs over urban economic development has also exacerbated spatial inequality by allowing the affluent to segregate themselves in well-manicured enclaves where they can then block others from enjoying the good schools and other municipal resources such enclaves enjoy. This "opportunity hoarding" may itself be an outcome of the decline of community Sandel decries, as the absence of a shared civic purpose and places where people can come together in a spirit of reciprocal obligation leads to increasingly selfish behavior.[40]

While the republican vision is a useful corrective, however, it is also seriously flawed because it too easily slips into the exclusion, scapegoating, and chauvinism of ethnic nationalism. Exclusion lies at the very core of republican ideology, which seeks to preserve the purity of the public sphere by banishing from that sphere whatever it defines as a corrupting influence. Historically, of course, women and foreigners were considered such corrupting influences, and were therefore strictly excluded from politics. Today, according to Sandel, it is creeping global consumerism that threatens to corrupt the public realm. But the troubling legacy of republicanism is not so easily expunged. It is perhaps no surprise, as Rich Schragger points out, that women and racial minorities were pointedly excluded from the citizenship of "small men and worthy dealers" that the anti-chain store advocates fought to salvage. Indeed, the rise of liberalism had a salutary impact on these groups, who gained the incidents of citizenship as they were "brought into the national economic marketplace through consumption." According to Schragger, "Access to chain stores and standardized goods freed blacks from fraught relationships with white and ethnic communities via consumerist anonymity, and allowed them to exercise the political power of the purse." Meanwhile, as women became the face of consumerism in America,

---

[40] On opportunity hoarding generally, see CHARLES TILLY, DURABLE INEQUALITY (1999). On opportunity hoarding in the specific context of racial inequalities in the provision of local resources, see, for example, R. L'HEUREUX LEWIS-MCCOY, INEQUALITY IN THE PROMISED LAND: RACE, RESOURCES AND SUBURBAN SCHOOLING 19–44 (2014).

empowering consumers meant that women "gained both economic and political power."[41]

Though Sandel attempts to revive republican citizenship in a way that excises the exclusionary aspects of its previous incarnation, he cannot do so without losing what is most fundamental to republican ideology – the idea that the public realm must be purified of corrupting foreign influences, especially commerce. Operationalized through the lens of place, this means that those perceived as foreign must be excluded in order to maintain the character of the place for the benefit of its preexisting inhabitants, who are defined as the true members of the community in contrast to the foreign agents who come after. In Simon's view, for example, the primary and indeed sole beneficiaries of community economic development are supposed to be the preexisting residents of the community.[42] By design or effect, devices like rent control and condominium conversion legislation make it harder for new people to gain entrance to the community. In lower-income communities experiencing or on the cusp of gentrification, new development is often treated as a zero-sum game in which developers profit and existing communities lose some non-commodifiable good such as "authenticity."[43] Market-rate housing, typically denounced as "luxury" housing, is a particular object of opprobrium, the term "luxury" indicating the invasion of both commerce and alien values into the community. New residents, likewise, are often condemned as "gentrifiers," a term denoting their foreignness and superficial relationship to the community.[44] Although there is little evidence that new market-rate housing actually contributes to gentrification or displacement, and is more likely to *prevent* it by lowering rents, the

---

[41] Schragger, *supra* note 30, at 1074–76; *see also* COHEN, *supra* note 10, at 31–41; 75–83 (on women's incorporation as citizens in new consumer economy); 41–53; 83–100 (on blacks' incorporation as citizens in new consumer economy). As Cohen notes, this incorporation was somewhat ambivalent, in that blacks and women were both advantaged and disadvantaged in different ways by the rise of the consumer economy. I addressed in Part II some of the ambiguities in liberal local citizenship's devotion to consumerism, a matter I return to in the conclusion.

[42] SIMON, *supra* note 18, at 69–76 . ("Community economic development connotes development for the benefit of the community – defined in terms of its residents at the time a project is undertaken.").

[43] On gentrification and the debate over "authenticity," see SHARON ZUKIN, NAKED CITY: THE DEATH AND LIFE OF AUTHENTIC URBAN PLACES (2010); JAPONICA BROWN-SARACINO, A NEIGHBORHOOD THAT NEVER CHANGES: GENTRIFICATION, SOCIAL PRESERVATION, AND THE SEARCH FOR AUTHENTICITY (2009).

[44] SCHLICHTMAN, ET AL., *supra* note 21, is a fascinating look at the multi-faceted aspects of the word gentrifier and what it means to be a gentrifier.

republican ideology of corruption nevertheless treats it as an alien that must be excluded.[45]

Ironically, the "gentrifiers" who are so often vilified for entering poor communities are usually themselves priced out of wealthier suburban neighborhoods due to the practice of exclusionary zoning that Sandel and Simon both condemn. On that note, despite the efforts of Sandel and Simon to distinguish CED from suburban zoning, there are some uncomfortable similarities. Like practitioners of CED, suburban homeowners seek to preserve the preexisting community against invasion by outsiders, and often express similar concerns about foreign financial influences corrupting the character of their communities, denouncing "greedy developers" for building "luxury" condos that snarl traffic and create parking nightmares. It is not uncommon for wealthy anti-development homeowners (sometimes derisively called NIMBYs, or "Not in My Backyard") to appropriate the rhetoric of anti-gentrification and displacement, perhaps apotheosized when a city council member from Beverly Hills argued that building more market-rate ("luxury") apartments in his city would displace many of the city's renters.[46] Of course, sometimes NIMBYs tip their hands about their actual motivations and complain that new apartments will bring "inner city values" into their tranquil suburban environs. Whatever rhetoric is used, the idea is the same: to prevent the foreign influence, especially commerce, from corrupting place.

Ultimately, Sandel's worry that liberalism "creates a moral void that opens the way for narrow, intolerant moralisms" such as ethnic nationalism leads him to embrace a solution that is itself not much different from ethnic nationalism. A core aim of ethnic nationalism is to confer economic self-sufficiency on a territorially defined community in order to purge the foreign element implicit in the liberal economic order. Nationalist movements are often bound up with campaigns for economic independence. Quebec's modern movement for secession from Canada gained steam after it obtained its own source of hydro-electric power with "Le Grande 2" and believed it was no longer economically dependent on Canada.[47] Similarly, after Egypt built

---

[45] *See, e.g.*, Vicki Been et al., *Supply Skepticism: Housing Supply and Affordability*, NYU Furman Center Working Paper (August 20, 2018), http://furmancenter.org/research/publication/supply-skepticismnbsp-housing-supply-and-affordability; John Mangin, *The New Exclusionary Zoning*, 25 Stan. L. & Pol'y Rev. 91, 108–13 (2014) (explaining the "supply skepticism" among anti-gentrification activists and scholars).

[46] https://twitter.com/JohnMirisch/status/987010314376900608; *see also* Henry Grabar, *Gentrification Got Gentrified*, Slate.com (May 3, 2019, 5:50 AM), https://slate.com/business/2019/05/gentrification-definition-housing-policy-methodology-cities-suburbs.html.

[47] *See* Michael Ignatieff, Blood and Belonging 143–75 (1993).

its own source of hydroelectric power, the Aswan Dam, it was emboldened to pursue a militantly nationalist project. Egypt withdrew from the postwar economic coalition, instituted a policy of import substitution to wean itself off economic ties to the west, and attempted to create a pan-Arab nationalist movement.[48] It is perhaps *because* local economic self-sufficiency raises a threat of internal nationalist secession movements that courts in the United States have been so insistent on a single, integrated national economic market.

In addition, the idea that citizenship should be rooted in a primordial connection to place and the related idea that those lacking such a connection should be treated as corrupting foreign influences are hallmarks of ethnic nationalism. Nationalist enterprises have often created a sense of shared identity by portraying some perceived foreign influence as the corrupt adversary against whom the nation is arrayed. Under Nasser, the Egyptians expelled all the Jews and other perceived foreigners. Here in the United States, nationalism, exemplified by the election of Donald Trump, has led to the scapegoating of various identifiably "different" groups, including immigrants, Muslims, black athletes, China, and others. As is true at the local level in the debate over development and neighborhood change, at the national level the community is rhetorically divided between its legitimate members with roots in place and the illegitimate foreigners who are simply moving through space. The latter are portrayed in terms that practically deny their very humanity and hence rationalize their political marginalization. The republican idea of citizenship rooted in place thus seems to lead, almost inexorably, to the scapegoating of visible, politically vulnerable people who can easily be stigmatized as foreign and corrupting agents of space.[49]

At the same time, the effort to insulate places against the imposition of space almost inevitably fails. Neither cities nor nation-states can wall themselves off against the regional and global economies of which they are a part, and their efforts to do so usually lead at best to their isolation, and at worst to economic ruin. According to Audrey McFarlane, the flaw in CED is that it sees the poor black neighborhood "as an autonomous, self-sustaining unit capable of articulating and protecting the interests of its residents" when in fact

---

[48] *See* DANIEL YERGIN, THE PRIZE: THE EPIC QUEST FOR OIL, MONEY & POWER 480–98, 508–09 (1992).

[49] The fate of the Jews of Egypt under Nasser is beautifully told in ANDRE ACIMAN, OUT OF EGYPT (2007) (focusing on the Jews of Alexandria) and LUCETTE LAGNADO, THE MAN IN THE WHITE SHARKSKIN SUIT: A JEWISH FAMILY'S EXODUS FROM OLD CAIRO TO THE NEW WORLD (2007) (focusing on the Jews of Cairo).

continued globalization has relocated manufacturing to the southern United States and the Third World; decentralization of the metropolitan area has taken jobs and retail services from central cities, and last but not least, middle class and affluent people have moved the peripheries of the metropolitan area such that there are now new urban areas called exurbs and other urban areas called edge cities.[50]

McFarlane's observation echoes Manuel Castell's lament about urban social movements: they are "aimed at transforming the meaning of the city without being able to transform society."[51] Thus, we must look elsewhere for a model of local citizenship that can serve as a suitable alternative to our predominant liberal model.

---

[50] *See* McFarlane, *supra* note 20, at 924.
[51] MANUEL CASTELLS, THE CITY AND THE GRASSROOTS 327 (1983).

10

Postmodern Citizenship

The previous chapter described how theorists such as Michael Sandel attempted to combat the predominant, consumer-oriented liberal model of local citizenship by reviving an ancient republican form of urban citizenship in which citizens are freed from dependence on the marketplace to deliberate on civic affairs in the city's public places. Sandel's account poses a fairly strict dichotomy between republican and liberal citizenship, in which republicanism appears as a model of communitarian harmony and civic engagement in contrast to liberalism's acquisitive individualism. But I described a dark side to republicanism – it purchases harmony and civic engagement at the price of exclusion and xenophobia. We thus seem to be presented with an unpleasant choice between the excessive commercialism and consumerism of liberal citizenship and the totalitarian conformity, exclusivity, and bigotry of republican citizenship. (Personally, the first one sounds better). In addition, the opposition Sandel constructs between liberal and republican conceptions of citizenship is mirrored by a similarly rigid dichotomy between space and place. Sandel eschews the notion of citizen-consumers indifferently moving through space in favor of a community of citizens bound together by their connections to a particular place. But I described how attachment to place can breed resentment of outsiders and a reactionary fixation on the status quo. Thus, it appears we are stuck between space, representing the coldness of liberalism, and place, representing the paranoid defensiveness of republicanism.

But perhaps we are not doomed to choose between two untenable options. In our global age, as I showed in Part I, many of the boundaries and distinctions on which citizenship has long seemed to depend, such as the public/private distinction, are melting away. Accordingly, some legal scholars have offered a "postmodern" view of urban citizenship that rejects facile dichotomies such as liberal/republican and space/place, seeing these things as existing along a spectrum rather than in clear opposition to each other. This chapter explores that postmodern view of citizenship and describes its similarities and contrasts with the republican view. Among those similarities is that postmodern citizenship's repudiation of firm distinctions has made it, like republican citizenship, unwelcome within our political and legal tradition, which insists that local citizenship be perceived as liberal and unmoored from place. I conclude that unlike republican citizenship, which fails because it too readily embraces closure, postmodern citizenship's critical flaw is its extreme openness.

10.1 GERALD FRUG ON COMMUNITY BUILDING AND POSTMODERN CITIZENSHIP

Gerald Frug has often spoken of a "postmodern" idea of local government,[1] and within his work, I find a clear articulation of a postmodern vision of urban citizenship. According to Frug, citizenship consists largely of accommodating oneself to the wide diversity and difference of urban life. To be a citizen is to be "introduced to a perspective broad enough to encompass 'the different races, differing religions, and unlike customs' that constitute American life."[2] Superficially, this view of citizenship shares many affinities with republican citizenship. Like Sandel, Frug envisions citizenship as bound up with and occurring in place, specifically the city. According to Frug, the city is a "fortuitous association" of strangers who proudly display their differences, and it is in the city that we learn to become citizens by experiencing difference.[3] Like Sandel, Frug lionizes the city schools and parks as the truly public places where people learn to accommodate difference. Hence, for Frug as for Sandel, urban citizenship is an activity rather than a status – the act of building community by being together with strangers in the city's public places.[4]

Another affinity that postmodern citizenship shares with republican citizenship is a deep opposition to the liberal conception of local citizenship. That conception, as I discussed in the first part, is exemplified by the "Tiebout model" of municipal government. Under the Tiebout model, residents are mobile consumer-voters who choose a city in which to settle the same way

---

[1] *See* GERALD FRUG, CITY MAKING: BUILDING COMMUNITIES WITHOUT BUILDING WALLS 92–112 (1999) (on the "postmodern subject" in local government law).
[2] Gerald E. Frug, *City Services*, 73 N.Y.U. L. Rev. 23, 46 (1998) (quoting JOHN DEWEY, DEMOCRACY AND EDUCATION 25 (1916)).
[3] *See id.* at 35–37 (on "fortuitous associations").
[4] *See id.* at 38–42 (schools and parks); 92–93 (on parks).

shoppers choose groceries at the store. The products for which consumers are shopping are the various municipal services cities offer – schools, policing, and so forth. Like any consumer good, these services are distributed based on an ability to pay, as the quality of local schools and other services are generally built into the purchase price of homes in the municipality. As a result, city services such as schools become de facto mechanisms for segregating people into communities that are socioeconomically homogenous. In Tiebout's consumerist municipality, "values commonly associated with democracy – notions of equality, of the importance of collective deliberation and compromise, of the existence of a public interest not reducible to personal economic concerns – are of secondary concern, or no concern at all ..."[5] The postmodern idea of citizenship, by contrast, uses public services to bring diverse people together. As Frug argues, any service worthy of the name "public," whether it is a school, a transit system, or simply a sidewalk, should "facilitate[] the daily experience of crossing paths with different kinds of people."[6] In essence, where the Tiebout model "privatizes" local government services, postmodern citizenship "public-izes" them.

Both Sandel and Frug, in short, reject the idea that citizenship in a local community is a voluntary association, chosen in the same way a person chooses goods in the marketplace. People cannot freely choose their associations because individuals are to a large extent constituted by the associations in which they find themselves "situated," making individual choice a mirage. In addition, real citizenship cannot occur in a voluntary association because a voluntary association constricts peoples' perspectives to their own self-interest as consumers, and enervates the spirit of civic engagement that only comes from fortuitous associations.[7]

Here, however, Frug's vision of citizenship begins to diverge from Sandel's, and this is where it becomes "postmodern." For Sandel, individual choice cannot be the basis of citizenship because individuals are defined by their group associations. For that reason, Sandel is suspicious of liberalism's emphasis on individual rights and would instead vindicate the claims of what he calls "constitutive communities," those groups in which people find themselves situated, even if that means suppressing individual rights. For instance, Sandel defends the right of the Amish to withdraw their children from public schools, even at the expense of depriving those children of the opportunity to

---

5   *See id.* at 25–35 (criticizing Tiebout model as a cramped, consumerist vision of local citizenship).
6   *See id.* at 91–92.
7   *See* FRUG, *supra* note 1, at 73–91 (discussing Sandel).

learn about the outside world and revise their own commitments. For Sandel, identity is more important than choice. Hence, in his view, a community's right to protect itself against global economic forces takes precedence over the individual freedom of mobility and choice in the market.[8]

Frug, though, implicitly points out a critical flaw in Sandel's analysis. Sandel assumes that although the individual is situated within the community, the community is an autonomous and "centered" subject. However, Frug shows that the community Sandel lionizes is just as "situated" as the individual. No community exists on an island or has the ability to isolate itself from the larger forces surrounding it. Though suburban communities attempt to deny their relationship with central cities by hoarding their tax revenue and using restrictive zoning to maintain racial and socioeconomic homogeneity, and cities retaliate with rent control and community economic development to reduce their dependence on macroeconomic forces, the reality is that these communities necessarily have an interdependent relationship. As Frug writes:

> Localities cause unemployment by attracting businesses from neighboring cities; they generate pollution that harms their neighbors as well as themselves; they zone for office complexes and shopping malls that change the lives of employees and customers in other towns; they educate people who move elsewhere in the area; they enact crime-control policies that cause criminals to move to new locations, thereby victimizing people who live across the border.[9]

In short, while Frug agrees with Sandel that liberal citizenship is inadequate because individual identities are constituted by group associations, he shows that republican citizenship is also inadequate because group identity is just as unstable as individual identity. Our identities are "postmodern" in that they do not conform with or respect any boundaries or firm referents.[10]

Accordingly, Frug rejects the idea that the law should privilege people with connections to a particular place, or ratify a fixed idea of community. In contrast to Sandel and others like William Simon, Frug argues that the law should encourage interlocal mobility, and that "those who want to move to a

---

[8]   *See* Michael Sandel, *Freedom of Conscience or Freedom of Choice, in* Articles of Faith, Articles of Peace 74 (Hunter & Guiness eds., 1990) (On the Amish); Michael Sandel, *Introduction, in* Liberalism and Its Critics 1 (Michael Sandel ed., 1984); Michael Sandel, Liberalism and the Limits of Justice (1982).

[9]   Frug, *supra* noteote 1, at 77.

[10]   *See id.* at 64–69 (on the city as a "centered subject"); 73–85 (on city as a "situated subject"); 92–105 (on city as a "postmodern subject").

neighborhood should not face community-imposed obstacles to doing so (the community should have no right to exclude them)."[11] While acknowledging concerns about gentrification and displacement, Frug is ambivalent about mechanisms to protect neighborhood stability such as rent control and condominium conversion legislation, seeing them, like suburban exclusionary zoning, as barriers to individual mobility. He even goes so far as to advocate a radical restructuring of local voting rights, decoupling the franchise from residence and empowering people to vote in *any* municipality they desire. Hence, Simon counts Frug among those who favor impersonal markets and bureaucracies across space rather than strong place-based policies and face to face collaboration.[12]

10.2 POSTMODERN CITIZENSHIP AND A GLOBAL SENSE OF PLACE

To say that Frug sides with space over place, however, falls right into the trap of assuming that places are centered rather than situated within a larger context. To be sure, Frug's vision of citizenship rejects a neat distinction between space and place, in which place represents fixity and space represents mobility. He offers instead a postmodern view of place as fluid and cosmopolitan, open to the introduction of difference, and bound up with mobility rather than antagonistic to it. On this view, place complements space rather than being distinct from it.

This way of thinking about place has been articulated most clearly by the geographer Doreen Massey in an important essay called *A Global Sense of Place*. Reflecting on the experience of walking down a main street in the Kilburn district of London, Massey observes that Kilburn indeed has a sense of place, that is, a distinctive character, a feeling that the location is imbued with meaning. This sense of place, however, is achieved by moving down the street, not from sitting still, and the sense one gets while moving down the street is not that of a stable community with a "seamless, coherent identity," but rather a meeting place of various "social relations, experiences and understandings." Alongside historical markers of the struggle for a free Ireland, she finds sari shops and advertisements for concerts to which "All Hindus are cordially invited," a Muslim vendor selling conservative tabloid newspapers, and of

---

[11] *See id.* at 83.
[12] *See id.* at 81–85 (on gentrification and anti-gentrification controls); 97–109 (on local voting rights and "the postmodern subject"); WILLIAM H. SIMON, THE COMMUNITY ECONOMIC DEVELOPMENT 224 (2001).

course, a traffic jam on the way into central London. According to Massey, places like Kilburn have a "progressive" or "global" sense of place, in contrast to the parochial republican view of place. These places are "extroverted," in that they are conscious of their links with the outside world, and do not seek "to shrink the world to the size of the community," as the republican idea of place does. Global places like Kilburn do not have boundaries, because boundaries create outsiders. At the same time, global places contain a profound sense of place, because they are not mere abstractions or constructions of global capital, but locations imbued with meaning by the constant display of difference there.[13]

The global sense of place described by Massey helps clarify what distinguishes postmodern citizenship from republican citizenship on one hand, and liberal citizenship on the other. Where the republican model of citizenship, much like the ethno-nationalist model described earlier, is predicated on a bounded, reactionary idea of place that severs the connection between the community and the world, the postmodern idea of citizenship emphasizes the connections between places and the ways that the local is tied to the global. And unlike the liberal, Tieboutian idea of citizenship, which sees municipalities as fungible places of consumption, postmodern citizenship offers a sense of place that is meaningful and liberated from global capitalism.

Postmodern citizenship, as reflected in Massey's global sense of place, is much more expansive and inclusive than any of the other conceptions of citizenship discussed thus far. Rather than segregating people based on their ability to pay (as in the liberal model) or unifying them based on their primordial connections to the territory (as in the republican and nationalist models), places become ways of bringing people together in all their diversity, without amalgamating or diminishing their differences. As a result, people who would otherwise be precluded from citizenship because they lack long-standing community ties, national identity, or consumer status are nevertheless incorporated into political life by displaying their diverse identities *in public places*. In CIVIC WARS, an important history of civic activity in public spaces in America, Mary Ryan reveals that even as power became more privatized and restricted to a privileged class during the postbellum period, those who were shut out of formal political participation used public space to assert their difference and push for greater access to politics. Women, blacks, and members of organized labor made their presence known by marching in

---

[13] Doreen Massey, A *Global Sense of Place*, in SPACE, PLACE, AND GENDER 146, 146–56 (1994).

public parades and holding mass meetings. According to Ryan, these displays were not simply public gatherings but rebellions by marginalized people against a public culture that excluded them. She writes: "As the major ceremonies of industrial America assumed a more universalizing and transcendent aspect . . . those excluded from public culture became more aggressive and forceful in their ceremonial offensives." These groups "defied the culture of transcendence and unity" by appropriating "the open spaces of America's cities as a place not just to display their separate cultures but also to make demands upon the state." These public appearances were "opportunities to construct identities around differences that were only dimly visible in everyday life or social statistics."[14]

The use of public space to display difference and exhibit citizenship remains evident in modern times. As Aihwa Ong describes, though female migrant domestic workers in China and Singapore are treated like a "subhuman underclass," maintained in a permanently subordinate and vulnerable legal status, denied even basic humanitarian protections against physical abuse, essentially "incarcerated" within the domestic sphere and prohibited from appearing in public, Filipina maids regularly resist their political exclusion by staging periodic street festivals. In doing so, these women challenge both the nationalist conception of citizenship as confined to ethnic Chinese, and the divide between the public and private spheres that confines many women to the domestic sphere of the home. Public space becomes a "place" for differentiated identities rather than an abstract and homogenous space for a manufactured societal unity.[15]

By asserting themselves in public places, marginalized people challenge the premise underlying the liberal, republican, and nationalist conceptions of citizenship that the public and private realms should be rigidly segregated and that private concerns necessarily "corrupt" the public realm when they are allowed to be articulated publicly. As Seyla Benhabib astutely observes, "All struggles against oppression in the modern world begin by redefining what had previously been considered nonpublic, private and nonpolitical issues as matters of public concern."[16] Rather than shrinking the public sphere to consumption or national identity, this conception enlarges it to encompass private concerns and identities.

---

[14] Mary Ryan, Civic Wars 256–57 (1997).
[15] Aihwa Ong, A *Biocartography: Maids, Neoslavery, and NGOs*, in Neoliberalism as Exception 202–03 (2006).
[16] Seyla Benhabib, *Models of Public Space*, in Habermas and the Public Sphere 73, 84 (Craig Calhoun ed., 1992).

10.3 THE STATE, SPACE, AND LIBERAL CITIZENSHIP

10.3.1 *The State Transforms the Meaning of Place*

Needless to say, the idea that local citizenship germinates through the display of difference in public places conflicts with the liberal idea that local citizenship occurs in sterile spaces that are stratified based on ability to pay. As a result, the state has often answered the efforts of marginalized groups to redefine citizenship through the appropriation of public places by reasserting a liberal vision of local citizenship based upon abstract, privatized space. Ryan explains that during the late nineteenth century, as women, minorities, and other marginalized groups were beginning to transform public spaces from sites of market activity into places for civic engagement, liberal reformers were simultaneously closing off the formal public sphere of the state by reconceptualizing it in liberal terms as a marketplace. The reformers sought to remove the politics from local government and make cities operate like private businesses, vesting power in expert commissions and professional city managers, stripping authority from elected officials, enacting strict spending and debt limits, conducting public business in private meetings, and attempting to limit the franchise to taxpayers. According to Ryan, the model of government was more the board meeting than the public meeting. These reforms, as Frug famously describes, reinforced the strict distinction between the public and private spheres at the very time that marginalized groups were challenging that distinction.[17]

As part of this movement to reinforce liberal hegemony, public space was also closed off and privatized. Reform governments established the first professional police forces to monitor the use of city spaces, and codified formal as well as informal zoning codes to control the movement of different populations through space. Public health experts used "germ theories" of hygiene to discourage public congregations by assigning negative moral and health connotations to public places like streets, and to urge the segregation of different populations to avoid "contamination," while sociologists articulated theories of the "natural" segregation of populations within the city. Designers and reformers further attempted to discourage street life by enlarging domestic spaces and lauding wholesome domestic

---

[17] *See* RYAN, *supra* note 14, at 183–222; 271–82; Gerald E. Frug, *The City as a Legal Concept*, 93 HARV. L. REV. 1057, 1083–90 (1980) (asserting that public/private distinction has been critical in establishing local governments' subordinate legal status).

culture, while re-directing public life into places of consumption like department stores.[18]

Considering that the appearance of women in public posed an especially important challenge to liberalism's separation of public and private, reformers were preoccupied with controlling women's movement. According to Mona Domosh and Joni Seager, "the presence of women on the street has always been seen as problematic."[19] The reformers' obsession with domestic culture was a means of tying women to the privatized sphere of the home and shaming them from participating in the public life of the street. Until the 1970s, many public accommodations such as bars, diners, and even airplanes refused to serve women, and women had no recourse under civil rights laws.[20] Department stores became feminized, controlled environments where women could appear in public in an unthreatening capacity as consumers.[21]

As Regina Austin has further described, black mobility and black leisure in public space have also been seen as threatening to a liberal, consumer-oriented social order, and so public spaces have been militantly guarded to exclude blacks. During the Jim Crow era, of course, black mobility was constrained by blacks' uncertain ability to access public accommodations and restaurants, and there were a variety of formal and informal social constraints that blacks had to expertly navigate – such as being careful not to pass white drivers on the road in certain towns. Highway and transit lines were often deliberately routed in such a way to make travel for black people very difficult (while also often routed in such a way to disrupt black neighborhoods).[22] Blacks were excluded from places of middle-class leisure and consumption because such prohibitions "enhanced the status of mass forms of leisure" by eliminating "association with persons who were vulgar and rowdy."[23] Even today, Austin notes, blacks' ability to access places of mass

---

[18] See RYAN, *supra* note 14, at 183–222; 276; *see also* WILLIAM LEACH, LAND OF DESIRE: MERCHANTS, POWER, AND THE RISE OF A NEW AMERICAN CULTURE (1994) (describing new culture of consumption embodied by the department store).

[19] MONA DOMOSH & JONI SEAGER, PUTTING WOMEN IN PLACE: FEMINIST GEOGRAPHERS MAKE SENSE OF THE WORLD 72 (2001).

[20] See Elizabeth Sepper & Deborah Dinner, *Sex in Public*, 129 YALE L.J. (forthcoming), https://papers.ssrn.com/sol3/papers.cfm?abstract_id=3344715.

[21] See DOMOSH AND SEAGER, *supra* note 19, at 88–93.

[22] See Regina Austin, *"Not Just for the Fun of It:" Governmental Restraints on Black Leisure, Social Inequality and the Privatization of Public Space*, 71 S. CAL. L. REV. 667, 681–84, 697 (1998); Allyson Hobbs, *Summer Road-Tripping While Black*, N.Y. TIMES (Aug. 31, 2018), https://www.nytimes.com/2018/08/31/opinion/sunday/summer-road-tripping-while-black.html.

[23] Austin, *supra* note 22, at 696.

leisure like movie theaters and parks is often restricted on "colorblind" rationales such as public safety.[24]

Genuine, uncommodified places in which fortuitous encounters could occur were thus transformed into carefully curated places of consumption. This transformation was apotheosized by the movement to the suburbs. Where public spaces like parks and schools were once open places where people of all classes mingled and freely displayed their difference, when the suburbs opened up for settlement by affluent urban dwellers, parks and schools became differentiated in Tieboutian fashion based on ability to pay. Instead of encountering difference, people in wealth-stratified suburbs experienced sameness – others who share their socioeconomic status and demand for public services. Suburban homes were largely placed off limits to the poor and people of color by restrictive zoning laws, while increasing dependence on the automobile and strict enforcement of trespassing laws ensured that access to private suburban shopping malls was limited to the affluent. As Lizabeth Cohen explains, just as blacks were succeeding in using their power as consumers to de-segregate public spaces like parks and swimming pools, they faced exclusion again as those spaces moved out to the suburbs and were placed off limits to nonresidents.[25] In addition, suburban shopping malls and the detached single family home became idealized domesticated spaces for women's consumption. Suburban zoning ordinances strictly separated residential from commercial areas in order to ensure that women's lives revolved around consumption in the home. As we saw in Chapters 4 and 7, women attained the right of suffrage, finally giving them the full rights of citizenship, only after it was clear that women had effectively been confined to the sphere of domestic consumption. In short, the global sense of place was overtaken by stultified places of consumption, and postmodern citizenship based on fortuitous association was overtaken by liberal citizenship in voluntary associations.[26]

---

[24] *See id.* at 673–82.
[25] *See* LIZABETH COHEN, A CONSUMERS' REPUBLIC: THE POLITICS OF MASS CONSUMPTION IN POSTWAR AMERICA 184–91; 265–67; 286–89 (2003).
[26] *See* COHEN, *supra* note 25, at 194–289; DOLORES HAYDEN, THE GRAND DOMESTIC REVOLUTION: A HISTORY OF FEMINIST DESIGNS FOR AMERICAN HOMES, NEIGHBORHOODS, AND CITIES 281–86 (1981) (describing efforts of reformers, government, and business to encourage settlement in single-family homes in the suburbs in order to boost consumption and to define women's roles as domesticated consumers); Margaret Crawford, *The World in a Shopping Mall*, in VARIATIONS ON A THEME PARK 3, 3–30 (Michael Sorkin ed. 1992) (on the culture of consumption embodied in the suburb and the suburban shopping mall); GWENDOLYN WRIGHT, BUILDING THE DREAM: A SOCIAL HISTORY OF HOUSING IN AMERICA 96–113, 193–214 (1981) (on the suburban "cult of domesticity").

For all of these reasons, advocates of postmodern citizenship like Frug are bitterly critical of exclusionary suburbs and their zoning laws.[27] But perhaps even more disturbing for them is the fact that, as cities have enjoyed a resurgence in recent decades after a long period of decline, many are now choosing not to dedicate public spaces to civic activity and fortuitous encounters, but are emulating the liberal suburban model and transforming their public places into places of consumption such as faux historic districts, urban shopping malls, and gentrified downtowns.[28] Critics have denounced the "disneyfication" of urban places, in which the unplanned mingling among strangers is replaced by the appearance of spontaneity in carefully controlled environments. In addition, the creation of urban "tourist bubbles" requires the exclusion of people deemed to detract from the consumer-oriented nature of the space, such as the homeless or political activists. According to Don Mitchell, urban places of consumption "narrow the list of people eligible to form 'the public.'"[29] At the same time, they obscure the reality of homelessness, poverty, and racial segregation from the consuming middle-class person's view.[30] In short, urban places are being deprived of the very qualities – openness, diversity, spontaneity – that would enable them to cultivate postmodern citizenship.

10.3.2 *The Business Improvement District as a Place of Consumption: The Case of* Kessler v. Grand Central District Management Association

As we saw in the last chapter on republican citizenship, the courts have played a key role in affirming local citizenship's liberal character by ratifying the transformation of public spaces into places of consumption. An exemplar of this approach is the case of *Kessler* v. *Grand Central District Management Association*,[31] discussed in Chapter 6. *Kessler* involved a Business Improvement District ("BID") created to manage public space around the Grand Central Terminal in New York. The BID had the power to charge mandatory assessments to landowners near Grand Central and then use the assessed

---

[27] *See, e.g.*, FRUG, *supra* note 1, at 76–81; Frug, *supra* note 2, at; 35–45; 53–60; 75–80.
[28] *See* DON MITCHELL, THE RIGHT TO THE CITY: SOCIAL JUSTICE AND THE FIGHT FOR PUBLIC SPACE 10 (2003) (deploring "suburbanization of downtown").
[29] *See* MITCHELL, *supra* note 28, at 139–41.
[30] On tourist bubbles, faux historic districts, and other aspects of urban areas' transformation into places of consumption, see GERALD E. FRUG & DAVID J. BARRON, CITY BOUND 165–84 (2008); M. Christine Boyer, *Cities for Sale: Merchandising History at South Street Seaport*, in VARIATIONS ON A THEME PARK, *supra* note 26, at 181 .
[31] 158 F.3d 92, 108 (2d Cir. 1998).

funds to make improvements and provide services in the area. The BID's governing board, called the Grand Central District Management Association ("GCDMA"), was elected through a process that gave the great majority of the voting power to the landowners subject to the assessment, and largely disfranchised residents and others affected by the BID's operations. The Second Circuit Court of Appeals held that the GCDMA governing structure was not subject to the constitutionally mandated "one person, one vote" rule because the landowners who enjoyed most of the voting power were disproportionately interested in the BID's governance. As the court stated: "The principal economic benefit from GCDMA's activities . . . plainly accrues to the property owners, who will enjoy an increase in the value of their property."[32]

In affirming the constitutionality of the BID's governing structure, the court was also placing its imprimatur on a mechanism that has been a critical part of the transformation of urban places into places of consumption like tourist bubbles and sanitized historic districts.[33] The very *raison d'etre* of the BID is to increase property values for landowners in urban areas by making those areas into pleasing destinations for middle-class consumers. BIDs regularly lobby city hall on zoning and land use matters to ensure that the spaces they manage are kept clear of undesirable land uses like street vendors and adult entertainment businesses. They have also used less formal mechanisms to keep their spaces clear of the homeless and panhandlers.[34] One BID in New York erected barriers to keep out the homeless, reasoning that "We're just trying to protect our own turf."[35] Several BIDs, including the GCDMA, have been accused of using "goon squads" to harass and intimidate the homeless. While many of these allegations have proven to be unfounded, there is a clear conflict of interest between the desire of homeless and other disadvantaged individuals to use public space for their basic daily needs and the desire of BIDs to make the space attractive for business and tourism. In short, as Richard Schragger argues, BIDs are actively engaged in "defining and delineating the contours of public space itself."[36]

---

[32] 158 F.3d at 108.

[33] *See, e.g.,* MICHAEL WARNER, THE TROUBLE WITH NORMAL: SEX, POLITICS AND THE ETHICS OF QUEER LIFE 161 (1999) (discussing role of Times Square BID in pushing for rezoning of Times Square to outlaw adult businesses and making the area desirable for middle-class tourists and consumers).

[34] Robert C. Ellickson, *Controlling Chronic Misconduct in City Spaces: Of Panhandlers, Skid Rows, and Public-Space Zoning,* 105 YALE L.J. 1165, 1199 (1996).

[35] *Quoted in* SHARON ZUKIN, NAKED CITY 145 (2010).

[36] Richard Schragger, *The Limits of Localism,* 100 MICH. L. REV. 371, 457 (2001). On the BID generally, and the ways in which it acts as a land use authority, see Kenneth A. Stahl, *Local Government, "One Person, One Vote," and the Jewish Question,* 49 HARV. C.R.-C.L. L. REV. 1,

Perhaps not surprisingly, the people who are most likely to be harmed by the BIDs' exercise of land use authority – street vendors, the homeless, long-term residents who may be displaced by higher rents as property values increase – are also disfranchised by the BID governing board. The reason they are disfranchised is because their interest in the governance of the BID is not commodifiable in the way a landowner's interest is. This is clear in the court's conclusion that the GCDMA may constitutionally deviate from "one person, one vote" and weight votes based on property ownership because "[t]he principal economic benefit from GCDMA's activities ... plainly accrues to the property owners, who will enjoy an increase in the value of their property."[37] Functionally, the BID operates to ensure that those individuals whose interests are not reducible to property values are excluded from both participation in its government *and* the public space the BID governs.[38] They are not part of the public that the BID is obligated to serve.

As a result, the public spaces subject to the BID's jurisdiction are sanitized of all but market interests, converted from genuine places into places of consumption. Such spaces can no longer serve as meeting places for "fortuitous associations," as Frug intends, or for the display of difference, as Ryan describes. Citizenship ceases to be the act of reconciling oneself to difference or asserting one's identity, and becomes instead a right to participate in the marketplace available only to those with sufficient financial means to purchase access. As Don Mitchell laments, BIDs suppress the *political* capacity of the places they control by ensuring that commerce is the only activity that can be conducted there. "Market and design considerations thus displace the idiosyncratic and extemporaneous interactions of engaged people in the

---

48–52 (2014); Kenneth A. Stahl, *Neighborhood Empowerment and the Future of the City*, 161 U. PA. L. REV. 939, 975–76; 993 (2013); Audrey McFarlane, *Preserving Community in the City: Special Improvement Districts and the Privatization of Urban Racialized Space*, 4 STAN. AGORA 5 (2003); Richard Briffault, *A Government for Our Time: Business Improvement Districts and Urban Governance*, 99 COLUM. L. REV. 365 (1999).

[37] *Kessler*, 158 F.3d at 108. The court also states that landowners are disproportionately interested in BID governance because they are the ones who pay the mandatory assessment that finances the BID's operation. *See id.* at 107. The hornbook rule on special assessments is that the assessment charged to each landowner may not exceed the particular benefit that landowner receives. Thus, the legitimacy of the assessment is directly tied to the anticipated increase in property values from overcoming the collective action problem.

[38] For another case with similar logic, see S. Cal. Rapid Transit Dist. v. Bolen, 822 P.2d 875, 883 (1992) (assessment districts to finance rail stations through assessments on nearby landowners could limit the franchise to assessed landowners because "it is they who will most directly feel both the beneficial economic effects of the transit station locations and bear the financial burden of the annual assessments").

determination of the shape of urban space in the contemporary world."[39] Further, marginalized people like the homeless are effectively denied citizenship because they are refused access to the places that have historically been the public fora in which democratic action takes place. Mitchell writes that the effort to bar the homeless from public spaces "re-creates the public sphere as intentionally exclusive, as a sphere in which the legitimate public includes only those who ... have a place governed by private property rules to call their own. Landed property thus again becomes a prerequisite for legitimate citizenship."[40]

For postmodernists, replacing the diversity and spontaneity of urban life with carefully controlled consumption destroys the fortuitous association that ought to characterize the city. As Frug describes his ideal city, for example, there is

> a reaction that is common among people who live in big cities – and quite different from the feelings of discomfort and alarm so often experienced by suburban residents – when the girl with green hair and multiple piercings, the African American kids blasting hip-hop on a boom box, the gay couple holding hands, the panhandler, and the mentally ill person pushing a shopping cart pass by. That reaction is: Whatever.[41]

10.4 CRITIQUE OF POSTMODERN CITIZENSHIP

Here, however, we come to the great flaw in the postmodern model. In an important critique of Frug's City Making, Richard Ford argues that the openness to difference Frug celebrates may ironically lead right back to the closed-mindedness Frug denounces. As Ford explains, urban dwellers in even the most progressive cities have a limited ability to tolerate aggressive panhandlers and hostile encounters with the homeless. When those limits are reached, people may flee to neighboring suburban communities where they can exercise more control over their environments.[42]

Ford's observation has long been echoed by sociologists, who have noted that the extreme openness and diversity of the city is so overwhelming that it may become impossible for citizens to engage in the civic-minded spirit Frug

[39] MITCHELL, *supra* note 28, at 140. Frug is also critical of BIDs in Gerald E. Frug, *The Seductions of Form*, 3 DREXEL L. REV. 11, 17 (2010).
[40] *Id.* at 183–84.
[41] FRUG, *supra* note 1, at 213.
[42] Richard Thompson Ford, *Bourgeois Communities: A Review of Gerald Frug's* City Making, 56 STAN. L. REV. 231, 241–45 (2003).

intends. Constantly being around strangers can be disorienting and unsettling, and it can lead to exploitation, harassment, and violence, or at least the fear of it. Robert Putnam's research shows that a racially and ethnically diverse community is associated with lower levels of trust and cooperation, higher population turnover and less civic participation, as well as less confidence and engagement in government, fewer friends, and less happiness. Conversely, ethnically and racially homogeneous groups have higher levels of trust, which confers all sorts of positive impacts on communities, including safer neighborhoods, better schools, healthier children, and more overall satisfaction with life.[43] Putnam and others have shown that over the long term, urban dwellers can develop the capacity to tolerate and enjoy diversity, but in the short term they may find that diversity so destabilizing that they never have a chance to develop a tolerance for it.[44]

As the early urban sociologists who studied the industrial city realized, coping with the bewildering diversity of urban life requires some form of defense mechanism. One such mechanism is the dividing up of urban space into particularized zones for specific ethnic groups or people with shared interests – like BIDs. According to the sociologist Lynn Lofland, city dwellers buffer themselves against the impersonality and diversity of the city at large by carving out enclaves or "urban villages," populated by individuals with shared norms and cultural backgrounds. As Lofland writes, "[w]e can live in the world of strangers only because we have found a way to eliminate some of the 'strangeness.'" This does not mean that urban dwellers avoid all interactions with strangers but that their interactions with strangers are made less threatening because strangers can be identified based on their location. A truly borderless or "global" citizenship of the type Frug and Massey advocate would make it impossible to create the normative subcommunities that enable urban diversity to flourish.[45]

Similarly, if cities have no ability to police their borders, they may lose what makes their openness desirable. Absent some closure or boundary, the difference that Frug embraces as the foundation of postmodern citizenship is inevitably ephemeral. For instance, Frug envisions the city as a mosaic of discrete and culturally distinct subcommunities, offering "a differentiation between neighborhoods, thereby producing a distinct sense of place when

---

[43] ROBERT D. PUTNAM, BOWLING ALONE 400 (2000); Robert D. Putnam, E Pluribus Unum: *Diversity and Community in the Twenty-First Century*, 30 SCANDINAVIAN POL. STUD. 137, 142–43, 149–50 (2007).

[44] Putnam, supra note 43, at 138–39.

[45] LYNN LOFLAND, A WORLD OF STRANGERS 66–91, 118–37, 176 (1973).

one travels from one location to another."[46] But such differentiation is hard to maintain if those neighborhoods have no ability to protect their character against change. As Rosabeth Kanter's study of nineteenth-century communes observes, "the community's distinctiveness and social isolation may be lost when boundaries are relatively permeable."[47] But Frug is so committed to openness that he is loath to permit any closure, even at the neighborhood level.

If one line of criticism is that postmodern citizenship is too open to be meaningful, another is that its openness is only superficial. Early urban sociologists like Georg Simmel and Louis Wirth realized that urban dwellers could only cope with the bewildering diversity of urban life by adopting a "blasé attitude" toward it.[48] Diversity becomes a kind of window dressing that we observe but do not engage with in a meaningful sense. According to Richard Sennett,

> in modern life we are all so immersed in our inner life that we pass by difference without soaking it in; we perceive difference but react to it with aloofness. We are unable or unwilling to communicate with those who are different, although we are surrounded by them and constantly in contact with them.[49]

The "whatever" attitude that urban dwellers demonstrate toward difference, in other words, is not a basis for genuine political activity.

Modern sociologists have likewise observed that the postmodern championing of diversity is a kind of "aestheticized difference," that is, "an appreciation of diversity as a picturesque scene that gives those who look on a sense of cultural capital – a sense of their own self-worth in being able to appreciate difference."[50] This "aestheticized" approach to diversity may lead cities to become the places of consumption that Frug and Massey see as antithetical to postmodern citizenship and a global sense of place. Urban diversity is now perceived as an amenity that has lured the wealthy back to cities, leading to concerns about gentrification of historically disadvantaged neighborhoods. Though there is some debate about the extent to which gentrification

---

[46] See FRUG, *supra* note 1, at 117.

[47] See ROSABETH MOSS KANTER, COMMITMENT AND COMMUNITY 148–61 (1972).

[48] See Georg Simmel, *The Metropolis and Mental Life*, in CLASSIC ESSAYS ON THE CULTURE OF CITIES 47, 51 (Richard Sennett ed. 1969); Louis Wirth, *Urbanism as a Way of Life*, in CLASSIC ESSAYS ON THE CULTURE OF CITIES, *supra*, at 143, 153.

[49] See RICHARD SENNETT, THE CONSCIENCE OF THE EYE 128–29 (1990).

[50] See TIM CRESWELL, PLACE: A SHORT INTRODUCTION 78 (2004) (*citing* Jon May, *Globalization and the Politics of Place: Place and Identity in an Inner London Neighborhood*, 21 TRANS. OF THE INST. OF BRITISH GEOG. 194, 208 (1996)).

increases rents and causes displacement of existing residents, there is no doubt that gentrification changes the character of existing neighborhoods, often causing unique local businesses to be displaced by global chains, or in other words, the displacement of urban difference with a kind of sameness. According to Sarah Schulman, gentrification imports the "suburban values" of "racial and class stratification, homogeneity of consumption, mass-produced aesthetics, and familial privatization" into the city.[51]

In short, where republican citizenship's embrace of closure leads it down a path to xenophobia and exclusion, postmodern citizenship's embrace of openness makes it so amorphous as to be self-defeating.

---

[51] Sarah Schulman, The Gentrification of the Mind 23–35 (2012).

11

Differentiated Citizenship

If republican citizenship (Chapter 9) fails because it is too closed, excluding all those who are perceived as inauthentically tied to the city's places, postmodern citizenship (Chapter 10) fails because it is too open, refusing to draw any boundaries around places at all. Between these two extremes, however, may lie a third option, "differentiated citizenship."[1] Like republican and postmodern citizenship, differentiated citizenship uses a commitment to place to challenge the liberal and ethno-nationalist models of local citizenship, but does so in a way that attempts to avoid the destructive choice between extreme openness and extreme closure. This chapter explores differentiated citizenship and what distinguishes it from postmodern and republican citizenship. Like these others, differentiated citizenship has not been particularly embraced by the guardians of our legal and political tradition, who see differentiated citizenship (correctly) as a threat to the predominant liberal model of local citizenship. Ultimately, I conclude that differentiated citizenship is also flawed because it wavers on its commitments in a way that renders it unintelligible.

11.1 THE CONCEPT OF DIFFERENTIATED CITIZENSHIP

As articulated by its main proponents Iris Young and Will Kymlicka, differentiated citizenship means the incorporation of people into political life not as individuals but as members of the different national, ethnic, or religious

---

[1] See WILL KYMLICKA, MULTICULTURAL CITIZENSHIP (1995); IRIS MARION YOUNG, JUSTICE AND THE POLITICS OF DIFFERENCE (1990); Will Kymlicka & Wayne Norman, *Return of the Citizen: A Survey of Recent Work on Citizenship Theory*, 104 ETHICS 352 (Jan. 1994); Iris Marion Young, *Polity & Group Difference: A Critique of the Ideal of Universal Citizenship*, 99 ETHICS 250 (Jan. 1989).

groups to which they belong. These groups would enjoy rights to maintain their cultural distinctiveness, including exemptions from generally applicable laws for religious practices, language rights, weighted representation in legislatures, and, most significantly from the place-based perspective, collective rights to own land or engage in territorial self-government. Kymlicka, for example, speaks favorably of many countries' policies of reserving lands for ownership by indigenous peoples. Title is held collectively by the group in order to prevent individual landowners from selling off tribal lands piecemeal. In this way, the integrity of the group is protected against the commodification of its land that individual ownership would promote.[2]

Differentiated citizenship challenges the very premise of liberal citizenship that the only meaningful political relationship is that between the individual and the state. The cultural group, intermediate between the individual and the state, becomes the basis of political organization. According to Kymlicka and Young, recognizing group rights is necessary to provide members of minority groups with the benefits of full citizenship because the supposed neutrality and universality of liberal citizenship is a myth that actually privileges the culture of the majority group at the expense of other cultural groups. As Young writes, "The attempt to realize an ideal of universal citizenship that finds the public embodying generality as opposed to particularity, commonness versus difference, will tend to exclude or to put at a disadvantage some groups, even when they have formally equal citizenship status."[3] This is so because there simply is no impartial, universal perspective, and so claiming to ignore "groupness" means that the culture of the existing dominant group will prevail. Indeed, as Kymlicka points out, citizenship in the liberal nation-state inherently demarcates the "in-group" from the "out-group" and is therefore itself a group-differentiated concept. Thus, recognizing minority group rights simply places them on equal footing with the privileged majority.[4]

Differentiated citizenship shares much in common with both republican and postmodern citizenship. Like postmodern citizenship, it builds citizenship on a foundation of difference rather than sameness. Like republican citizenship, it gives groups the right to maintain their distinctiveness against the pressures of liberal cultural and economic homogeneity.[5] It shares with both conceptions a mistrust of the consumer-oriented vision of citizenship and

---

[2] See KYMLICKA, *supra* note 1, at 26–33; 43; 174–87 (on tribal land rights); YOUNG, *supra* note 1, at 156–91; Kymlicka & Norman, *supra* note 1, at 370–77; Young, *supra* note 1, at 258–67; 270–74.

[3] YOUNG, *supra* note 1, at 256–57; *see also* KYMLICKA, Note 1, at 124–25.

[4] YOUNG, *supra* note 1, at 256–57; KYMLICKA, *supra* note 1, at 124–25.

[5] YOUNG, *supra* note 1, at 15–38 (on liberal orientation of the "distributive paradigm").

a rejection of the liberal belief that the self is fully constituted in the individual.[6] And, like the other two conceptions, differentiated citizenship is based on an idea of the city as a place where citizens can be free from the market-orientation of liberalism and space to express their differences in public. Young, for instance, denounces the way that municipal economies have become hostage to mobile capital, resulting in "an abstract space of efficiency and Cartesian rationality that often comes to dominate and displace the lived space of human movement and interaction."[7] In this "abstract space," group differences are amalgamated or neglected, often resulting in the exploitation and displacement of marginalized groups, while at the same time cities are segregated based on race and class. Young favors instead an ideal of "social differentiation without exclusion," where groups come together in public places to celebrate their differences. "In this ideal groups do not stand in relations of inclusion and exclusion, but overlap and inter-mingle without becoming homogenous."[8] In her view, the city reinforces and encourages the formation of group identities, especially among marginalized and "deviant" groups who find "both a cover of anonymity and a critical mass unavailable in the smaller town."[9]

11.2 THE MYTH OF COMMUNITY

At the same time, differentiated citizenship also diverges from the republican and postmodern citizenship models in important ways. Initially, Young and Kymlicka both assail Sandel's republican vision of citizenship as incompatible with a citizenship based on difference. Sandel's vision, as we recall, was that of a closed "constitutive community" with rights to wall itself off from the impositions of the outside world. Such constitutive communities share "a common vocabulary of discourse and a background of implicit practices and understandings within which the opacity of the participants is reduced if never fully dissolved."[10] Young denounces what she calls Sandel's "myth of commu-nity," which "expresses a longing for harmony among persons, for consensus and mutual understanding ... "[11] This longing will inevitably go unrequited because "[f]eelings, desires, and commitments do not cease to exist and motivate just because they have been excluded from the definition of moral

---

[6] *See id.* at 45 ("The self is a product of social processes, not their origin.")

[7] *See id.* at 242–43.

[8] *See id.* at 238–39.

[9] *Id.* at 238.

[10] MICHAEL SANDEL, LIBERALISM AND THE LIMITS OF JUSTICE 172–73 (1982).

[11] *See* YOUNG, *supra* note 1, at 229.

reason. They lurk as inarticulate shadows, belying the claim to comprehensiveness of universalist reason."[12]

The troubling implication of the "myth of community," like ethnonationalism, is that it justifies the suppression of difference and the exclusion of those deemed different. According to Young, "[t]he most serious political consequence of the desire for community, or for copresence and mutual identification with others, is that it often operates to exclude or oppress those experienced as different. Commitment to an ideal of community tends to value and enforce homogeneity." And, to return to the theme of place, Young goes on to observe that this homogenous vision of community often manifests as a reactionary effort to preserve cherished places against change and difference: "pressuring the Black family that buys a house on the block to leave; beating up the black youths who come into 'our' neighborhood; zoning against the building of multiunit dwellings."[13]

Like Frug and Massey's idea of postmodern citizenship, differentiated citizenship defines place far more expansively than the republican vision. For Young, as for Frug, citizenship is a celebration of group difference that occurs in the city's places. Indeed, Young defines the city itself as the "being together of strangers," the confluence of differences in physical space. According to Young, "as a normative idea, city life instantiates social relations of difference without exclusion. Different groups dwell in the city alongside one another, of necessity interacting in city spaces." This being together of strangers "entails some common problems and common interests, but they do not create a community of shared final ends, of mutual identification and reciprocity." The city, as Young sees it, has its ethnic neighborhoods but their borders are porous. "In the good city one crosses from one distinct neighborhood to another without knowing precisely where one ended and the other began. In the normative ideal of city life, borders are open and undecidable."[14]

11.3 RECOGNITION FOR GROUP DIFFERENCE

Though Young's vision of differentiated citizenship seems quite similar to Frug and Massey's idea of postmodern citizenship, they diverge in that, where postmodern citizenship assumes that all identities are inherently unstable and therefore that the state should steer clear of shoring up particular identifications, Young and Kymlicka both call for affirmative measures to

---

[12] *See id.* at 103.
[13] *Id.* at 234–35.
[14] *Id.* at 227, 237–39.

protect group difference, particularly representation for groups in legislatures.[15] According to Young, "blindness to difference disadvantages groups
whose experiences, culture, and socialized capacities differ from those of
privileged groups." A political system that fails to recognize difference
therefore marginalizes groups outside the privileged majority culture. "The
solution lies at least in part in providing institutionalized means for the
explicit recognition and representation of oppressed groups," such as collective representational rights for those groups in political bodies and veto
power over decisions that affect them.[16]

Unlike postmodern citizenship, then, differentiated citizenship treats group
differences as stable rather than ephemeral, and therefore entitled to political
recognition. According to Kymlicka, our membership in particular cultural
groups, "affects how others perceive and respond to us, which in turn shapes
our self-identity."[17] For Kymlicka, cultural groups serve as a central focal point
in self-identification because they are based on belonging rather than accom-
plishment. As Frug himself acknowledges, postmodern citizenship lacks this
sense of belonging. "Being connected everywhere seems the equivalent of
being connected nowhere (and to no one). Not only 'I' but 'we' becomes a
word with no particular meaning."[18]

As we recall, one of the perils of providing groups with political recognition is that it may create a sense of national identity that then leads to calls
for secession from the wider polity, thereby dissolving society's differences
into a balkanized geography of homogenous cultures. But neither Young nor
Kymlicka see differentiated citizenship that way. For them, it is a means of
integrating subgroups into political society. Marginalized groups have been
excluded from full participation in the larger society because of their cultural differences, so they can only be included in that society by recognizing
those differences.[19]

11.4 DIFFERENTIATED CITIZENSHIP IN PLACE

At the time Young and Kymlicka wrote, an age when cities were in decline
and suburbs were synonymous with an affluent white middle class, the idea

---

[15] KYMLICKA, *supra* note 1, at 26–33; 131–51; 174–87 (on self-government and special
  representational rights); YOUNG, 164; 183–91 (on need for special representation rights).
[16] YOUNG, *supra* note 1, at 183–91; KYMLICKA, *supra* note 1, at 138–49; Young, *supra* note 1,
  at 257–59.
[17] *See* KYMLICKA, *supra* note 1, at 89.
[18] GERALD FRUG, CITY MAKING: BUILDING COMMUNITIES WITHOUT BUILDING WALLS 110 (1999).
[19] *See* KYMLICKA, *supra* note 1, at 176–81.

that cities would be sites of differentiated citizenship might have seemed like a utopian fantasy. In our age of globalization, however, that vision is increasingly being realized. As the world has become more globalized, borders more porous, and people more mobile, cities as well as many suburbs have emerged as enclaves for particular ethnic and racial groups. Groups that are minorities at the state or national level may be a majority in particular localities or neighborhoods, giving them leverage to make political demands. For example, blacks are highly concentrated in many cities in the northeast and south; Hispanics in the sunbelt, and Asians in cities along the west coast. In addition, many cities today contain multiple ethnic and racial groupings. As Richard Ford notes, "Immigration has literally produced a third world within the metropole: for example, Los Angeles, California now has the largest Spanish-speaking population in the world outside Mexico City, and the largest Korean-speaking population outside Seoul."[20]

Mass migration has caused the emergence of huge diasporic enclaves within cities that often recreate entire "old world" communities with which they maintain close contacts. William Sites and Rebecca Vonderlack-Navarro describe how several Mexican immigrant neighborhoods in Chicago created "hometown associations" to foster political and cultural ties with their places of origin in Mexico.[21] Samuel Huntington observes that two-thirds of the families in the village of Miraflores in the Dominican Republic have relatives in the neighborhood of Jamaica Plain in Boston. Jamaica Plain has become a virtual extension of Miraflores as people and information are constantly flowing back and forth between them. "As a result, when someone is ill, cheating on his spouse, or finally granted a visa, the news spreads as quickly in Jamaica Plan as it does on the streets of Miraflores."[22] This is an incredibly interesting example of how space and place are closely intertwined – the rapid movement of people across borders enables the creation of a real, authentic place in Jamaica Plain.

The relationship between particular racial or ethnic groups and places has enabled those groups to organize and push for policies that meet their collective demands, and often for direct political control over the territory

---

[20] Richard T. Ford, *City-States and Citizenship, in* CITIZENSHIP TODAY 209, 217 (T. Alexander Aleinikoff & Doiglas Klusmeyer eds., 2001).

[21] *See* William Sites & Rebecca Vonderlack-Navarro, *Tipping the Scale: State Rescaling and the Strange Odyssey of Chicago's Mexican Hometown Associations, in* REMAKING URBAN CITIZENSHIP: ORGANIZATIONS, INSTITUTIONS AND THE RIGHT TO THE CITY 151 (Michael Peter Smith & Michael McQuarrie eds. 2012).

[22] *See* SAMUEL HUNTINGTON, WHO ARE WE? THE CHALLENGE TO AMERICA'S NATIONAL IDENTITY 206 (2004).

they inhabit. This process began in the 1960s, when historically disadvantaged black and Hispanic communities organized to fight urban renewal schemes that targeted those communities. What began as project-specific neighborhood organizing led to broader demands that minority communities be more fully incorporated into city government. Aided by the enactment of a federal Voting Rights Act, community organizations forced many cities, especially in the sunbelt, to change their method of electing city council members from "at-large" systems in which all of the council members are elected in a single, citywide election, to district or "ward" elections in which council members are elected from specific geographic areas within the city. District elections allowed ethnic groups that were highly concentrated in specific neighborhoods to have legislators who represented the interests of those neighborhoods. The switch to district elections ushered in a "new style of politics" for many sunbelt cities, in which traditional power brokers now had to reckon with the power of neighborhood-based organizations. According to Carl Abbott, after 1965 minority communities in sunbelt cities "all learned to use spatial concentration and neighborhood networks as political resources." They "created city council districts, neighborhood organizations, and community groups that could use their geographic bases to articulate a variety of public interests."[23] The Sunbelt cities that converted from at-large to district elections during the 1970s and 1980s all experienced increased attentiveness to neighborhood and minority concerns, such as land-use siting, provision of city services, and relations with the police.[24] Empirical studies also show that district systems lead to increased minority representation.[25]

---

[23] CARL ABBOTT, THE METROPOLITAN FRONTIER: CITIES IN THE MODERN AMERICAN WEST 102 (1993).

[24] *See* CARL ABBOTT, THE NEW URBAN AMERICA: GROWTH AND POLITICS IN SUNBELT CITIES 214–15, 241–43 (rev. ed. 1987) (discussing "new style of politics" in Sunbelt cities that have switched to ward voting, in which cities are forced to pay attention to concerns of slow-growth neighborhood groups and minority neighborhoods); AMY BRIDGES, MORNING GLORIES: MUNICIPAL REFORM IN THE SOUTHWEST 204–06 (1997) (noting improvement in equitable provision of city services after switch to ward voting); DENNIS R. JUDD & TODD SWANSTROM, CITY POLITICS: PRIVATE POWER AND PUBLIC POLICY 217–18, 384, 390 (4th ed. 2004) (noting improvements in police relations, neighborhood involvement in city planning and development, and minority hiring in cities that switched to ward voting); Milton D. Morris, *Black Electoral Participation and the Distribution of Public Benefits, in* MINORITY VOTE DILUTION 271, 283–84 (Chandler Davidson ed., 1984) (noting increased responsiveness to needs for community services, increased municipal jobs held by African Americans, and shifts in governmental priorities).

[25] *See, e.g.,* Chandler Davidson & George Korbel, *At-Large Elections and Minority Group Representation, in* MINORITY VOTE DILUTION, *supra* note 24, at 65; Jerry L. Polinard et al., *The Impact of District Elections on the Mexican American Community: The Electoral Perspective,* 72

In addition to organizing for quotidian demands such as improved city services, many racial and ethnic groups have used their "spatial concentration" in particular places to obtain recognition of collective cultural rights as well. A vivid example is Monterey Park, a small city in Los Angeles County's San Gabriel Valley. During the 1980s, Monterey Park was rapidly shifting from a majority white city to a diverse municipality with large Asian and Hispanic populations. Members of the existing white community formed an organization called RAMP (Resident Association of Monterey Park), which had the traditional NIMBY purpose of slowing the city's growth, but coupled with a nativist goal of preventing a "Chinese takeover" of the town. After a city council election in which RAMP's preferred candidates defeated a handful of minority candidates, the city council adopted an ordinance requiring Chinese businesses to include English translations on their storefronts.[26]

In the aftermath of the ordinance and the 1990 census, an organization of Asian American citizens petitioned the California state assembly to create a new assembly district that represented Asian Americans in the area around Monterey Park. The organization argued that "there was such an entity as an 'Asian American' community." Former Monterey Park Mayor and City Council member Judy Chu testified that, "[w]ithout concentrated districts, the ability for Asian Americans to express their concern about issues will be diluted." As an example, Chu cited "attempts to restrict languages other than English from being spoken in public, from being written on any city materials that went to the public, and from being on commercial signs ... [and] attempts to prevent foreign-language materials from being in [the Monterey Park] library."[27] Ultimately, the state agreed to create a new district that included the areas with the largest Asian populations in the San Gabriel Valley and the places with the heaviest Asian population growth. As Robert Chang and Keith Aoki explain, the redistricting has caused many Asian Americans to think of themselves as part of a distinct "Asian American" voting bloc.[28]

Soc. Sci. Q. 608, 611–14 (1991); Jeffrey S. Zax, *Election Methods and Black and Hispanic City Council Membership*, 71 Soc. Sci. Q. 339, 353–54 (1990).

[26] *See* Robert S. Chang & Keith Aoki, *Centering the Immigrant in the Inter/National Imagination*, 85 Calif. L. Rev. 1395, 1431–42 (1997); *see also* Keith Aoki, *A Tale of Three Cities: Thoughts on Asian American Electoral and Political Power after 2000*, 8 Asian Pac. Am. L.J. 1, 15–22 (2002).

[27] *See* Chang & Aoki, *supra* note 26, at 1431–32.

[28] *See id.*

Other marginalized groups have also used their connection to places to claim a right of collective cultural citizenship. Benjamin Forest's incisive analysis of the incorporation of West Hollywood, California, makes this clear.[29] In the 1980s, West Hollywood was an unincorporated part of Los Angeles County with a large gay population. When residents of the area organized to incorporate West Hollywood as a city, Forest explains that the gay community quickly took up the incorporation cause as a way to achieve recognition as a legitimate social and political group. The gay press in West Hollywood used the incorporation campaign "to construct an alternative, positive identity" for gays, "one that accepted and co-opted some existing stereotypes" about gays.[30] For example, the gay press emphasized West Hollywood's status as a hub for creative activity, entertainment, and progressive values. According to Forest, because place is seen as a natural and pre-political way of organizing people, tying gay identity to the physical space of West Hollywood through incorporation was a way of legitimizing gay political organization, analogous to the way ethnic groups organize politically in places. "[T]he use of place encourages the common-sense perception that gays are a social group as natural, and therefore as legitimate, as ethnicities."[31] Thus, Forest concludes that "it is possible to see the incorporation campaign as an attempt by gays to achieve the entitlements of citizenship by (symbolically) creating themselves as a social group."[32]

11.5 THE STATE REJECTS DIFFERENTIATED CITIZENSHIP

As we have seen before, however, efforts to implement differentiated citizenship in place have run straight into the nation-state's insistence on individualism, a single national identity, and undifferentiated space. As an initial matter, the courts have been wary at best of allowing legislative districts to be based on group identity. In adopting the "one person, one vote" principle in the 1960s, the Supreme Court rejected the argument that states should be permitted to recognize group difference by weighting votes territorially to accommodate people's attachments to particular places. In response to claims by dissenting justices that "representative government is a process of accommodating group

---

[29] Benjamin Forest, *West Hollywood as a Symbol: The Significance of Place in the Construction of a Gay Identity*, 13 ENVI. & PLAN. D: SOCIETY & SPACE 133 (1995).
[30] *Id.* at 141.
[31] *Id.* at 151.
[32] *Id.* at 150.

interests,"[33] the Court answered that "the rights allegedly impaired are individual and personal in nature."[34]

In recent years, the Supreme Court has been especially vigilant to ensure that districts are drawn to represent individuals and not groups, especially racial groups. In *Shaw v. Reno*, the Court struck down a districting system designed to provide greater political representation for blacks in North Carolina, arguing that crafting districts to provide direct representation for racial groups "bears an uncomfortable relationship to political apartheid" and "threatens to carry us further from the goal of a political system in which race no longer matters."[35] Electoral districts are not supposed to be organic communities of people with shared interests, but random and arbitrary groupings of individuals. According to Benjamin Forest, "the placement of a voter in a district reflects the optimal solution to an allocation problem, not a normative judgment about the membership of that voter in a particular community."[36]

The Court's hostility toward race-based districting is part of a broader skepticism on the Court's part about any "affirmative action" mechanisms that threaten to elevate group rights over individual rights. Cristina Rodriguez observes, for example, a similar judicial reluctance to recognize collective language rights, which is another key component of Kymlicka and Young's differentiated citizenship model. According to Rodriguez, "courts generally have treated linguistic difference as a barrier to overcome" in furtherance of a unitary national identity.[37] One court, for example, held that schools were not required by federal law to provide bilingual education programs, stating that "linguistic and cultural diversity within the nation state, whatever may be its advantages from time to time, can restrict the scope of the fundamental compact."[38]

---

[33] Lucas v. Forty-Fourth Gen. Assembly of Colorado, 377 U.S. 713, 749 (1964) (Stewart, J., dissenting); *see also id.* at 750 ("Legislators do not represent faceless numbers. They represent people, or more accurately, the majority of the voters in their districts – people with identifiable needs and interests which require legislative representation, and which can often be related to the geographical areas in which these people live.") Reynolds v. Sims, 377 U.S. 533, 623–24 (1964) ("[L]egislators can represent their electors only by speaking for their interests – many of which do reflect the place where the electors live.")

[34] Reynolds, 377 U.S. at 561.

[35] 509 U.S. 630, 647, 657 (1993).

[36] Benjamin Forest, *Mapping Democracy: Racial Identity and the Quandary of Political Representation*, 91 ANNALS OF ASS'N OF AMER. GEO. 143, 156 (2001).

[37] *See* Cristina M. Rodriguez, *Accommodating Linguistic Difference: Toward a Comprehensive Theory of Language Rights in the United States*, 36 HARV. C.R.C.L. L. REV. 133, 209 (2001).

[38] Guadalupe Organization, Inc. v. Tempe Elementary School District No. 3, 587 F.2d 1022, 1027 (9th Cir. 1978); Rodriguez, *supra* note 37, at 211.

Differentiated citizenship has proven most threatening to the national "compact" in circumstances where groups have attempted to assert collective control over particular places in a way that challenges the predominant judicial idea of local citizenship as liberal, based on mobility and money and unmoored from places. Take the case of *City of Chicago* v. *Morales*.[39] The city of Chicago enacted a "gang congregation ordinance" that prohibited individuals identified as "criminal street gang members" from "'loitering' with one another or with other persons in any public place."[40] According to Dan Kahan and Tracey Meares, this law and others like it were properly understood not as top-down mandates, but as organic products of the local black community.[41] Unlike historical vagrancy laws that often targeted minorities, Chicago's gang congregation law was championed by black political and religious leaders as a way of protecting the safety of their communities and promoting their collective values. As a result of the Voting Rights Act and effective community organizing, blacks now possess "considerable political influence" in many urban areas.[42] Community leaders see gang congregation ordinances as ways of shoring up the internal cultural foundations of the community, so that the community can effectively police itself.[43] Kahan and Meares emphasize that gang congregation laws were not designed to punish young gang members, but to protect them against the far harsher consequences of the drug war – lengthy incarceration, inability to vote or find work, lives of violence and death. According to Kahan and Meares, black communities strongly believe in the idea of "linked fate," that is, "the sense in which many African Americans measure their individual well-being by assessing the

---

[39]   527 U.S. 41 (1997).

[40]   *See id.* at 45–46.

[41]   *See, e.g.,* Dan M. Kahan & Tracey L. Meares, *Foreword: The Coming Crisis of Criminal Procedure,* 86 Geo. L .J. 1153, 1160–61 (1998); Tracey L. Meares & Dan Kahan, *The Wages of Antiquated Procedural Thinking: A Critique of Chicago v. Morales,* 1998 U. Chi. Legal F. 197 [hereinafter *Wages*]; Tracey L. Meares & Dan M. Kahan, *Law and (Norms of) Order in the Inner City,* 32 Law & Soc. Rev. 805 (1998) [Herainafter *Norms*]; Brief Amicus Curiae of the Chicago Neighborhood Organizations in Support of Petitioner, City of Chicago v. Morales, 1998 WL 328366 (U.S.) [hereinafter *Morales Amicus Brief*].

[42]   *Morales Amicus Brief, supra* note 41, at *10.

[43]   *See* Kahan & Meares, *supra* note 41, at 1164, 1168 (inner-city minority communities "seek policing methods that will assist them in the project of restoring community life"); 1175–76 (advocates of gang-congregation laws see gang members targeted by the laws as members of their own communities); Meares & Kahan, *Wages, supra* note 41, at 208 (minority communities seek "to establish law enforcement policies that will help them reinforce weak social structures that accompany neighborhood poverty") *id.* at 210 (gang members are part of the community); *See* Richard C. Schragger, *The Limits of Localism,* 100 Mich. L. Rev. 371, 411 (2001) (noting how community policing emphasizes "the sociological infrastructure of the city neighborhood itself").

well-being of African Americans as a group."[44] For that reason, the framers of the gang congregation law saw themselves as working for the protection and redemption of the young men subject to the gang law. "Inner city supporters of the new community policing do not seek to exclude and cast out offenders; rather they seek policing methods that will assist them in the project of restoring community life."[45] The gang protection ordinance thus reflects the unique and collective "local knowledge" of the black community, as opposed to the universalizing and individualizing abstractions of liberalism.[46] In short, Meares and Kahan see the Chicago gang congregation law as a law enforcement strategy that emerges through the community's internal social norms rather than imposed from the outside.[47]

The aim of the gang congregation law to knit Chicago's black community into a cultural entity exercising a form of collective citizenship in place may have been precisely what doomed it in the Supreme Court. The Court rejected the gang congregation ordinance, observing that, in restricting the ability of suspected gang members to loiter, the ordinance violated "the right to move 'to whatsoever place one's own inclination may direct',"[48] which the Court held to be a protected "liberty" interest under the due process clause.[49] As we recall, one principal feature of liberal local citizenship today is the right to travel. State and local governments have no power to enact immigration regulations or otherwise to limit population mobility. The porosity of local borders is what enables them to be rational associations freely chosen by individual consumer-voters. In retarding population movement, Chicago thus offended the liberal nature of local citizenship unmoored from place.

Of course, to return to a paradox explored in the first two parts of this book, the Supreme Court's affirmation of a right to travel rests uneasily alongside its longstanding indulgence of local zoning regulations that restrict the development of housing and thereby make it exceedingly difficult for people (especially of lesser means) to establish residence in wealthier communities. And indeed, Chicago's gang congregation law can readily be seen as a type of zoning regulation. The city of Chicago defended the law in just those terms, arguing that it was attempting to regain control over city spaces from street

---

[44] *See* Meares & Kahan, *Wages*, *supra* note 41, at 210; Kahan & Meares, *supra* note 41, at 1176.

[45] Kahan & Meares, *supra* note 41, at 1168.

[46] *Id.* at 1177–80.

[47] *See* Meares & Kahan, *Norms*, *supra* note 41, at 827.

[48] *Morales*, 527 U.S. at 54 (*quoting* 1 WILLIAM BLACKSTONE, COMMENTARIES ON THE LAWS OF ENGLAND 130 [1765]).

[49] *See id.* at 53–54.

gangs in the same way suburban municipalities use zoning laws to keep out unwanted land uses.[50] As Richard Schragger puts it,

> [P]roponents of the Gang Congregation Ordinance support Chicago's inner-city neighborhoods' decision to defend themselves as do many wealthy, suburban neighborhoods: By excluding (through zoning or otherwise) undesirable uses of space, and, by extension, undesirables. The theoretical bases for local autonomy that ground the inner-city residents' claims to govern are similar to those that ground the 'rights' of suburban municipalities, gated communities, homeowners associations, and business improvement districts to exclude, police, and regulate themselves.[51]

In a few important ways, however, Chicago's gang congregation law is *not* like suburban zoning, and therefore did not meet with the Court's approval in the same way zoning laws have. First, it is a more direct, coercive restriction on mobility, whereas zoning impedes mobility only indirectly through the mechanism of the market. From the liberal perspective, zoning is not a restraint on mobility at all because mobility is a function of ability to pay, the resident a "consumer-voter" who votes with their wallet. Courts have consistently held that zoning regulations do not interfere with the Constitutional right to travel because they "merely make[] it more difficult for the outsider to establish his residence in the place of his choosing."[52] Second, and as discussed in Chapter 2, insofar as zoning makes the acquisition of residence in a community a market transaction, it makes local citizenship a matter of individual choice rather than shared identity. According to Richard Ford, zoning facilitates a view of municipalities "as marketplace commodities into which anyone with enough cash can buy entry, and the political process is understood to occur in a neutral political space and to consist of individuals who form groups for purely strategic purposes."[53] The advocates of Chicago's gang congregation law, on the other hand, envisioned

---

[50] *See* Meares & Kahan, *Wages, supra* note 41, at 199. ("The council noted that street gangs often exert control over physical space by loitering: they intimidate members of other gangs and non-gang-involved neighborhood residents, preventing entrance into controlled areas. Thus, an obvious solution was a policy that allowed police to break a gang's grip on certain public spaces."); *see also* NICOLE STELLE GARNETT, ORDERING THE CITY: LAND USE, POLICING, AND THE RESTORATION OF URBAN AMERICA 27 (2010) (noting that Chicago's anti-gang law had "zoning" characteristics and the city defended it using zoning analogies).

[51] *See* Schragger, *supra* note 43, at 374–75.

[52] *See* Assoc. Homebuilders v. City of Livermore, 557 P.2d 473, 484 (1976); *see also* Vill. of Belle Terre v. Boraas, 416 U.S. 1, 7 (1973).

[53] Richard Thompson Ford, *The Boundaries of Race: Political Geography in Legal Analysis*, 107 HARV. L. REV. 1841, 1888–89 (1994).

citizenship as a collective enterprise, focused on the "linked fate" of the community and its young men caught up in the drug trade. In other words, where zoning facilitates a view of local citizenship as liberal and local citizens as footloose and mobile, Chicago's gang law appears to resemble ethno-nationalism, fetishizing a relationship between a people and its territory. For that reason, courts cannot tolerate it.

Under Kymlicka and Young's model, however, Chicago's law is not ethno-nationalist but an example of differentiated citizenship, because what the proponents of the law seek is not to separate or constitute themselves as a separate nation, but to place themselves on an equal footing with middle-class suburbanites. As Schragger's quote illustrates, all the law was intended to do was to give Chicago's black community the same power to control its character that wealthy suburban communities enjoy as a matter of course. Wealthy communities can control disorder through zoning laws that exclude undesirable uses and ensure their members have uniformly high socioeconomic status. But zoning provides little protection against the kinds of externalities associated with concentrated poverty, like high crime and incarceration rates, low levels of trust, and so forth. Hence, poorer communities of color do not have the luxury of using money as a means of social control the way affluent suburban communities do. Poorer communities do, however, have the ability to use more direct coercive power to accomplish the same ends. A paradox of segregation is that the geographic concentration of minorities in certain places, often as a result of suburban zoning laws, deprives those communities of economic power but simultaneously gives them a source of political power. In the case of Chicago's gang law, the black community was attempting to use its new political power to compensate for its lack of economic power – to effectively coerce the social control that affluent suburbanites can "purchase" through zoning. In other words, this is exactly the sort of situation in which Kymlicka and Young would argue that a degree of group differentiation is necessary to realize the liberal ideal of equality among citizens. Nevertheless, the courts are suspicious of any local citizenship that recognizes group identity fixed to particular places, choosing to enshrine instead a thin citizenship of money and shared economic interests unmoored from place.

11.6 THE CRITIQUE OF DIFFERENTIATED CITIZENSHIP: PERILS OF MULTICULTURALISM

According to many commentators, there is good reason for courts to be wary of differentiated citizenship. Rogers Smith warns, for example, that the "multiculturalism" championed by differentiated citizenship is dangerous because it can lead directly to the ethnic nationalism that is now prevalent in our political culture. Smith argues that differentiated citizenship, by fracturing society into multiple groupings, undermines the sense of belonging to a single "people" or nation.[54] Because such belonging is a deeply felt human need, its deprivation will cause people to turn to a darker "ascriptive" nationalism, including calls for stricter immigration limits, opposition to affirmative action, racial tensions, and the like. In short, he argues that by stripping away the sense of a unitary national identity, Kymlicka and Young's ideas "may produce morally culpable complicity in malevolent forms of national community."[55]

Indeed, Kymlicka himself acknowledges that differentiated citizenship can "weaken the bonds with the larger political community, and indeed question its very authority and permanence."[56] The basic premise of differentiated citizenship is that society is composed of distinct groups, and does not constitute a single nation. From Kymlicka's perspective, however, it is preferable to acknowledge this fact and construct a sense of national unity out of our many identities – *E Pluribus unum* – than create a fictitious unitary identity that acts to subordinate minority groups to the majority culture.[57]

This argument, however, leads to a criticism from a somewhat different direction. Recognizing the distinctiveness of minority communities by giving them control over their territory may simply reinforce their marginalization. It legitimizes the idea of defining space in racial terms and thus justifies the decision of white middle-class suburbanites to create their own segregated environments in which they can hoard their tax base and limit access to quality schools, jobs, and appreciating home values. As Richard Ford writes, "separate territorial status rarely delivers on its promise of autonomy. Often, the subordinate group unwittingly conspires in its own continued subordination and participates in its own quarantine."[58] This occurs because "the position of security that the dominant group enjoys requires the subjugation of a subordinate group. No group can entirely control its own fate without also controlling other groups around it. The coveted position in question is not autonomy, but hegemony – a position that, by definition, everyone cannot occupy."[59]

---

[54] *See* ROGERS M. SMITH, CIVIC IDEALS: CONFLICTING VISIONS OF CITIZENSHIP IN U.S. HISTORY 473–75; 485–88 (1997); *see also* HUNTINGTON, *supra* note 22, at 141–77.
[55] SMITH, *supra* note 54, at 474.
[56] *See* KYMLICKA, *supra* note 1, at 181.
[57] *See id.* at 181–95.
[58] *See* Ford, *supra* note 20, at 909.
[59] *Id.*

In addition, territorial separation facilitates the "othering" of marginalized groups, which can heighten racial tensions and further intensify the desire for separation. Audrey McFarlane writes:

> Racializing space effectively demarcates particular areas not only based on racial identity but also imposes popular stereotypes, anxieties, and concerns on these places. The role of these places in the popular imagination justifies their subordination and oppression. The ghetto is a place that makes the places outside of it (whether affluent central-city neighborhoods, the suburbs, or exurbs) a desirable refuge and a safe haven.[60]

Ironically, though differentiated citizenship attempts to navigate between the openness of postmodern citizenship and the closure of republican citizenship, in doing so it actually takes on the flaws of each. On one hand, its openness to difference creates an amorphous idea of citizenship that leaves people desperate for meaningful human connections, a desperation that may lead down the path to ethnic nationalism. On the other hand, its embrace of territorial autonomy for subordinated groups traps those groups in their subordination.

In addition, in attempting to avoid the perils of both postmodern and republican citizenship, differentiated citizenship becomes practically incoherent on its own terms. For instance, both Kymlicka and Young claim to champion difference without exclusion, recognizing that group identities are not immutable and that the members of all different groups are part of a common civic society. However, they also both advocate for group rights that will inevitably lead to territorial separation. Kymlicka, for example, advocates for indigenous peoples to have collective land rights that would include veto power over land use changes, extensive residency requirements, and prohibitions on individual ownership and alienation of land. Young says that in her "normative idea of city life, borders are open and undecidable," but she also favors distinct legislative representation for marginalized groups, which would likely facilitate group claims for territorial exclusion or separation.[61]

Young and Kymlicka's hedging of their commitments makes a certain sense. Their ideal is a society that is open but where differences flourish.

---

[60] *See* Audrey G. McFarlane, *Race, Space and Place: The Geography of Economic Development*, 36 SAN DIEGO L. REV. 295, 339–40 (1999); *see also* Schragger, *supra* note 43, at 429 (criticizing Chicago gang-loitering ordinance for "reinforc[ing] the isolation of inner-city, minority neighborhoods in their particular geography – a geography of diluted rights and racially identified space ... ").

[61] YOUNG, *supra* note 1, at 239, 240.

Rather than choose between openness and closure, they want to have a bit of both. They can hardly be faulted for their refusal to choose. The tension between withdrawal into the familiar and engagement with the strange – and our reluctance to choose between them – are fundamental parts of the urban condition and, indeed, fundamental parts of modern citizenship. The conclusion that follows will address that tension and, alas, make some choices.

Conclusion

C.1 THE UNIVERSAL AND THE EXCLUSIONARY

One of the central dilemmas explored in this book has been how to reconcile a vision of citizenship that recognizes the basic rights of persons with a vision that affirms the fundamental attachment of a people to its territory. The more widely we extend the scope of our political community, the more we attenuate the bonds that unite citizens, but the more we limit the protections of citizenship to a privileged class, the more exposed and vulnerable we render the noncitizens who reside, often permanently, within our borders. As Linda Bosniak writes, citizenship involves "conflicting normative commitments" to two competing "legal and moral worlds." One is the "world of borders, sovereignty and national community membership" and the other is "the world of social relationships among territorially present people."[1] But we cannot choose between these two "worlds" because they both make up fundamental parts of our national character. So we have chosen not to choose. According to Bosniak, citizenship is "segmented and divided" between "universalist and exclusionary commitments."[2] The American legal and political tradition, as described in Parts I and II of this book, has resolved this conundrum by dividing its commitments jurisdictionally, with the local being the "universalist," or liberal, sphere of mobility and choice, and the national the "exclusionary," or ethno-nationalist, sphere of identity and attachment.

That we have looked to the local to resolve the paradox of citizenship is unsurprising considering that the very concept of citizenship was born in the city. The ancient Athenians were the first to wrestle with balancing "universalist and exclusionary commitments," creating for foreigners the special status

---

[1] LINDA BOSNIAK, THE CITIZEN AND THE ALIEN 38 (2006).
[2] *Id.* at 81.

of *metic* that gave them the right of residence but forbade them and their descendants from ever becoming citizens. One of the fundamental dilemmas of urban life has long been the tension between the desire to engage with the outside world, and the desire to withdraw into the intimacy of the familiar. William Thomas, one of the early sociologists to study the modern American city, observed that urban living is characterized by two contradictory impulses: "the desire for new experience" and "the desire for security."[3] On one hand, the very reason people come together in cities is to be among strangers. It allows us to find people who share our tastes and interests, to experience new ideas and cultures, and to enjoy the thrill of the crowd and the pleasures of anonymity.[4] It makes exchange more efficient by matching consumers with producers and labor with capital.[5] From an economic perspective, cities provide the advantages of "agglomeration" that enable innovation through economies of scale and the sharing of ideas.[6] On the other hand, constantly being around strangers can be disorienting and unsettling, and it can lead to exploitation, harassment, and violence, or at least the fear of it. As I described in Chapter 10, research shows a correlation between racial and ethnic diversity and lower levels of trust and cooperation, higher population turnover, less civic participation, less confidence and engagement in government, fewer friends, and less happiness.[7] Conversely, ethnically and racially homogeneous groups have higher levels of social capital, which confers all sorts of positive impacts on communities, including safer neighborhoods, better schools, healthier children, and more overall satisfaction with life.[8]

As such, just as our thinking about citizenship attempts to balance nation-hood with universality, urban residents often simultaneously desire both the

---

[3] WILLIAM I. THOMAS I, THE POLISH PEASANT IN EUROPE AND AMERICA 72–73 (1918–19) (describing the "four wishes" of the immigrant, including the two contradictory impulses of "the desire for new experience" and "the desire for security").

[4] *See* IRIS MARION YOUNG, JUSTICE AND THE POLITICS OF DIFFERENCE 236–41 (1990).

[5] *See* RICHARD SENNETT, THE FALL OF PUBLIC MAN 23 (1974) ("Out in public was where moral violation occurred and was tolerated; in public one could break the laws of respectability."); Louis Wirth, *Urbanism as a Way of Life*, in CLASSIC ESSAYS ON THE CULTURE OF CITIES 143, 150 (Richard Sennett ed. 1969) ("[The city] has brought together people from the ends of the earth *because* they are different and thus useful to one another, rather than because they are homogeneous and like-minded.")

[6] David Schleicher, *The City as a Law and Economics Subject*, 2010 U. ILL. L. REV. 1507, 1509 (explaining agglomeration economies in large cities).

[7] ROBERT D. PUTNAM, BOWLING ALONE 400 (2000); Robert D. Putnam, *E Pluribus Unum: Diversity and Community in the Twenty-First Century*, 30 SCANDINAVIAN POL. STUD. 137, 142–43, 149–50 (2007).

[8] *See* PUTNAM, *supra* note 7, at 400 ("[S]ocial capital is inevitably easier to foster within homogeneous communities ... ").

intimacy of a community of shared values and the impersonality of the exciting world of strangers.[9] And just as we have declined to choose between the two conflicting approaches to citizenship, the inherent contradiction in urban life is similarly unresolvable. Gerald Frug acknowledges this openly, candidly refusing to take sides between engagement and withdrawal. "To me the two positions may be irreconcilable, but they both are indispensable ... [T]hey replicate the contradictory experience of community: the desire for connection with others and the desire for the feel of the modern metropolis."[10] He goes on to say that "city life is a compromise between withdrawal from strangers and engagement with them. The exact nature of this compromise constantly has to be negotiated and renegotiated."[11]

The tension Frug describes between withdrawal and engagement, like the tension Bosniak describes between citizenship's inclusionary and exclusionary commitments, recalls the dynamic of space and place described in Part III. Where space, understood as the ability to move across borders, evokes freedom, it also undermines people's attachments to places. But as people attain refuge in the comfort of place, they come to feel confined, and again seek to move. As Yi-Fu Tuan writes, we need both space and place because "human lives are a dialectical movement between shelter and venture, attachment and freedom."[12]

Thus, a key feature of the various conceptions of urban citizenship described in Part III has been an effort to negotiate between space and place, engagement and withdrawal. The advocates of republican citizenship, seeing a robust sense of community rooted in place diminished by the homogenizing pressures of space and globalization, have attempted to revitalize the face-to-face connections of a community of meaning by building walls to insulate the community against the outside world. Postmodernist citizenship, by contrast, embraces the enhanced freedom engagement promises by rejecting borders, finding meaning and a deepened appreciation for place in the connections that globalization creates among people. Finally, differentiated citizenship stands for inclusion without differentiation, a city defined by engagement among strangers that also offers security and recognition for the thick groups in which people find themselves embedded.

---

[9] *See* SENNETT, *supra* note 5, at 294–95 (explaining the assumption that "impersonality is a summation, a result, a tangible effect of all the worst evils" of modernity that makes "face-to-face contacts in a territorial community seem so important").

[10] GERALD FRUG, CITY MAKING: BUILDING COMMUNITIES WITHOUT BUILDING WALLS 112 (1999).

[11] *Id.* at 141.

[12] YI-FU TUAN, SPACE AND PLACE 54 (1977).

All three conceptions ran into the same problem, which is the resistance of policymakers and the courts to a re-calibration of local citizenship. In our political and legal tradition, as we saw in Parts I and II, the boundary between space and place, between engagement and withdrawal, between universality and particularism, has not been something to be "negotiated and re-negotiated" but to be firmly assigned by the courts. According to Michael Walzer, the liberal-nationalist tradition has generally neglected the "popular character" of boundary-definition, putting all its faith in courts to "define and patrol the circle of rights."[13] The preference for judicial rather than popular line-drawing is a vestige of a "classical" era of jurisprudence, during which jurists posited that institutions had distinct spheres of activity and that "[t]he role of the judiciary (its sphere of absolute power) was the application of a single, distinctively legal, analytic apparatus to the job of policing the boundaries of these spheres."[14] Determining the boundaries between the spheres was, moreover, not a political or democratic task, but an "objective, quasi-scientific one."[15] The state of citizenship federalism today bears the mark of this classical era of jurisprudence. It has been the courts who have determined that immigration is an exclusively federal power, that local public education and other benefits must be open to all regardless of immigration status, and that our national economic system requires free mobility of population and goods within national borders. In making those determinations, the courts have also necessarily determined the contours of local citizenship, and the boundaries between local and federal citizenship. Local citizenship is liberal, determined by money and mobility, whereas federal citizenship is ethno-nationalist, determined by identity and linked fate.

In articulating this vision of local citizenship, the courts have necessarily precluded communities from positing their own, alternative visions. According to Robert Cover, judge-made law is "jurispathic"; it denies normative communities within the state the right to make their own laws. "Confronting the luxuriant growth of a hundred legal traditions, they [the courts] assert that *this one* is law and destroy or try to destroy the rest."[16] Cover finds an alternative to the "jurispathic" mode, as Sandel did in Chapter 9, in Louis D. Brandeis's notion of federalism. Brandeis sought to "decentralize" law, to locate it in "an uncoerced politics, a free public space."[17] That is, in short,

---

[13] *See* Michael Walzer, *Liberalism and the Art of Separation*, 12 POL. THEORY 315, 328 (1984).

[14] *See* Duncan Kennedy, *Toward an Historical Understanding of Legal Consciousness: The Case of Classical Legal Thought in America, 1850–1940*, 3 RES. LAW & SOC. 3, 5, 7 (1980).

[15] *Id.* at 7.

[16] Robert Cover, *Foreword:* Nomos *and* Narrative, 97 HARV. L. REV. 4, 53 (1983).

[17] *Id.* at 48.

what the three models discussed in Part III have sought to do. In essence, they have claimed that determining the boundaries of citizenship is, as Michael Walzer argues, "a popular, not an esoteric art." As Walzer continues, "Believers, scholars, workers and parents establish the lines – and then the citizens as a body do so, through the political process."[18]

As it happens, the judicial monopoly on defining citizenship may have run its course. The judicial structure of consciousness that segregated different ideas about citizenship into different spheres is now collapsing under the weight of globalization, as described in Chapter 7. Liberalism has burst out of its sphere and increasingly exercised influence over the ethno-nationalist sphere of federal citizenship. A void has opened up that is increasingly being filled by reactionary nationalist sentiments. The republican, postmodern, and differentiated citizenship models all offered different ways of filling that void, a "third way" that avoids the extremes of both liberalism and nationalism. As we have seen, however, their boundary-drawing efforts also proved problematic. Republican citizenship's attempt to erect walls around the community led it down a path to xenophobia and nativism, at the same time that it failed to actually protect cities against the imposition of global forces. Advocates of postmodern and differentiated citizenship attempted to create an urban citizenship based on difference without exclusion, but the inherent contradictions in that idea resulted in an amorphous construct incapable of inspiring loyalty and also toothless in the face of globalization, opening the door for a more potent and sinister form of belonging to take its place.

It seems almost inevitable that any effort at line-drawing will fail because citizenship, like urban life, is a series of contradictions that resists easy classification. The judicial structure of consciousness that is now collapsing was the product of a lengthy evolution and worked well for a long time to paper over those contradictions. The void left behind cannot be hastily filled, and it will take a similarly long and painful process to determine what form of membership will take its place.

C.2 EMBRACING LIBERAL CITIZENSHIP IN A GLOBAL AGE

Nevertheless, the discussion in this book gives some indication as to how local citizenship may be re-constructed in a manner that is both equitable and suitable for a global age. In particular, as liberalism has become an increasingly dominant part of our citizenship, it may be that we should embrace it – while also reforming it – instead of trying to wall it off from civic life. It is not simply

---

[18] Walzer, *supra* note 13, at 328.

that liberalism has become so entrenched that efforts to reverse it will be fruitless but also that liberalism properly understood may do a better job than many alternatives of articulating a coherent and just theory of membership in a globalizing world where borders and sovereignty are diminishing.

As an initial matter, liberalism is so bound up with local citizenship that attempting to excise it makes little sense. For example, in celebrating the city's places where people come together in all their differences, Iris Young states offhandedly that such places "should be open to all activities, *except perhaps selling things* ... "[19] But this exception is hard to square with the fact that the very reason many cities exist is because of "selling things," and many of the public places in which people gather to participate in politics and display their differences started their lives as marketplaces in which things were bought and sold. The same places where the ancient Athenians engaged in politics were places where they also engaged in trade. The medieval and early modern cities made no distinction whatsoever between politics and commerce. Though the modern nation-state attempted to impose the public/private distinction on cities as a way of subjecting them to state sovereignty, cities have always resisted this easy categorization, especially in their use of public places. According to Don Mitchell, the modern city is a contradictory "hybrid of commerce and politics" in which "the anarchy of the market meets the anarchy of politics to create an interactive, democratic public."[20]

The anarchy of the market and the medium of money may, indeed, provide the preconditions for urban democracy and citizenship to exist. The urban sociologist Georg Simmel observed that in the anonymous city, money allows us to manage our relations with strangers. It enables us to have the kind of abstract and impersonal relations that make diversity tolerable and enjoyable.[21] Even the Marxian geographer David Harvey agrees that the only places that have succeeded in creating authentic communities capable of restraining the forces of global capital have done so "by an accommodation to the power of money, to commodification and capital accumulation and to modern technologies."[22] Every effort "to establish difference in the

---

[19] IRIS MARION YOUNG, JUSTICE AND THE POLITICS OF DIFFERENCE 255 (1990) (emphasis added).

[20] DON MITCHELL, THE RIGHT TO THE CITY: SOCIAL JUSTICE AND THE FIGHT FOR PUBLIC SPACE 137 (2003).

[21] *See* Georg Simmel, *The Metropolis and Mental Life*, in CLASSIC ESSAYS ON THE CULTURE OF CITIES 47, 49 (Richard Sennett ed. 1969) (describing how money economy replaced personal with impersonal relationships); John Allen, *On Georg Simmel: Proximity, Distance and Movement*, in THINKING SPACE 54, 61 (Mike Crang & Nigel Thrift eds. 2000) ("medium of money" provided way for city dwellers to reduce relationships to an abstraction).

[22] DAVID HARVEY, JUSTICE, NATURE, AND THE GEOGRAPHY OF DIFFERENCE 318 (1996).

contemporary world has to do so through social practices that engage with the power of money."[23] Ultimately, Harvey argues that "we cannot reject the world of sociability which has been achieved by the interlinking of all people and places into a global economy ... " Instead, we should "build upon this achievement and seek to transform it in socially constructive ways."[24]

There is little doubt that liberal ideas about citizenship have managed to make society more inclusive and accepting of diversity. Lizabeth Cohen demonstrates that during the postwar period, as citizenship increasingly merged with consumerism, marginalized groups like women and blacks were able to use their power as consumers to obtain political rights they had previously been denied.[25] Anke Ortlepp's recent book JIM CROW TERMIN-ALS likewise demonstrates how the era of air travel ushered in a new "mobile integrationist nationwide culture" in which blacks had agency as "citizen-consumers."[26] Although courts have been hostile to the idea of "differentiated citizenship," or the effort to recognize group difference as a means of incorp-orating marginalized groups into our political culture, multinational corporations have created segmented consumer markets that foster distinct identities among groups within society while also tying them into the broader consumer culture.[27] They have succeeded so well, in fact, that multicultural-ism is actually declining and more groups that were once distinct markets, especially Hispanics, are now assimilating toward the lifestyle traditionally associated with the white middle class.[28] It is for this very reason that cancer-ous right-wing bloviator Tucker Carlson has recently gone from singing the praises of global capitalism to denouncing it, because global capital has played a role in weakening white Christian males' stranglehold on political and cultural power.[29]

---

[23] *Id.* at 319.

[24] *Id.* at 314.

[25] *See* LIZABETH COHEN, A CONSUMERS' REPUBLIC: THE POLITICS OF MASS CONSUMPTION IN POSTWAR AMERICA 31–41; 75–83 (2003); *id.* at 41–53; 83–100 (on blacks' incorporation as citizens in new consumer economy).

[26] ANKE ORTLEPP, JIM CROW TERMINALS: THE DESEGREGATION OF AMERICAN AIRPORTS 2–3 (2017).

[27] *See* GARY GERSTLE, AMERICAN CRUCIBLE: RACE AND NATION IN THE TWENTIETH CENTURY 356–57 (2001); COHEN, *supra* note 25, at 309–31.

[28] *See* JODY VALLEJO, BARRIOS TO BURBS: THE MAKING OF THE MEXICAN AMERICAN MIDDLE CLASS (2012); Noah Smith, *Hispanics are Like Everyone Else Who Comes to America*, BLOOMBERG.COM (Jan. 30, 2019 4:30 AM), https://www.bloomberg.com/opinion/articles/2019-01-30/sorry-mr-brokaw-but-hispanics-have-blended-right-in.

[29] *See* Eric Levitz, *Why Tucker Carlson Plays a Critic of Capitalism on TV*, NYMAG.COM (Jan. 8, 2019), http://nymag.com/intelligencer/2019/01/tucker-carlson-romney-monologue-capitalism-social-conservatives-fox-news.html.

In this light, perhaps the biggest blind spot that the various proponents of urban citizenship share is their utter disdain for the suburbs as embodiments of the liberal local citizenship they abhor. The very idea of urban citizenship rests on a perception of cities as the public "places" where real citizenship happens, where fortuitous associations occur, where differences are displayed. The urban citizenship literature treats suburbs as deadened places of consumption where atomized consumers drive alone in their SUVs to the McMansions where they stare blankly at their iPads.

The reality, however, is that the suburbs are now the most authentic sites of local citizenship. While the urban citizenship theorists praise cities for their diversity and decry the homogeneity and exclusivity of suburbs, suburbs are now far more diverse than cities. Thirty-five percent of suburban residents today are minorities, which equals their share of the population nationwide. Poverty has also moved to the suburbs – there are now more poor people in suburbs than in cities. In increasing numbers, immigrants are eschewing the central cities where they once resided and settling directly in suburban communities where there are job opportunities and lower housing costs.[30] Not surprisingly, suburban communities like Tacoma Park, Maryland, are choosing to become sanctuary cities or to enfranchise noncitizens. Others, like Monterey Park, have become ethnic enclaves where particular social groups can practice differentiated citizenship.[31] Cities, on the other hand, are becoming monocultural enclaves for the wealthy, as zoning restrictions and an influx of capital place housing out of reach for people of modest means. As Margaret Crawford writes: "difference may actually be the defining characteristic of suburbia, rather than the sameness consistently attributed to it. In fact, currently, in an inversion of conventional wisdom, cities are becoming more homogenous while suburbs grow more diverse."[32]

It is undoubtedly true, as the critics contend, that suburbs in general still lack the sense of "place" evident in cities. Despite the best efforts of "new urbanist" designers to introduce walkable places into the suburbs where fortuitous encounters can occur, by and large the suburbs remain sprawling

---

[30] *See, e.g.*, AUDREY SINGER ET AL., TWENTY-FIRST CENTURY GATEWAYS: IMMIGRANT INCORPORATION IN SUBURBAN AMERICA (2008).

[31] *See* Susan W. Hardwick, *Toward a Suburban Immigrant Nation*, in SINGER ET AL., *supra* note 30, at 31, 45.

[32] *See* MARGARET CRAWFORD, MAKING SUBURBIA: NEW HISTORIES OF EVERYDAY AMERICA 382 (2015). There are a number of excellent recent sources revisiting the conventional view of suburbs. *See, e.g.*, AMANDA KOLSON HURLEY: RADICAL SUBURBS: EXPERIMENTAL LIVING ON THE FRINGES OF THE AMERICAN CITY (2019); THE NEW AMERICAN SUBURB: POVERTY, RACE AND THE ECONOMIC CRISIS (Katrin B. Anacker ed. 2015).

and automobile-focused, with few centers and few opportunities for spontaneous interactions outside of consumer-oriented spaces like shopping malls. The irony thus is that our cities have places but lack diversity, while suburbs have diversity without places.[33]

A much more serious problem with suburbia – and the liberal consumer society more generally – is its legacy of exclusion and segregation. Historically, one of the main reasons people initially moved to the suburbs was to create enclaves of wealth and race, and suburbs became synonymous with racial segregation. Today, even as suburbs have become more diverse, they remain as segregated as ever. And the liberal ideology of consumerism undoubtedly bears some of the blame. For one thing, as I have discussed at length, liberalism replaces the stratification of identity with the stratification of money, a state of affairs that was practically perfected in the suburbs. As Lizabeth Cohen explains, the postwar suburbs were rigidly segregated by wealth and income, establishing "new kinds of hierarchies" and subtle gradations even within the middle class, as residents furiously sought to trade up to bigger homes in better neighborhoods at the same time as those neighborhoods enacted ever stricter zoning regulations to rigidify existing class distinctions.[34] Racial segregation was perhaps the defining characteristic of the suburbs, as zoning, racially restrictive covenants, mortgage lending practices, and highway building policies mixed with private racial prejudice to keep blacks and other minorities out of the suburbs.[35] Furthermore, as discussed earlier, the courts' persistent belief in liberal local citizenship blinded them to the reality of segregation, as they insisted on seeing racial separation as a result of private choice rather than governmental coercion. Policymakers and courts encouraged suburbanites to believe that racial segregation was an economic imperative, and to defend suburban racial homogeneity in the liberal language of markets and rights rather than the ethno-nationalist language of white supremacy.[36]

---

[33] *See* ALAN EHRENHALT, THE GREAT INVERSION AND THE FUTURE OF THE AMERICAN CITY 205–17 (2012) (describing challenges suburbs face in trying to create authentic places); ROBERT E. LANG & JENNIFER B. LEFURGY, BOOMBURBS: THE RISE OF AMERICA'S ACCIDENTAL CITIES 11, 13–18, 82–83 (2007) (describing lack of place in large sunbelt suburban cities, called "boomburbs").

[34] *See* COHEN, *supra* note 25, at 200–4.

[35] *See id.* at 212–27; RICHARD ROTHSTEIN, THE COLOR OF LAW: A FORGOTTEN HISTORY OF HOW OUR GOVERNMENT SEGREGATED AMERICA (2017).

[36] *See, e.g.,* David M. P. Freund, *Marketing the Free Market: State Intervention and the Politics of Prosperity in Metropolitan America,* in THE NEW SUBURBAN HISTORY 11, 11–13; 29; 31–32 (Kevin M. Kruse & Thomas J. Sugrue eds. 2006).

Liberalism has never been a monolith, however. The language of markets and rights can and has been used to expand the circle of members as well as to contract it. The liberal market economy promises to break the immutable bonds of identity and replace it with equality of opportunity and individual freedom. As such, liberalism has inspired artisans to demand an end to indentured servitude, landless people to mobilize against the property qualification for voting, and women to demand suffrage and "the promise of a life without hierarchy and illegitimate constraints."[37] Liberalism has fueled the argument that those who are fully integrated into our economic and social life must also be included within our political community, an argument that has led to expanding protections for immigrants regardless of their immigration status. Consumers today are using the power of their wallets to force corporations to take stands on controversial social issues.[38] Historically marginalized groups like women and blacks have used their power as consumers to assert their rights as citizens. Perhaps for all these reasons, scholars in the critical race tradition like Kimberle Crenshaw have emphasized "the transformative potential that liberalism offers." Despite its flaws, liberalism is "receptive to some aspirations that are central to Black demands, and may also perform an important function in combating the experience of being excluded and oppressed."[39] Reflecting on the legacy of the Civil Rights movement, Crenshaw notes that the articulation of activists' demands in the liberal language of rights

> exposed a series of contradictions – the most important being the promised privileges of American citizenship and the practice of absolute racial subordination. Rather than using the contradictions to suggest that American citizenship was itself illegitimate or false, civil rights protestors proceeded as if American citizenship were real, and demanded to exercise the 'rights' that citizenship entailed.[40]

---

[37] See Hendrik Hartog, *Imposing Constitutional Traditions*, 29 WM. & MARY L. REV. 75, 78–79 (1987).

[38] See Tom C. W. Lin, *Incorporating Social Activism*, 98 B. U. L. REV. 1535, 1547 (2018) (describing how consumers are placing more pressure on businesses to engage in social activism); LAWRENCE B. GLICKMAN, BUYING POWER: A HISTORY OF CONSUMER ACTIVISM IN AMERICA 203 (2009) (describing how "Americans used their pocketbooks to achieve their social and political goals").

[39] See Kimberle Williams Crenshaw, *Race, Reform and Retrenchment: Transformation and Legitimation in Antidiscrimination Law*, 101 HARV. L. REV. 1331, 1358 (1988); *see also* LAURA KALMAN, THE STRANGE CAREER OF LEGAL LIBERALISM 177–80 (1996) (discussing responses of critical race theorists to republican critiques of liberalism).

[40] *Id.* at 1368.

If the liberal language of "rights" empowers blacks to fight segregation, however, it also raises a paradox, because, as just mentioned, suburban racial segregation has also long been framed in terms of the "rights" of suburban communities to exclude. When two competing sides both frame their arguments in liberal terms as a matter of rights, who wins? This question cuts to the heart of local citizenship. Who are a city's citizens, entitled to the rights of local citizenship?

The courts have found themselves caught in this dilemma. On one hand, it has been a staple of local citizenship that local borders must be open. Liberalism requires that local citizenship be a matter of mobility and choice; as such, we have seen courts frequently affirm the rights of individuals to establish residence, and therefore citizenship, in the municipality of their choosing. On the other hand, courts have been extremely deferential toward local zoning regulations that impede population mobility, generally on the grounds that such regulations do not *directly* restrict mobility but merely make mobility a function of one's ability to pay to acquire residence – another staple of liberalism. For example, the California Supreme Court held that zoning regulations do not interfere with the right to travel because they "merely make it more difficult for the outsider to establish his residence in the place of his choosing."[41]

As I have argued, however, globalization is weakening the judiciary's ability to define citizenship. The new global knowledge-based economy is causing jobs to cluster in certain hubs of innovation – like California – and the resulting demand for housing is placing pressure on those places' zoning regulations. Due largely to restrictive zoning laws throughout the state that limit housing growth way below the level of job growth, California is 49th out of the 50 states in homes per capita, and so along with the state's tremendous job growth has come skyrocketing home prices, rents, homelessness, and gentrification of minority communities. For those caught up in this housing crisis, the court's claim that zoning laws do not affect population mobility rings hollow.

As globalization has made it increasingly difficult for the judiciary to meaningfully define the contours of citizenship, the people must take back the reins, and engage in that painful process of "negotiating and re-negotiating" the boundaries between engagement and withdrawal. Of course, the people have had no easier a time than the judiciary has in drawing those boundaries. When "progressive" cities like San Francisco claim that "all are

---

[41] *See* Assoc. Homebuilders v. City of Livermore, 557 P.2d 473, 484 (1976).

welcome here" while their residents angrily protest shelters that would house the city's exploding homeless population, it is clear that there is a lot of confusion about who counts as a member of the community.[42] A quandary posed by social science research is that people are initially hostile to the introduction of diversity into their communities, but develop "ego strength" to tolerate and embrace it over time.[43] The problem this creates is that the initial hostility causes people to fight hard against the introduction of diversity, which then makes it impossible for them to ever develop ego strength. We are desperately in need of a broad and deep political movement that seeks to break down zoning barriers and introduce diversity into exclusionary communities, using the same liberal language of mobility and rights often mustered by community residents mouthing "Not in My Backyard" sentiments. Fortunately, a "Yes in My Backyard" (YIMBY) movement is now underway, and it has scored some important victories, including pushing places like California, Oregon, and Minneapolis to reform their exclusionary zoning policies and change the conversation regarding the role of zoning in affecting housing prices. Several Presidential candidates are talking openly, for the first time in decades, about zoning reform and other land use policies to increase housing production and lower housing costs in exclusionary communities.[44]

The premise of the YIMBY movement is simply that liberalism should meet its promise of enabling people to have the option of social and geographic mobility. Exclusionary zoning, much like ethnic nationalism, is based on a destructive fantasy that we can wall out danger and uncertainty. Ironically, this fantasy only increases our sense of vulnerability and anxiety, as danger and uncertainty can never be completely banished; "they threaten to enter consciousness at any moment."[45] Indeed, in our age of globalization, there is no way to turn back the tide of increasing population mobility. Paradoxically, as

---

[42] *See* Dominic Fracassa, *Neighbors Appeal Controversial Embarcadero Navigation Center as Fight Grinds on*, S.F. CHRONICLE (May 24, 2019, 9:23 PM), https://www.sfchronicle.com/bayarea/article/Neighbors-appeal-controversial-Embarcadero-13895073.php?psid=bonTl.

[43] Robert D. Putnam, E Pluribus Unum: *Diversity and Community in the Twenty-First Century*, 30 SCANDINAVIAN POL. STUD. 137, 138–44 (2007); on "ego strength," see FRUG, *supra* note 10, at 120–21.

[44] On the YIMBY movement, see Kenneth A. Stahl, *"Yes in My Backyard:" Can a New Pro-housing Movement Overcome the Power of NIMBYs?*, 41 ZONING & PLANNING LAW REPORT 1 (2018); Erin McCormick, *Rise of the Yimbys: The Angry Millennials with a Radical Housing Solution*, THE GUARDIAN (Oct. 2, 2017, 2:15 PM), https://amp.theguardian.com/cities/2017/oct/02/rise-of-the-yimbys-angry-millennials-radical-housing-solution; Alana Semuels, *From 'Not in My Backyard' to 'Yes in My Backyard,'* THE ATLANTIC (July 5, 2017), https://www.theatlantic.com/business/archive/2017/07/yimby-groups-pro-development/532437/.

[45] FRUG, *supra* note 10, at 120.

Frug notes, "giving up the idea that the world can be purified or controlled" can reduce one's anxiety and enable one to live a fuller life as one develops "an ability to cope with whatever surprises and conflicts one encounters, a confidence that one won't be overwhelmed by complexity or disorder, a feeling that one can live with, even learn to enjoy, otherness."[46] The liberal-nationalist idea of a citizenship bounded by walls will thus only lead to its own demise; we must embrace mobility and the expansive conception of membership that comes with it.

[46] *Id.* at 120–21.

Bibliography

ABBOTT, CARL, THE METROPOLITAN FRONTIER: CITIES IN THE MODERN AMERICAN WEST (1993).

THE NEW URBAN AMERICA: GROWTH AND POLITICS IN SUNBELT CITIES (rev. ed. 1987).

ACIMAN, ANDRÉ, OUT OF EGYPT (2007).

ACKERMAN, BRUCE, WE THE PEOPLE: FOUNDATIONS (1991).

Agnew, John A., *Space and Place*, in THE SAGE HANDBOOK OF GEOGRAPHICAL KNOWLEDGE 316 (John A. Agnew & David N. Livingstone eds., 2011).

PLACE AND POLITICS (1987).

Allen, John, *On Georg Simmel: Proximity, Distance and Movement*, in THINKING SPACE 54 (Mike Crang & Nigel Thrift eds., 2000).

ANDERSON, BENEDICT, IMAGINED COMMUNITIES (1983).

Aoki, Keith, *A Tale of Three Cities: Thoughts on Asian American Electoral and Political Power After 2000*, 8 ASIAN PAC. AM. L.J. 1 (2002).

Applebaum, Binyamin, *In City Built by Immigrants, Immigration Is the Defining Issue*, N.Y. TIMES (Oct. 12, 2016), https://www.nytimes.com/2016/10/13/business/econ omy/hazleton-pennsylvania-donald-trump-immigrants.html?_r=0.

ARENDT, HANNAH, ON REVOLUTION (1963).

THE HUMAN CONDITION (1958).

THE ORIGINS OF TOTALITARIANISM (2nd ed. 1958).

ARIES, PHILLIPE, 3 A HISTORY OF PRIVATE LIFE 9 (1989).

Austin, Regina, *"Not Just for the Fun of It:" Governmental Restraints on Black Leisure, Social Inequality and the Privatization of Public Space*, 71 S. CAL. L. REV. 667 (1998).

Badger, Emily, *Metropolitan Areas Are Now Fueling Virtually All of America's Population Growth*, WASH. POST (Mar. 27, 2014), https://www.washingtonpost.com/ news/wonk/wp/2014/03/27/metropolitan-areas-are-now-fueling-virtually-all-of-amer icas-population-growth/ [https://perma.cc/9ENF-LHDJ].

Baker, Lynn A., & Daniel B. Rodriguez, *Constitutional Home Rule and Judicial Scrutiny*, 86 DENV. U. L. REV. 1337 (2009).

Baker, Paula, *The Domestication of Politics: Women and American Political Society, 1780–1920*, 89 AMER. HIST. REV. 620 (1984).

Barber, Benjamin R., *In the Age of Donald Trump, the Resistance Will Be Localized*, NATION (Jan. 18, 2017), https://www.thenation.com/article/in-the-age-of-donald-trump-the-resistance-will-be-localized/.

IF MAYORS RULED THE WORLD: DYSFUNCTIONAL NATIONS, RISING CITIES (2013).

Constitutional Faith, in FOR LOVE OF COUNTRY 30 (Martha C. Nussbaum & Joshua Cohen eds., 2002).

JIHAD V. MCWORLD (1995).

Barron, David J., *Reclaiming Home Rule*, 116 HARV. L. REV. 2257 (2003).

Baubock, Rainer, *Expansive Citizenship: Voting beyond Territory and Membership*, 38 PS: POLITICAL SCIENCE & POLITICS 683 (2005).

Reinventing Urban Citizenship, 7 CIT. STUD. 139 (2003).

BAUMAN, ZYGMUNT, GLOBALIZATION (1998).

Been, Vicki, et al., *Supply Skepticism: Housing Supply and Affordability*, NYU FURMAN CENTER WORKING PAPER (Aug. 20, 2018), http://furmancenter.org/research/publication/supply-skepticismnbsp-housing-supply-and-affordability.

Bender, Thomas, *Intellectuals, Cities, and Citizenship in the United States: The 1890s and 1990s*, in CITIES AND CITIZENSHIP 21 (James Holston ed., 1999).

Benhabib, Seyla, *Models of Public Space*, in HABERMAS AND THE PUBLIC SPHERE 73 (Craig Calhoun ed., 1992).

Benn, Stanley I. & Gerald F. Gaus, *The Liberal Conception of the Public and the Private*, in PUBLIC AND PRIVATE IN SOCIAL LIFE 31 (S. I. Benn & G. F. Gaus eds., 1983).

BENNETT, SUSAN, et al., COMMUNITY ECONOMIC DEVELOPMENT LAW (2012).

BERMAN, HAROLD J., LAW AND REVOLUTION: THE FORMATION OF THE WESTERN LEGAL TRADITION (1983).

BERRY, JEFFREY M. et al., THE REBIRTH OF URBAN DEMOCRACY (1993).

BICKEL, ALEXANDER, THE MORALITY OF CONSENT 33 (1975).

THE SUPREME COURT AND THE IDEA OF PROGRESS (1970).

Blank, Yishai, *Spheres of Citizenship*, 8 THEORETICAL INQUIRIES L. 411 (2007).

Borjas, George, *Welfare Reform and Immigrant Participation in Welfare Programs*, 36 INT'L MIG. REV. 1093 (2002).

Bosniak, Linda, *Being Here: Ethical Territoriality and the Rights of Immigrants*, in CITIZENSHIP BETWEEN PAST AND FUTURE 123 (Engin Isin et al. eds., 2008).

Citizenship Denationalized, 7 IND. J. GLOBAL LEGAL STUD. 447 (2000).

BOSNIAK, LINDA, THE CITIZEN AND THE ALIEN (2006).

Boyer, M. Christine, *Cities for Sale: Merchandising History at South Street Seaport*, in VARIATIONS ON A THEME PARK 181 (Michael Sorkin ed., 1992).

BRIDGES, AMY, MORNING GLORIES: MUNICIPAL REFORM IN THE SOUTHWEST (1997).

Briffault, Richard, *A Government for Our Time: Business Improvement Districts and Urban Governance*, 99 COLUM. L. REV. 365 (1999).

Who Rules at Home?: One Person/One Vote and Local Governments, 60 U. CHI. L. REV. 339 (1993).

Our Localism: Part II: Localism and Legal Theory, 90 COLUM. L. REV. 346 (1990).

Brown-Saracino, Japonica, A Neighborhood That Never Changes: Gentrification, Social Preservation, and the Search for Authenticity (2009).

Brubaker, William Rogers, *Citizenship and Naturalization: Policies and Politics*, in Immigration and the Politics of Citizenship 99 (William Rogers Brubaker ed., 1989).

Introduction, in Immigration and the Politics of Citizenship in Europe and North America 1 (William Rogers Brubaker ed., 1989).

Castañeda, Ernesto, *Urban Citizenship in New York, Paris, and Barcelona: Immigrant Organizations and the Right to Inhabit the City*, in Remaking Urban Citizenship: Organizations, Institutions and the Right to the City 57 (Michael Peter Smith & Michael McQuarrie eds., 2012).

Castells, Manuel, The City and the Grassroots (1983).

Chang, Robert S. & Keith Aoki, *Centering the Immigrant in the Inter/National Imagination*, 85 Calif. L. Rev. 1395 (1997).

Chi. Pub. Schs., Office of Local Sch. Council Relations, 2018 Local School Council Election Guide (2018) [https://perma.cc/LM62-SV2S].

Clark, LaToya Baldwin, *Education as Property*, 105 Va. L. Rev. 397 (2019).

Clausing, Kimberly, Open: The Progressive Case for Free Trade, Immigration and Global Capital (2019).

Cohen, Lizabeth, A Consumers' Republic: The Politics of Mass Consumption in Postwar America (2003).

Condon, Jenny-Brooke, *The Preempting of Equal Protection for Immigrants*, 73 Wash. & Lee L. Rev. 77 (2016).

Cong. Research Serv., R43221, Noncitizen Eligibility for Public Benefits: Legal Issues (2013), https://www.everycrsreport.com/files/20130909_R43221_6b375b0965db2c6cac9515d87d8d7b4b65ebbd10.pdf.

Cover, Robert, *Foreword: Nomos and Narrative*, 97 Harv. L. Rev. 4 (1983).

Cramer, Katherine J., The Politics of Resentment (2016).

Crawford, Margaret, Making Suburbia: New Histories of Everyday America (2015).

The World in a Shopping Mall, in Variations on a Theme Park 3 (Michael Sorkin ed., 1992).

Crenshaw, Kimberle Williams, *Race, Reform and Retrenchment: Transformation and Legitimation in Antidiscrimination Law*, 101 Harv. L. Rev. 1331 (1988).

Creswell, Tim, Place: A Short Introduction (2004).

Cummings, Scott L., *Community Economic Development as Progressive Politics: Toward a Grassroots Movement for Economic Justice*, 54 Stan. L. Rev. 399 (2001).

Dahl, Robert S., Democracy and Its Critics (1989).

Davidson, Chandler & George Korbel, *At-Large Elections and Minority Group Representation*, in Minority Vote Dilution 65 (Chandler Davidson ed., 1984).

Do, Anh, *In Fighting Homeless Camp, Irvine's Asians Win, but at a Cost*, L.A. Times (Apr. 1, 2018, 5:00 AM), https://www.latimes.com/local/lanow/la-me-homeless-asians-20180401-story.html.

Domosh, Mona & Joni Seager, Putting Women in Place: Feminist Geographers Make Sense of the World (2001).

Douglas, Joshua A., *The Right to Vote under Local Law*, 85 GEO. WASH. L. REV. 1039 (2017).

Dudley, David, *The GOP Is Afraid of My City*, CITYLAB (July 22, 2016), http://www .citylab.com/crime/2016/07/the-gop-is-afraid-of-baltimore-chicago-detroit-st-louis/ 492671 [https://perma.cc/PWG3-QDUQ].

Eagly, Ingrid V., *Immigrant Protective Policies in Criminal Justice*, 95 Tex. L. Rev. 245 (2016).

EHRENHALT, ALAN, THE GREAT INVERSION AND THE FUTURE OF THE AMERI-CAN CITY (2012).

Elias, Stella Burch, *The New Immigration Federalism*, 74 OHIO ST. L.J. 703 (2013).

Ellickson, Robert C., *Controlling Chronic Misconduct in City Spaces: Of Panhandlers, Skid Rows, and Public-Space Zoning*, 105 YALE L.J. 1165 (1996).

Elshtain, Jean Bethke, PUBLIC MAN, PRIVATE WOMAN: WOMEN IN SOCIAL AND POLITICAL THOUGHT (1993).

EWEN, ELIZABETH, IMMIGRANT WOMEN IN THE LAND OF DOLLARS: LIFE AND CULTURE ON THE LOWER EAST SIDE, 1890–1925 (1985).

The Federalist No. 10, at 64 (James Madison) (Jacob E. Cooke ed., 1961).

The Federalist No. 2, at 9 (John Jay) (Jacob E. Cooke ed., 1961).

FISCHEL, WILLIAM A., THE HOMEVOTER HYPOTHESIS (2001).

ZONING RULES! (2015).

FISHMAN, ROBERT, BOURGEOIS UTOPIAS: THE RISE AND FALL OF SUBURBIA (1987).

Florida, Richard, *Geographic Inequality Is Swallowing the Recovery*, CITYLAB (May 23, 2016), http://www.citylab.com/politics/2016/05/there-are-more-losers-than-winners-in-americas-economic-recovery-due-to-geographic-inequality/483989/ [https://perma .cc/56XL-WZFU].

FLORIDA, RICHARD, WHO'S YOUR CITY (2008).

Ford, Richard T., *City-States and Citizenship*, in CITIZENSHIP TODAY 209 (T. Alexander Aleinikoff & Douglas Klusmeyer eds., 2001).

Law's Territory (A History of Jurisdiction), 97 MICH. L. REV. 843 (1999).

Ford, Richard Thompson, *Bourgeois Communities: A Review of Gerald Frug's City Making*, 56 STAN. L. REV. 231 (2003).

Geography and Sovereignty: Jurisdictional Formation and Racial Segregation, 49 STAN. L. REV. 1365 (1997).

The Boundaries of Race: Political Geography in Legal Analysis, 107 HARV. L. REV. 1841 (1994).

Forest, Benjamin, *Mapping Democracy: Racial Identity and the Quandary of Political Representation*, 91 ANNALS OF ASS'N OF AMER. GEO. 143 (2001).

West Hollywood as a Symbol: The Significance of Place in the Construction of a Gay Identity, 13 ENV'T & PLAN. D: SOCIETY & SPACE 133 (1995).

Fortner, Michael Javen, *Urban Autonomy and Effective Citizenship*, in URBAN CITI-ZENSHIP AND AMERICAN DEMOCRACY 23 (Amy Bridges & Michael Javen Fort-ner eds., 2016).

Fracassa, Dominic, *Neighbors Appeal Controversial Embarcadero Navigation Center as Fight Grinds On*, S.F. CHRON. (May 24, 2019, 9:23 PM), https://www.sfchronicle .com/bayarea/article/Neighbors-appeal-controversial-Embarcadero-13895073.php? psid=bonTl.

Freund, David M. P., *Marketing the Free Market: State Intervention and the Politics of Prosperity in Metropolitan America*, in THE NEW SUBURBAN HISTORY 11 (Kevin M. Kruse & Thomas J. Sugrue eds., 2006).

FRIEDMAN-KASABA, KATHIE, MEMORIES OF MIGRATION: GENDER, ETHNICITY AND WORK IN THE LIVES OF JEWISH AND ITALIAN WOMEN IN NEW YORK, 1870–1924 (1996).

FRUG, GERALD E. & DAVID J. BARRON, *The Seductions of Form*, 3 DREXEL L. REV. 11 (2010).

CITY BOUND 141 (2008).

CITY MAKING: BUILDING COMMUNITIES WITHOUT BUILDING WALLS (1999).

City Services, 73 N.Y.U. L. Rev. 23 (1998).

The City as a Legal Concept, 93 HARV. L. REV. 1057 (1980).

Frug, Jerry, *Decentering Decentralization*, 60 U. CHI. L. REV. 253 (1993).

Fuller, Thomas, *The Loneliness of Being Black in San Francisco*, N.Y. TIMES (JULY 20, 2016), https://www.nytimes.com/2016/07/21/us/black-exodus-from-san-francisco.html.

Garfield, Leanna, *Mark Zuckerberg Once Made a $100 Million Investment in a Major U.S. City to Help Fix Its Schools – Now the Mayor Says the Effort "Parachuted" in and Failed*, BUS. INSIDER (May 12, 2018, 11:00 AM), https://www.businessinsider.com/mark-zuckerberg-schools-education-newark-mayor-ras-baraka-cory-booker-2018-5.

Garnett, Nicole Stelle, *Affordable Private Education and the Middle Class City*, 77 U. CHI. L. REV. 201 (2010).

ORDERING THE CITY: LAND USE, POLICING, AND THE RESTORATION OF URBAN AMERICA (2010).

THE GENTRIFICATION DEBATES (Japonica Brown-Saracino ed., 2010).

THE GENTRIFICATION READER (Loretta Lees et al. eds., 2010).

Gerda, Nick, *OC Supervisors Back Off New Homeless Shelters, Make Promise to Work with Cities*, Voice of OC (Mar. 28, 2018), https://voiceofoc.org/2018/03/oc-supervisors-back-off-new-homeless-shelters-make-promise-to-work-with-cities/.

GERSTLE, GARY, AMERICAN CRUCIBLE: RACE AND NATION IN THE TWENTIETH CENTURY (2001).

GLAESER, EDWARD, TRIUMPH OF THE CITY (2011).

Glass, Maeve, *Citizens of the State*, 85 U. CHI. L. REV. 865 (2018).

GLICKMAN, LAWRENCE B., BUYING POWER: A HISTORY OF CONSUMER ACTIVISM IN AMERICA (2009).

GOETZ, EDWARD G., THE ONE-WAY STREET OF INTEGRATION: FAIR HOUSING AND THE PURSUIT OF RACIAL JUSTICE IN AMERICAN CITIES (2018).

Gordon, Jennifer, *Immigration as Commerce: A New Look at the Federal Immigration Power and the Constitution*, 93 IND. L.J. 653 (2018).

Gordon, Sarah Barringer, *"The Liberty of Self-Degradation": Polygamy, Woman Suffrage, and Consent in Nineteenth-Century America*, 83 J. AMER. HIST. 815 (1996).

Grabar, Henry, *Gentrification Got Gentrified*, SLATE (May 3, 2019, 5:50 AM), https://slate.com/business/2019/05/gentrification-definition-housing-policy-methodology-cities-suburbs.html.

Granovetter, Mark S., *The Strength of Weak Ties*, 78 AM. J. SOC. 1360 (1973).

Green, Erica L., *Lebron James Opened a School That Was Considered an Experiment. It's Showing Promise*, N.Y. TIMES (Apr. 12, 2019), https://www.nytimes.com/2019/04/12/education/lebron-james-school-ohio.html.

GREENFELD, LIAH, NATIONALISM: FIVE ROADS TO MODERNITY 399–400 (1992).

HALL, PETER, CITIES OF TOMORROW (1988).

Hamilton, Bruce W., *Zoning and Property Taxation in a System of Local Governments*, 12 URB. STUD. 205 (1975).

Hardwick, Susan W., *Toward a Suburban Immigrant Nation*, in Audrey Singer et al., TWENTY-FIRST CENTURY GATEWAYS: IMMIGRANT INCORPORATION IN SUB-URBAN AMERICA 31 (2008).

Harper-Ho, Virgina, *Noncitizen Voting Rights: The History, the Law, and Current Prospects for Change*, 18 L. & INEQUALITY 271 (2000).

Hartog, Hendrik, *Imposing Constitutional Traditions*, 29 WM. & MARY L. REV. 75 (1987).

PUBLIC PROPERTY AND PRIVATE POWER: THE CORPORATION OF THE CITY OF NEW YORK IN AMERICAN LAW 1730–1870 (1983).

HARVEY, DAVID, JUSTICE, NATURE, AND THE GEOGRAPHY OF DIFFERENCE (1996).

Money, Time, Space and the City, in CONSCIOUSNESS AND THE URBAN EXPERI-ENCE 1 (1989).

HAYDEN, DOLORES, REDESIGNING THE AMERICAN DREAM: GENDER, HOUSING AND AMERICAN LIFE (2002).

THE GRAND DOMESTIC REVOLUTION: A HISTORY OF FEMINIST DESIGNS FOR AMERICAN HOMES, NEIGHBORHOODS, AND CITIES (1981).

HAYDUK, RON, DEMOCRACY FOR ALL: RESTORING IMMIGRANT RIGHTS IN THE UNITED STATES (2006).

Hays, Samuel P., *The Politics of Reform in Municipal Government in the Progressive Era*, 55 PAC. NORTHWEST Q. 157 (1964).

Heater, Derek, CITIZENSHIP (1990).

Hing, Bill Ong, *Immigration Sanctuary Policies: Constitutional and Representative of Good Policing and Good Public Policy*, 2 U.C. IRVINE L. REV. 247 (2012).

Hobbs, Allyson, *Summer Road-tripping While Black*, N.Y. TIMES (Aug. 31, 2018), https://www.nytimes.com/2018/08/31/opinion/sunday/summer-road-tripping-while-black.html.

HOBSBAWM, E. J., NATIONS AND NATIONALISM SINCE 1780: PROGRAMME, MYTH, REALITY (1990).

HOFSTADTER, RICHARD, THE AGE OF REFORM (1955).

Holston, James ed., CITIES AND CITIZENSHIP (1999).

HONIG, BONNIE, DEMOCRACY AND THE FOREIGNER (2001).

Honohan, Iseult, *Liberal and Republican Conceptions of Citizenship*, in THE OXFORD HANDBOOK OF CITIZENSHIP 83 (Ayelet Shachar et al. eds., 2017).

Horwitz, Morton J., *Republicanism and Liberalism in American Constitutional Thought*, 29 WM. & MARY L. REV. 57 (1987).

Santa Clara Revisited: The Development of Corporate Theory, 88 W. VA. L. REV. 173 (1986).

The History of the Public/Private Distinction, 130 U. PA. L. REV. 1423 (1982).

Hovenkamp, Herbert, *The Classical Corporation in American Legal Thought*, 76 GEO. L.J. 1593 (1988).

Huntington, Clare, *The Constitutional Dimension of Immigration Federalism*, 61 VAND. L. REV. 787 (2008).

HUNTINGTON, SAMUEL, WHO ARE WE? THE CHALLENGE TO AMERICA'S NATIONAL IDENTITY (2004).

HURLEY, AMANDA KOLSON, RADICAL SUBURBS: EXPERIMENTAL LIVING ON THE FRINGES OF THE AMERICAN CITY (2019).

IGNATIEFF, MICHAEL, *The Myth of Citizenship*, in THEORIZING CITIZENSHIP 53 (Ronald Beiner ed., 1995).

BLOOD AND BELONGING (1993).

Isin, Engin ed., DEMOCRACY, CITIZENSHIP AND THE GLOBAL CITY (2000).

Jackson, Kenneth T., CRABGRASS FRONTIER: THE SUBURBANIZATION OF THE UNITED STATES (1985).

Jackson, Kenneth T. & David S. Dunbar eds., *Remonstrance of the Inhabitants of the Town of Flushing* (1657), *reprinted in* EMPIRE CITY: NEW YORK THROUGH THE CENTURIES 33 (2002).

Jackson, Vicki C., *Citizenship and Federalism*, in CITIZENSHIP TODAY: GLOBAL PERSPECTIVES AND PRACTICES 127 (T. Alexander Aleinikoff & Douglas Klusmeyer eds., 2001).

JACOBSON, DAVID, RIGHTS ACROSS BORDERS: IMMIGRATION AND THE DECLINE OF CITIZENSHIP (1996).

JANOWITZ, MORRIS, THE COMMUNITY PRESS IN AN URBAN SETTING (1952).

JARDINA, ASHLEY, WHITE IDENTITY POLITICS (2019).

JONES, MARTHA S., BIRTHRIGHT CITIZENS: A HISTORY OF RACE AND RIGHTS IN ANTEBELLUM AMERICA (2018).

JUDD, DENNIS R. & TODD SWANSTROM, CITY POLITICS: PRIVATE POWER AND PUBLIC POLICY (4th ed. 2004).

Kahan, Dan M. & Tracey L. Meares, *Foreword: The Coming Crisis of Criminal Procedure*, 86 GEO. L .J. 1153 (1998).

Kaiman, Beth, *Takoma Park Weighs Noncitizen Vote*, WASH. POST, Oct. 31, 1991, at M2.

KALMAN, LAURA, THE STRANGE CAREER OF LEGAL LIBERALISM (1996).

KANTER, ROSABETH MOSS, COMMITMENT AND COMMUNITY (1972).

Kennedy, Duncan, *Toward an Historical Understanding of Legal Consciousness: The Case of Classical Legal Thought in America, 1850–1940*, 3 RES. LAW & SOC. 3 (1980).

Kerber, Linda K., *The Paradox of Women's Citizenship in the Early Republic: The Case of* Martin v. Massachusetts, 1805, 97 AMER. HIST. REV. 349 (1992).

Separate Spheres, Female Worlds, Woman's Place: The Rhetoric of Women's History, 75 J. AMER. HIST. 9 (1988).

KEYSSAR, ALEXANDER, THE RIGHT TO VOTE: THE CONTESTED HISTORY OF DEMOCRACY IN THE UNITED STATES (2000).

Khalidi, Muhammad Ali *Al-Farabi on the Democratic City*, 11 BRIT. J. HIST. PHIL. 379 (2003).

KOTLER, MILTON, NEIGHBORHOOD GOVERNMENT (1969).

Kraditor, Aileen, The Ideas of the Woman Suffrage Movement, 1890–1920 (1965).

KRANE, DALE et al., HOME RULE IN AMERICA: A FIFTY-STATE HANDBOOK (2001).

KYMLICKA, WILL, MULTICULTURAL CITIZENSHIP (1995).

Kymlicka, Will & Wayne Norman, *Return of the Citizen: A Survey of Recent Work on Citizenship Theory*, 104 ETHICS 352 (Jan. 1994).

LAGNADO, LUCETTE, THE MAN IN THE WHITE SHARKSKIN SUIT: A JEWISH FAMILY'S EXODUS FROM OLD CAIRO TO THE NEW WORLD (2007).

LANG, ROBERT E. & JENNIFER B. LeFURGY, BOOMBURBS: THE RISE OF AMERICA'S ACCIDENTAL CITIES (2007).

LEACH, WILLIAM, LAND OF DESIRE: MERCHANTS, POWER, AND THE RISE OF A NEW AMERICAN CULTURE (1994).

Levinson, Sanford, *Suffrage and Community: Who Should Vote?* 41 FLA. L. REV. 545 (1989).

Levitz, Eric, *Why Tucker Carlson Plays a Critic of Capitalism on TV*, N.Y. INTELLIGENCER (Jan. 8, 2019), http://nymag.com/intelligencer/2019/01/tucker-carlson-romney-monologue-capitalism-social-conservatives-fox-news.html.

LEWIS-MCCOY, R. L'HEUREUX, INEQUALITY IN THE PROMISED LAND: RACE, RESOURCES AND SUBURBAN SCHOOLING (2014).

Lin, Tom C. W., *Incorporating Social Activism*, 98 B.U. L. REV. 1535 (2018).

LIPPMAN, WALTER, DRIFT AND MASTERY (1914).

LISTER, RUTH, CITIZENSHIP: FEMINIST PERSPECTIVES (2003).

LOFLAND, LYNN, A WORLD OF STRANGERS (1973).

Maas, Willem, *Multilevel Citizenship*, in THE OXFORD HANDBOOK OF CITIZENSHIP 644 (Ayelet Shachar et al. eds., 2017).

Mangin, John, *The New Exclusionary Zoning*, 25 STAN. L. & POL'Y REV. 91 (2014).

Markowitz, Peter L., *Undocumented No More: The Power of State Citizenship*, 67 STAN. L. REV. 869 (2015).

Marshall, T. H., *Citizenship and Social Class*, in CLASS, CITIZENSHIP, AND SOCIAL DEVELOPMENT 65 (1964).

MARX, KARL, *On the Jewish Question*, in THE MARX-ENGELS READER 26 (Robert C. Tucker ed., 2nd ed. 1978).

MARX, KARL & FRIEDRICH ENGELS, THE GERMAN IDEOLOGY (Prometheus Books 1998) (1845).

THE HOLY FAMILY (1956) (1844).

Massey, Doreen, *A Global Sense of Place*, in SPACE, PLACE, AND GENDER 146 (1994). RACE, PLACE AND GENDER (1994).

MCCONNAUGHY, CORRINE M., THE WOMAN SUFFRAGE MOVEMENT IN AMERICA: A REASSESSMENT (2013).

McCormick, Erin, *Rise of the Yimbys: The Angry Millennials with a Radical Housing Solution*, GUARDIAN (Oct. 2, 2017, 2:15 PM), https://amp.theguardian.com/cities/2017/oct/02/rise-of-the-yimbys-angry-millennials-radical-housing-solution.

McFarlane, Audrey G., *When Inclusion Leads to Exclusion: The Uncharted Terrain of Community Participation in Economic Development*, 66 BROOK. L. REV. 861 (2001). *Race, Space and Place: The Geography of Economic Development*, 36 SAN DIEGO L. REV. 295 (1999).

McFarlane, Audrey, *Preserving Community in the City: Special Improvement Districts and the Privatization of Urban Racialized Space*, 4 Stan. Agora 5 (2003).

Mead, Rebecca J., How the Vote Was Won: Woman Suffrage in the United States, 1868–1914 (2004).

Meares, Tracey L. & Dan Kahan, The Wages of Antiquated Procedural Thinking: A Critique of Chicago v. Morales, 1998 U. Chi. Legal F. 197.

Law and (Norms of) Order in the Inner City, 32 Law & Soc. Rev. 805 (1998).

Meckler, Laura & Dante Chinni, *City vs. Country: How Where We Live Deepens the Nation's Political Divide*, Wall St. J. (Mar. 21, 2014, 7:45 AM), http://www.wsj.com/articles/SB10001424052702303636404579395532755485004 [https://perma.cc/9AEQ-556E].

Michelman, Frank, *Law's Republic*, 97 Yale L.J. 1493 (1988).

Michener, Jamila, Fragmented Democracy: Medicaid, Federalism, and Unequal Politics (2018).

Miller, Gary J., Cities by Contract: The Politics of Municipal Incorporation (1981).

@JohnMirisch, Twitter (April 19, 2018, 9:49 AM), https://twitter.com/JohnMirisch/status/987010314376900608.

Mitchell, Don, The Right to the City: Social Justice and the Fight for Public Space (2003).

Monkkonen, Eric H., America Becomes Urban: The Development of U.S. Cities & Towns 1780–1980 (1988).

Morris, Milton D., *Black Electoral Participation and the Distribution of Public Benefits*, in Minority Vote Dilution 271 (Chandler Davidson ed., 1984).

Motomura, Hiroshi, *Whose Immigration Law? Citizens, Aliens and the Constitution*, 97 Colum. L. Rev. 1567 (1997).

Muggah, Robert & Misha Glenny, *Populism is Poison. Plural Cities are the Antidote*, World Econ. Forum (Jan. 4, 2017), https://www.weforum.org/agenda/2017/01/populism-is-poison-plural-cities-are-the-antidote/.

Mumford, Lewis, The City in History: Its Origins, Its Transformations, and Its Prospects (1961).

Nelson, Robert H., Private Neighborhoods and the Transformation of Local Government (2005).

Neuman, Gerald L., Strangers to the Constitution: Immigrants, Borders, and Fundamental Law (1996).

The New American Suburb: Poverty, Race and the Economic Crisis (Katrin B. Anacker ed., 2015).

Newkirk II, Vann R., *Mayors vs. Trump*, CityLab (July 27, 2016), http://www.citylab.com/politics/2016/07/cities-mayors-trump/493211 [https://perma.cc/DQ9F-43V6].

The New Suburban History (Kevin M. Kruse & Thomas J. Sugrue eds., 2006).

Ngai, Mae M., Impossible Subjects: Illegal Aliens and the Making of Modern America (2004).

Oldfield, Adrien, *Citizenship and Community*, in The Citizenship Debates 75 (Gershon Shafir ed., 1998).

Olsen, Frances E., *The Family and the Market: A Study of Ideology and Legal Reform*, 96 Harv. L. Rev. 1497 (1983).

Ong, Aihwa, *A Biocartography: Maids, Neoslavery, and NGOs*, in NEOLIBERALISM AS EXCEPTION (2006).

FLEXIBLE CITIZENSHIP: THE CULTURAL LOGICS OF TRANSNATIONALITY (1999).

ORTLEPP, ANKE, JIM CROW TERMINALS: THE DESEGREGATION OF AMERICAN AIRPORTS (2017).

PARK, EDWARD J. W. & JOHN S. W. PARK, PROBATIONARY AMERICANS: CONTEMPORARY IMMIGRATION POLICIES AND THE SHAPING OF ASIAN AMERICAN COMMUNITIES (2005).

Park, Madison, *Noncitizens in San Francisco Can Register to Vote, but Only for School Board Elections*, CNN.COM (July 20, 2018, 12:00 AM), https://www.cnn.com/2018/07/20/us/noncitizens-vote-san-francisco/index.html.

Park, Robert E., *The City: Suggestions for the Investigation of Human Behavior in the Urban Environment*, in THE CITY 1 (Robert E. Park et al. eds., 1925).

PARKER, KUNAL M., MAKING FOREIGNERS: IMMIGRATION AND CITIZENSHIP LAW IN AMERICA, 1600–2000 (2015).

PHELAN, SHANE, SEXUAL STRANGERS: GAYS, LESBIANS, AND DILEMMAS OF CITIZENSHIP (2001).

PIERCE, SARAH & ANDREW SELEE, MIGRATION POLICY INSTITUTE, IMMIGRATION UNDER TRUMP: A REVIEW OF POLICY SHIFTS IN THE YEAR SINCE THE ELECTION (2017), https://www.migrationpolicy.org/research/immigration-under-trump-review-policy-shifts.

Pindell, Ngai, *Home Sweet Home? The Efficacy of Rental Restrictions to Promote Neighborhood Stability*, 29 ST. LOUIS U. PUB. L. REV. 41 (2009).

PITKIN, HANNA FENICHEL, FORTUNE IS A WOMAN: GENDER AND POLITICS IN THE THOUGHT OF NICCOLO MACHIAVELLI (1984).

Pocock, J. G. A., *The Ideal of Citizenship since Classical Times*, in THE CITIZENSHIP DEBATES 31 (Gershon Shafir ed., 1998).

THE MACHIAVELLIAN MOMENT: FLORENTINE POLITICAL THOUGHT AND THE ATLANTIC REPUBLICAN TRADITION (1975).

Polinard, Jerry L. et al., *The Impact of District Elections on the Mexican American Community: The Electoral Perspective*, 72 SOC. SCI. Q. 608 (1991).

Pritchett, Wendell E., *The "Public Menace" of Blight: Urban Renewal and the Private Uses of Eminent Domain*, 21 YALE L. & POL. REV. 1 (2003).

Purcell, Mark, *Citizenship and the Right to the Global City*, 27.3 INT'L. J. URB. & REGIONAL RESEARCH 564 (2003).

PUTNAM, ROBERT D., *E Pluribus Unum: Diversity and Community in the Twenty-First Century*, 30 SCANDINAVIAN POL. STUD. 137 (2007).

BOWLING ALONE (2000).

Radin, Margaret Jane, Residential Rent Control, Phil. & Pub. Aff. 350 (1986).

Ramakrishnan, S. Karthick & Allan Colbern, *The California Package: Immigrant Integration and the Evolving Nature of State Citizenship* 6 POL. MATTERS 1 (2015).

Raskin, Jamin B., *Legal Aliens, Local Citizens: The Historical, Constitutional, and Theoretical Meanings of Alien Suffrage*, 141 U. PA. L. REV. 1391 (1993).

RELPH, EDWARD, PLACE AND PLACELESSNESS (1974).

Renshon, Stanley, *The Value of Citizenship*, N.Y. Sun (Sep. 15, 2003).

Report of the National Advisory Commission on Civil Disorders (1968) (Kerner Commission Report).

Ritzer, George, Globalization: A Basic Text (2010).

Rodriguez, Cristina M., *The Significance of the Local in Immigration Regulation*, 106 Mich. L. Rev. 567 (2008).

Accommodating Linguistic Difference: Toward a Comprehensive Theory of Language Rights in the United States, 36 Harv. C.R.C.L. L. Rev. 133 (2001).

Rosenblum, Darren, *The Futility of Walls: How Traveling Corporations Threaten State Sovereignty*, 93 Tulane L. Rev. 645 (2019).

Roseneil, Sasha ed., Beyond Citizenship: Feminism and the Transformation of Belonging (2013).

Rothstein, Richard, The Color of Law: A Forgotten History of How Our Government Segregated America (2017).

Rousseau, Jean-Jacques III, Emilius, or, A Treatise on Education (1768).

Roy, Nilanjana, *Cities Offer Sanctuary against the Insularity of Nationalism*, Fin. Times (Apr. 4, 2017), https://www.ft.com/content/b54093f0-191f-11e7-9c35-odd2cb31823a.

Rubinstein, David S. & Pratheepan Gulasekaram, *Immigration Exceptionalism*, 111 N. W.U. L. Rev. 583 (2017).

Rumore, Kori, *When Trump Talks about Chicago, We Track It*, Chi. Tribune (March 28, 2019, 8:10 AM), https://www.chicagotribune.com/news/local/break ing/ct-trump-tweets-quotes-chicago-htmlstory.html.

Ryan, Mary P., Civic Wars (1997).

Womanhood in America (1983).

Sack, Robert, Place, Modernity and the Consumer's World (1992).

Sampson, Robert J., Great American City (2012).

Sandel, Michael, Democracy's Discontent: America in Search of a Public Philosophy (1996).

What Money Can't Buy (2013).

Liberalism and the Limits of Justice (2nd ed. 1998).

Freedom of Conscience or Freedom of Choice, in Articles of Faith, Articles of Peace 74 (James Davison Hunter & Os Guinness eds., 1990).

Introduction, in Liberalism and its Critics 1 (Michael Sandel ed. 1984).

Liberalism and the Limits of Justice (1982).

Sassen, Saskia, Territory, Authority, Rights (updated ed. 2008).

Territory, Authority, Rights (2006).

The Global City (1989).

Saunders, John, *Non-citizens' Politics*, in Acts of Citizenship 292 (Engin F. Isin & Greg M. Nielsen eds., 2008).

Saunders, Peter, Social Theory and the Urban Question (2nd. ed. 1986).

Saxonhouse, Arlene W., Fear of Diversity: The Birth of Political Science in Ancient Greek Thought (1992).

Schleicher, David, *The City as a Law and Economics Subject*, U. Ill. L. Rev. 1507 (2010).

Schlichtman, John Joe et al., Gentrifier (2017).

Schragger, Richard C., *Rethinking the Theory and Practice of Local Economic Development*, 77 U. Chi. L. Rev. 311 (2010).
    Cities, Economic Development, and the Free Trade Constitution, 94 Va. L. Rev. 1091 (2008).
    The Anti-chain Store Movement in Localist Ideology, and the Remnants of the Progressive Constitution, 1920–1940, 90 Iowa L. Rev. 1011 (2005).
    The Limits of Localism, 100 Mich. L. Rev. 371 (2001).
Schuck, Peter H. & Rogers M. Smith, Citizenship without Consent: Illegal Aliens in the American Polity (1985).
Schulman, Sarah, The Gentrification of the Mind (2012).
Scott, James C., Seeing Like a State (1998).
Semuels, Alana, *From "Not in My Backyard" to "Yes in My Backyard,"* Atlantic (July 5, 2017), https://www.theatlantic.com/business/archive/2017/07/yimby-groups-pro-development/532437/.
    The Graying of Rural America, CityLab (Jun. 2, 2016), http://www.citylab.com/hous ing/2016/06/the-graying-of-rural-america/485288/ [https://perma.cc/9MAQ-TFN8].
Sennett, Richard, The Conscience of the Eye (1990).
    The Fall of Public Man (1974).
Sepper, Elizabeth & Deborah Dinner, *Sex in Public*, 129 Yale L.J. (forthcoming), https://papers.ssrn.com/sol3/papers.cfm?abstract_id=3344715.
Serwer, Adam, *The Cruelty is the Point*, Atlantic (Oct. 3, 2018), https://www.theatlantic.com/ideas/archive/2018/10/the-cruelty-is-the-point/572104/.
Shachar, Ayelet, *Citizenship for Sale?*, in The Oxford Handbook of Citizenship 789 (Ayelet Shachar et al. eds., 2017).
Sharkey, Patrick, Stuck in Place: Urban Neighborhoods and the End of Progress Toward Racial Equality (2013).
Sherry, Suzanna, *Civic Virtue and the Feminine Voice in Constitutional Adjudication*, 72 Va. L. Rev. 543 (1986).
Shimura, Tomoya, *About 250 Irvine Residents Convene to Oppose Proposed Homeless Camp Next to Great Park*, O.C. Reg. (Mar. 23, 2018, 4:39 PM), https://www.ocregister.com/2018/03/23/about-250-irvine-residents-convene-to-oppose-proposed-homeless-camp-next-to-great-park/?fbclid=IwAR3SnvfOqsO6852AWI1cjoY8cftgtCWO8rxcHpjWzB9R79X1J4Wpt6awfjo.
Siegel, Reva B., *"The Rule of Love": Wife Beating as Prerogative and Privacy*, 105 Yale L.J. 2117 (1996).
Simmel, Georg, *The Metropolis and Mental Life*, in Classic Essays on the Culture of Cities 47 (Richard Sennett ed., 1969).
Simon, William H., The Community Economic Development (2001).
Singer, Audrey et al., Twenty-First Century Gateways: Immigrant Incorporation in Suburban America (2008).
Sites, William & Rebecca Vonderlack-Navarro, *Tipping the Scale: State Rescaling and the Strange Odyssey of Chicago's Mexican Hometown Associations*, in Remaking Urban Citizenship: Organizations, Institutions and the Right to the City 151 (Michael Peter Smith & Michael McQuarrie eds., 2012).
Smith, Michael Peter & Michael McQuarrie eds., Remaking Urban Citizenship: Organizations, Institutions and the Right to the City (2012).

Smith, Noah, *Hispanics are Like Everyone Else Who Comes to America*, Bloomberg (Jan. 30, 2019, 4:30 AM), https://www.bloomberg.com/opinion/articles/2019-01-30/sorry-mr-brokaw-but-hispanics-have-blended-right-in.

Smith, Rogers M., *American Cities and American Citizenship*, in Urban Citizenship and American Democracy 211 (Amy Bridges & Michael Javen Fortner eds., 2016).

Civic Ideals: Conflicting Visions of Citizenship in U.S. History (1997).

"One United People": Second-Class Female Citizenship and the American Quest for Community, 1 Yale J. L. & Hum. 229 (1989).

Smith, Zadie, *Northwest London Blues*, in Feel Free 12 (2018).

Sorkin, Michael, *Introduction*, in Variations on a Theme Park xi (Michael Sorkin ed., 1992).

Sorkin, Michael ed., Variations on a Theme Park: The New American City and the End of Public Space (1992).

Soysal, Yasemin Nuhoğlu, Limits of Citizenship (1994).

Spar, Debora L. & David B. Yoffie, *A Race to the Bottom or Governance from the Top*, in Coping with Globalization 31 (Aseem Prakish & Jeffrey A. Hart eds., 2000).

Spiro, Peter J., *Formalizing Local Citizenship*, 37 Fordham Urb. L.J. 559 (2010).

Beyond Citizenship: American Identity after Globalization (2008).

Stahl, Kenneth A., *"Yes in My Backyard:" Can a New Pro-housing Movement Overcome the Power of NIMBYs?*, 41 Zoning & Planning Law Report 1 (2018).

The Challenge of Inclusion, 89 Temple L. Rev. 487 (2017).

Preemption, Federalism and Local Democracy, 44 Fordham Urb. L.J. 133 (2017).

Preemption, Federalism and Local Democracy, 44 Fordham Urb. L.J. 133 (2017).

Local Home Rule in the Time of Globalization, 2016 BYU L. Rev. 177 (2016).

Local Government, "One Person, One Vote," and the Jewish Question, 49 Harv. C.R.-C.L. L. Rev. 1 (2014).

Mobility and Community: An Essay on Great American City by Robert J. Sampson, 46 Urb. L.J. 625 (2014).

Neighborhood Empowerment and the Future of the City, 161 U. Pa. L. Rev. 939 (2013).

Reliance in Land Use, BYU L. Rev. 949 (2013).

The Suburb as a Legal Concept: The Problem of Organization and the Fate of Municipalities in American Law, 29 Cardozo L. Rev. 1193 (2008).

Steinfeld, Robert J., *Property and Suffrage in the Early American Republic*, 41 Stan. L. Rev. 335 (1989).

Stephens, Josh, *Trump to Cities: You're Dead to Me*, Planetizen (July 26, 2016, 8:00 AM), http://www.planetizen.com/node/87620/trump-cities-you're-dead-me [https://perma.cc/ANF8-NR57].

Stumpf, Juliet, *States of Confusion: The Rise of State and Local Power over Immigration*, 86 N.C. L. Rev. 1557 (2008).

Su, Rick, *Urban Politics and the Assimilation of Immigrant Voters*, 21 Wm. & Mary Bill Rts. J. 653 (2012).

Local Fragmentation as Immigration Regulation, 47 Hous. L. Rev. 367 (2010).

Sunstein, Cass R., *Interest Groups in American Law*, 38 STAN. L. REV. 29 (1985).
Surowiecki, James, *Losers!*, NEW YORKER (June 6 & 13, 2016), http://www.newyorker
.com/magazine/2016/06/06/losers-for-trump [https://perma.cc/VS6F-4QMR].
TAMIR, YAEL, LIBERAL NATIONALISM (1993).
TEACHOUT, ZEPHYR, CORRUPTION IN AMERICA: FROM BENJAMIN FRANKLIN'S
SNUFF BOX TO CITIZENS UNITED (2014).
TEAFORD, JON C., THE MUNICIPAL REVOLUTION IN AMERICA (1975).
THOMAS, WILLIAM I. I, THE POLISH PEASANT IN EUROPE AND AMERICA
(1918–19).
Tiebout, Charles M., *A Pure Theory of Local Expenditures*, 64 J. POL. ECON. 416
(1956).
TILLY, CHARLES, DURABLE INEQUALITY (1999).
TOLL, SEYMOUR I., ZONED AMERICAN (1969).
TROUNSTINE, JESSICA, SEGREGATION BY DESIGN: LOCAL POLITICS AND
INEQUALITY IN AMERICAN CITIES (2018).
TUAN, YI-FU, SPACE AND PLACE (1977).
UNDERKUFFLER, LAURA S., CAPTURED BY EVIL: THE IDEA OF CORRUPTION IN
LAW (2013).
VALLEJO, JODY, BARRIOS TO BURBS: THE MAKING OF THE MEXICAN AMERICAN
MIDDLE CLASS (2012).
Varsanyi, Monica W., *Documenting Undocumented Migrants: The* Matriculas Con-
sulares *as Neoliberal Local Membership*, 12 GEOPOLITICS 299 (2007).
Interrogating "Urban Citizenship" vis-à-vis Undocumented Migration, 10 CIT. STUD.
229 (2006).
Villazor, Rose Cuison, *American Nationals and Interstitial Citizenship*, 85 FORDHAM
L. REV. 1673 (2017).
"Sanctuary Cities" and Local Citizenship, 37 FORDHAM URB. L.J. 573 (2010).
What Is a "Sanctuary"? 61 SMU L. REV. 133 (2008).
Vogel, David & Robert A. Kagan, *Introduction*, in DYNAMICS OF REGULATORY
CHANGE: HOW GLOBALIZATION AFFECTS NATIONAL REGULATORY POL-
ICIES 1 (David Vogel & Robert A. Kagan eds., 2004).
Volpp, Leti, *Feminist, Sexual and Queer Citizenship*, in THE OXFORD HANDBOOK
OF CITIZENSHIP 153 (Ayelet Shachar et al. eds., 2017).
Citizenship Undone, 75 FORDHAM L. REV. 2579 (2007).
Walzer, Michael, *Spheres of Affection*, in FOR LOVE OF COUNTRY 125 (Martha C.
Nussbaum & Joshua Cohen eds., 2002).
Citizenship, in POLITICAL INNOVATION AND CONCEPTUAL CHANGE 211 (Ter-
ence Ball et al. eds., 1989).
Liberalism and the Art of Separation, 12 POL. THEORY 315 (1984).
SPHERES OF JUSTICE (1983).
WARNER, MICHAEL, THE TROUBLE WITH NORMAL: SEX, POLITICS AND THE
ETHICS OF QUEER LIFE (1999).
Weber, Max, *Citizenship in Ancient and Medieval Cities*, in THE CITIZENSHIP
DEBATES 43 (Gershon Shafir ed., 1998).
Weintraub, Jeff, THE THEORY AND POLITICS OF THE PUBLIC/PRIVATE DISTINC-
TION, IN PUBLIC AND PRIVATE IN THOUGHT AND PRACTICE 1 (Jeff Weintraub
& Krishan Kumar eds., 1997).

Weintraub, Jeff & Krishan Kumar eds., PUBLIC AND PRIVATE IN THOUGHT AND PRACTICE (1997).

White, Andrew, *The Government of American Cities*, 10 The Forum 357 (Dec. 1890).

WHITE, MORTON & LUCIA PERRY WHITE, THE INTELLECTUAL VERSUS THE CITY: FROM THOMAS JEFFERSON TO FRANK LLOYD WRIGHT (1962).

Williams, Joan, *The Development of the Public/Private Distinction in American Law*, 64 TEX. L. REV. 225 (1985).

WILLIAMSON, FISHER, ABIGAIL, WELCOMING NEW AMERICANS? LOCAL GOVERNMENTS AND IMMIGRANT INCORPORATION (2018).

WINKLER, ADAM, WE THE CORPORATIONS: HOW AMERICAN BUSINESSES WON THEIR CIVIL RIGHTS (2018).

Wirth, Louis, *Urbanism as a Way of Life*, in CLASSIC ESSAYS ON THE CULTURE OF CITIES 143 (Richard Sennett ed. 1969).

WOOD, GORDON S., THE RADICALISM OF THE AMERICAN REVOLUTION (1991).

WRIGHT, GWENDOLYN, BUILDING THE DREAM: A SOCIAL HISTORY OF HOUSING IN AMERICA (1981).

MORALISM AND THE MODEL HOME: DOMESTIC ARCHITECTURE AND CULTURAL CONFLICT IN CHICAGO, 1873–1913 (1980).

YERGIN, DANIEL, THE PRIZE: THE EPIC QUEST FOR OIL, MONEY & POWER (1992).

Young, Ernest A., *Dual Federalism, Concurrent Jurisdiction, and the Foreign Affairs Exception*, 69 GEO. WASH. L. REV. 139 (2001).

Young, Iris Marion, JUSTICE AND THE POLITICS OF DIFFERENCE (1990).

Polity and Group Difference: A Critique of the Ideal of Universal Citizenship, 99 ETHICS 250 (Jan. 1989).

Zaleski, Andrew, *Why Domino's Pizza Is Fixing Potholes Now*, CITYLAB (Jun. 14, 2018), https://www.citylab.com/transportation/2018/06/dominos-pizza-is-fixing-potholes-now-and-thats-fine/562829/.

Zax, Jeffrey S., *Election Methods and Black and Hispanic City Council Membership*, 71 SOC. SCI. Q. 339 (1990).

ZUKIN, SHARON, NAKED CITY: THE DEATH AND LIFE OF AUTHENTIC URBAN PLACES (2010).

ZUNZ, OLIVIER, THE CHANGING FACE OF INEQUALITY: URBANIZATION, INDUSTRIAL DEVELOPMENT, AND IMMIGRANTS IN DETROIT, 1880–1920 (1982).

Index

CPSIA information can be obtained
at www.ICGtesting.com
Printed in the USA
LVHW011942190821
695611LV00003B/355